APPLYING YOUR GENERALIST TRAINING

A Field Guide for Social Workers

 Brooks/Cole Empowerment Series

D1410819

Shelagh J. Larkin

BROOKS/COLE
CENGAGE Learning·

Australia • Brazil • Japan • Korea • Mexico • Singapore • Spain • United Kingdom • United States

BROOKS/COLE
CENGAGE Learning·

Applying Your Generalist Training:
A Field Guide for Social Workers
Shelagh J. Larkin

Senior Publisher: Jon-David Hague

Executive Editor: Jaime Perkins

Acquisitions Editor: Seth Dobrin

Assistant Editor: Suzanna Kincaid

Media Editor: Elizabeth Momb

Senior Brand Manager: Elizabeth Rhoden

Senior Market Development Manager:
Kara Kindstrom

Art and Cover Direction, Production
Management, and Composition:
PreMediaGlobal

Manufacturing Planner: Judy Inouye

Rights Acquisitions Specialist: Tom
McDonough

Text Researcher: Pablo D'Stair

Copy Editor: Maki Wiering

Cover Image: photobank.ch/iStockphoto

For product information and technology assistance, contact us at
Cengage Learning Customer & Sales Support, 1-800-354-9706.

For permission to use material from this text or product,
submit all requests online at **www.cengage.com/permissions.**
Further permissions questions can be e-mailed to
permissionrequest@cengage.com

Library of Congress Control Number: 2012944052

ISBN-13: 978-1-133-60076-3

ISBN-10: 1-133-60076-X

Brooks/Cole
20 Davis Drive
Belmont, CA 94002-3098
USA

Cengage Learning is a leading provider of customized learning solutions with office locations around the globe, including Singapore, the United Kingdom, Australia, Mexico, Brazil, and Japan. Locate your local office at **www.cengage.com/global.**

Cengage Learning products are represented in Canada by Nelson Education, Ltd.

To learn more about Brooks/Cole, visit **www.cengage.com/** brooks/cole

Purchase any of our products at your local college store or at our preferred online store **www.cengagebrain.com.**

Printed in the United States of America
1 2 3 4 5 6 7 16 15 14 13 12

ABOUT THE AUTHOR

SHELAGH LARKIN is a Licensed Independent Social Worker who obtained her MSW at the University of Kentucky in 1988. She has 24 years of experience in practice and social work education. Her practice experience is in the areas of mental health, child welfare and eating disorders. For the last 14 years she has been the Director for Field Education at Xavier University. In the role of field director, she is responsible for all aspects of the field program including recruiting sites, placing students, training field instructors, conducting liaison site visits, and teaching the integrative seminar course. All of these duties have provided her with a comprehensive and unique view of the needs of students and field instructors. She has published and presented at numerous national conferences in the areas of generalist field education, spiritually sensitive professional development, and interprofessional teaming. Lastly, she has also been awarded several grants most notable being CSWE's Gero-Ed Center Curriculum Development Institute grant.

ACKNOWLEDGEMENTS

I would like to thank my husband, Doug, and my daughters Maddie and Sarah for all their support during the process of writing this book. I would also like to thank my dean, department, and the students and field instructors I have worked with, because without them, this book would not have been possible. In addition, I would like to thank all the reviewers who provided excellent feedback and suggestions. I especially want to thank Lauren Hendrickson, who served as the research assistant while I was researching generalist practice, and Karen Kirst-Ashman, with whom I consulted.

CONTENTS

INTRODUCTION

Welcome to field education. Field is the most challenging and rewarding part of your social work education. As a field director for over 14 years, I have walked many students through this process. In fact, one of the things I love most about being a field director is that I get to be a part of an amazing transformation. I cannot adequately describe what it is I witness each year as I watch students go from their first day in field, unsure of what to do or what to expect, to their last day, confidently exiting field, prepared to enter their chosen profession or move on to their advanced education. But what I can say is that it is significant.

As I stated earlier, field is both challenging and rewarding. It is challenging in that you will exist in two worlds simultaneously: the world of the classroom and the world of practice in an agency. This is challenging because it is your responsibility to not only navigate successfully between both worlds but also integrate those worlds while moving seamlessly back and forth. Also, the demands of field education can be an overwhelming part of your education. On top of your classroom responsibilities, you will also be expected to work competently with clients in an agency while juggling other responsibilities in your life, such as work and family. I'm sure as you got ready to enter field you asked yourself, "OK, how am I supposed to do this?" Field can also be stressful because it is not controlled; that is, you will be exposed to what I like to call the good, the bad, and the ugly. There can be a great many experiences you will need to process. Some you will realize are not necessary for you to attend to, while others will become important learning experiences. So you will have some rough days. As I tell my students, the learning comes in many unexpected ways.

On the other hand, field education is extremely rewarding. I have seen students accomplish amazing things at their field agencies. For instance, students have translated forms into foreign languages to better serve their clients; developed policies for a treatment group that was being run by the agency in a host setting; designed, implemented, and ensured the sustainability of a program they developed; and redone the agency's assessment form to better reflect a strength-based philosophy. I have had students tell me they have been forever and profoundly changed as a result of their work with one particular client. Furthermore, field is often where students solidify their belief that they have chosen the right profession and are excited to begin their professional life. Finally, field will provide you with invaluable skills that students tell me they would never have gained had they not been in field. At the end of your field experience, you will see that it was more than worth it.

WHO AM I?

Well, first and foremost, I'm a social worker and have been for over 24 years. Regardless of where I have worked or what I have done at my jobs, whenever anyone asks me what I do, I say, "I'm a social worker." I received my BS in psychology from Xavier University in 1985. During my senior year, when I took cultural anthropology, social psychology, and sociology, I realized I was far more interested in the interaction between people and their social environments than solely considering the individual. As I began exploring graduate programs, my father, a professor at Xavier University, suggested I look into social work and talk to Dr. Dennis Long, who was on faculty in the social work department at Xavier. After meeting with Dennis, I realized that social work was the right fit for me. I then went to the University of Kentucky and received my master of social work (MSW) degree in 1988. I have over 24 years of social work experience in practice and social work education. The first 12 years of my professional life, I practiced in the areas of mental health, child welfare, and eating disorders, with individuals, families, groups, and organizations and have spent the last 14 years in social work education as the director for field education. My first two years in social work education I was also practicing.

As I reflect on my professional life, one thing that stands out is the fact that I have been involved with field in one way or another throughout my entire career. I worked with students in all of my jobs, and in fact, at my first job, I developed and ran a volunteer/student program. So I have been a field student, a field instructor, and now a field director. This means I have sat where you are today; I have sat across from many students as their field instructor, some of whom went on to become field instructors in my program; and for the last 14 years, I have managed students' field experiences as a field director. I even recently had a student tell me she wanted to be a field instructor. I consider the work I have done and will continue to do and the role that I play in the development of future social workers to be a privilege and an honor.

WHY I WROTE THIS BOOK

I wrote this book for two reasons. First, I have developed an approach to field education that is grounded in generalist practice called the *Generalist Field Education Approach* that I feel will add a great deal to your field experience and professional training as a generalist practitioner. Second, I believe this book will offer you the resources necessary to not only help you get through field, but also make field a wonderful learning and professional development experience. In my program, I fulfill many different roles as a field director, which has provided me with a unique perspective. This perspective enables me to have a deeper understanding of what students need as they navigate through their field experience, as well as illuminate the gaps that can exist between the classroom and field.

HOW TO USE THIS BOOK

This book is geared toward BSW students who are in their senior field courses and MSW foundation students. However, many of the principles can also be applied at the MSW advanced level. Each chapter will provide you with information that is important to your understanding of field education. Also, the book offers guided reflection questions and integrative activities to assist you in applying your generalist training to your field experience.

It has been important to me that this book strike a balance between content and process. That is, I do not want to repeat content you have already studied in your courses; instead, I hope to provide the necessary amount of relevant content regarding a topic so you can conceptualize that content area in the context of field education and provide resources so you can integrate that content area with your practice experiences in field.

The reflection questions in each chapter provide an opportunity to explore various content and process areas and experiences of field. I encourage you to start a reflection journal to record your answers to the reflection questions, as well as jot down questions for discussion.

The chapters also offer integrative activities for you to complete while in field. Some you will complete on your own and others you will work on with your field instructor during supervision or may even bring to class to discuss. The purpose of the integrative activities is to provide a way for you to directly link your generalist training to your practice experiences in field. So I encourage you to take your book with you to your field agency to use as a resource.

Last, it is my belief that the content and resources in this book will provide you with the tools necessary to develop and demonstrate competence in the 41 practice behaviors that operationalize the ten core competencies necessary for professional practice as outlined in the Council on Social Work Education, *Educational Policy and Accreditation Standards*, (*EPAS*, 2008). This, however, is not always a clear-cut process; so you will notice the "Helping Hands" icon located within the text that link the chapter content to the corresponding core competency and practice behavior(s). The practice behaviors have been alphabetized for clarity. In addition, at the end of each chapter, a section called Competency Notes will identify the location by page number of each practice behavior and provide a brief explanation of how the content in the chapter relates to the specific practice behavior. Finally, to gain an understanding of the specific tasks you can engage in field to develop and demonstrate the specific core competencies and practice behaviors, a list of suggested field tasks that reflect that chapter's content appears at the end of each chapter.

CHAPTER 1

Field Education: A Generalist Approach

This chapter will provide an overview of social work education with an emphasis on field and introduce you to the generalist field education approach. The purpose is to ground you in an understanding of the role that field plays in your education and training and better prepare you to be successful in your field placement.

SOCIAL WORK EDUCATION

Social work education is organized along multiple levels, and each level has its own educational outcomes and scope of practice. At the baccalaureate level, a student can obtain a bachelor's degree in social work (BSW). The purpose of undergraduate social work education as accredited by the Council on Social Work Education (CSWE) is to develop generalist practitioners. At the graduate level a person can obtain a master of social work (MSW) degree, which is considered the terminal degree of the profession. Master's level students are trained to be advanced practitioners. Both undergraduate (BSW) and graduate (MSW) social work programs use field education as an important part of a student's curriculum. Many graduate programs offer advanced standing for students who have a BSW degree, are within 5 years of receiving their degree, and meet the academic standards for admissions. Advanced standing means that the student is exempt from much of the foundation and often enters the MSW program in the concentration year. The last level of social work education is a doctorate-level Ph.D. (DSW) degree and is usually for individuals interested in conducting research or working as a professor in a university.

FIELD IN SOCIAL WORK EDUCATION

Field education has been a part of social work training and education since its inception. In fact, the first training program in 1898 was a 6-week program that involved lectures, agency visits, and field work. That training program went on to become The Columbia School of Social Work in New York (Fortune, 1994).

In the history of social work education, there were two early types of programs, agency based and university based, and each had its own focus and expected outcomes. The agency-based training programs were grounded in the idea of learning by doing with the student modeling a primary practitioner and focusing on common elements that defined social work methods. On the other hand, the university-based programs focused on social work's purpose in social reform and emphasized research and academic-based knowledge. Interestingly enough, field work in the early university-based programs consisted of "field excursions to observe rather than through actual work" (Fortune, 1994, p. 153). Thus the emphasis was on learning by observing and thinking rather than on doing.

A third type of education that emerged was undergraduate public education, mostly located in Midwestern rural areas that prepared people for public service. According to Fortune, "The legacy of the undergraduate state schools includes the public service and rural missions, responsiveness to localized service needs, and a detachment from the developments and strictures of field education in the other streams" (1994, p. 153).

It was not until 1970 that field became a required part of undergraduate social work education. Since then models and theories emerged to shape today's field experience (Schneck, Grossman and Glassman, 1991). Some social work programs emphasized the "doing" and saw field as the last part of a sequence of learning that began in the classroom, while others took a different approach, emphasizing the integration of classroom and field.

In fact, the struggle to define the role and place of field in the curriculum and in the development of professionals continues today (Wayne, Bogo, and Raskins, 2006). The current conceptualization of field education as articulated by the CSWE is that it "represents the central form of instruction and learning," described in the following excerpt from CSWE's *Educational Policies and Accreditation Standards (EPAS),* 2008.

Educational Policy 2.3—Signature Pedagogy: Field Education

Signature pedagogy represents the central form of instruction and learning in which a profession socializes its students to perform the role of practitioner. Professionals have pedagogical norms with which they connect and integrate theory and practice. In social work, the signature pedagogy is field education. The intent of field education is to connect the theoretical and conceptual contribution of the classroom with the practical world of the practice setting. It is a basic precept of social work education that the two interrelated components of curriculum—classroom and field—are of equal importance within the curriculum, and each contributes to the development of the requisite competencies of professional practice. Field education is systematically designed, supervised, coordinated, and evaluated based on criteria by which students demonstrate the achievement of program competencies. (p. 8)

In other words, for today's social work education programs, field education is the primary vehicle for training and socializing students for the profession. The training and socialization of students reflect the belief that both the classroom and field curriculum are critical to ensuring that students become competent practitioners. *EPAS* (2008) identifies field as the point of intersection and integration of the classroom and practice.

Finding oneself at that intersection of the classroom learning, field training, and professional socialization can be challenging for students. I have seen students struggle to meet the often competing academic and practice demands of field, feeling pulled in multiple directions. Furthermore, students often struggle with their own conceptualizations of what they think field should be and then are left feeling confused and overwhelmed. Yet the integration of classroom curriculum into real-life practice experiences and bringing field experiences back to the classroom is the reason you are in field. Thus field is much more than simply working in an agency. You will form and strengthen the connections between your existing knowledge and practical experience at this intersection of classroom learning, field training, and professional socialization, resulting in deeper understanding and an expected level of competence.

In terms of the structure of field, *EPAS* (2008) outlines specific guidelines regarding the structure and number of hours. The *EPAS* (2008) states that students at the undergraduate level are responsible to complete a minimum of 400 hours in an organization working under the supervision of a social worker. At the graduate level students must complete a minimum of 900 hours, although many schools require more. The 900 hours for MSW is for both the foundation and concentration years, thus students who qualify for advanced standing may do less than 900 because they will receive some credit for their BSW field hours. However, the exact number varies program to program, so you will want to check with your program to determine the number of required hours. Field is a significant commitment of time, as reflected in the clock hours, as well as when you consider the expectations for the outcomes of field. Thus I always ask my students to reflect on why they think field is such an important part of their social work education.

REFLECTION QUESTION 1.1

Now that you have a beginning understanding of field, why do you think field education is an important component of your social work education, and what role do you think field should play in your education and training as a social worker? Write your answer in your journal. Additional information will be provided on this later in the chapter.

THE GENERALIST FIELD EDUCATION APPROACH

This book is grounded in a conceptualization of field that considers the history and evolution of field education and captures the best of all the early approaches. This is accomplished by emphasizing "doing," mentorship with a field instructor, professional development, critical thinking, and the conscious and deliberate integration of field training and classroom learning. Furthermore, to assist you in the goal of developing your competence as a generalist practitioner, this text utilizes the generalist field education approach. First, from a conceptual standpoint, generalist field education is defined as a field experience that is grounded in, integrates, and impacts curriculum; takes place in organizations under the supervision of a field instructor; and requires students to engage in multilevel field tasks and the foundational roles of social work; and emphasizes ethical practice, diversity and social justice, critical thinking, and the application of the planned change process, with specific emphasis on multilevel assessment, planning, and implementation. Second, from a practical standpoint, this book offers integrative activities that will help you put the conceptual aspects of the approach into practice while in field. These integrative activities can be found throughout the book, and they coincide with various field-related activities.

Table 1.1 provides an overview of generalist field education. The table identifies each element of the generalist field education approach, corresponding supplemental resources, integrative activities that relate specifically to that element, and the

TABLE 1.1 The Generalist Field Education Approach

Element Generalist Field Education is:	Supplemental Resources	Integrative Activity	Field Activity/ Paperwork Time Frame
1. grounded in, integrates, and impacts curriculum	CSWE 2008 *EPAS* Department curriculum Course syllabi	**2.3 Curriculum Review** **13.1 Curriculum Analysis**	Orientation Weeks 1–3 End of year
2. takes place in organizations	Agency-based orientation materials	**2.1 Orientation and Training** **2.2 Agency Analysis** **3.2 Identifying Foundational Roles of Social Work in Field** **4.1 Field Safety Assessment**	Orientation Training Weeks 1–3
3. under the supervision of the field Instructor		**5.1 The Supervision Outline** **5.2 The Supervision Agenda** **5.3 Documenting Your Supervision Session**	Establish supervision time Week 1 or 2 Weeks 3–15
4. requires students engage in multilevel tasks and the foundational roles of social work	Agency job description	**3.1 Identifying Multilevel Learning Tasks** **3.2 Identifying Foundational Roles of Social Work in Field** **3.3 Constructing the Field Learning Plan**	Learning plan Weeks 3–5
5. emphasizes ethical practice, diversity, social justice, and critical thinking	NASW Code of Ethics Agency Code of Ethics	**7.1 The Agency Ethics Audit** **7.2 Resolving Ethical Dilemmas** **8.1 Developing an Understanding of Diversity, Culture, and Cultural Competence in Field: A Multilevel Approach** **8.2 Developing Culturally Competent Practice Skills in Field** **8.3 Identifying Social and Economic Injustice in Field** **8.4 Policy Analysis and Practice** **1.1 Translating Core Competencies into Field Competencies and Tasks** **1.2 The Field Portfolio** **1.3 The Field Journal** **9.1 Task Analysis** **9.2 The Literature Review** **12.1 Professional Development of Self Capstone Paper** **13.2 Pulling It All Together**	Orientation Weeks 1–3 Weeks 6–15
6. and the application of the planned change process with specific emphasis on multilevel assessment, planning, and implementation	Agency intakes and assessments Agency service plans Agency interventions	**10.1 The Phases of the Planned Change Process in Field** **10.2 The Multidimensional/Multilevel Assessment** **10.3 Identifying Theoretical Perspectives, Practice Models, and Commonly Utilized Interventions in Field** **10.4 Developing and Implementing Multilevel Plans** **10.5 The Planned Change Case Analysis**	Week 4 Weeks 6–15

corresponding activities or paperwork of field and suggested time frame for their completion. Note: the following time frame is based on a general 16-week semester; thus your particular time frame may vary depending on your program and agency requirements. Also, not all chapter activities are included in this table; only those that directly relate to the elements reflected in the generalist field education approach.

DEVELOPING AND DEMONSTRATING COMPETENCE IN FIELD

The outcome of field education is the ability to develop and demonstrate competence as a social worker. The *Educational Policy and Accreditation Standards* (*EPAS*, 2008) written by CSWE outlines a set of core competencies and defines them in the following way:

> Competency-based education is an outcome performance approach to curriculum design. Competencies are measurable practice behaviors that are comprised of knowledge, values, and skills. The goal of the outcome approach is to demonstrate the integration and application of the competencies in practice with individuals, families, groups, organizations, and communities. (p. 3)

EP 2.1.1–10

EPAS (2008) outlines 10 core competencies with corresponding practice behaviors that students must be able to demonstrate in their course work and in the field. The core competencies, corresponding knowledge values and skills, and practice behaviors are outlined in Integrative Activity 1.1: Translating Core Competencies into Field Competencies and Tasks. It is important to consider how each core competency can be demonstrated in field. The following is a list of field competencies organized into five overarching categories that relate specifically to field education. They are:

1. **Socialization and professional development as a social worker in field.**
   a. Develop skills for lifelong learning while in field.
   b. Apply knowledge of organization, specifically relating history of the organization, to history of the profession, to practice in field.
   c. Apply understanding of how the organization impacts services and the profession, and in turn how the organization is impacted by societal issues.
   d. Demonstrate understanding of the role and function of supervision in field.
   e. Use supervision effectively in field.
   f. Identify roles of professional social worker and student in field.
   g. Appropriately utilize professional social work roles in field.
   h. Demonstrate ability to reflect on practice and professional development in field.

2. **Ethical practice and consideration of diversity and social justice in field.**
   a. Engage in ethical practice in field.
   b. Utilize an ethical decision-making process to resolve ethical dilemmas in field.
   c. Demonstrate an understanding of the impact of diversity and difference on clients.
   d. Develop culturally competent practice skills in field.
   e. Demonstrate ability to advance social justice in field.

3. **Integration of knowledge, values, and skills acquired in the classroom with the practice experiences of field.**
   a. Demonstrate ability to link and utilize specific knowledge, values, and skills from courses with practice in field.
   b. Demonstrate ability to analyze field tasks using critical-thinking skills.

  c. Utilize understanding of the role of policy and policy development in practice at field agency.

  d. Apply analysis of client systems from the perspective of human development and the person and environment construct in field.

  e. Apply research findings to practice in field.

4. **Effective communication skills in field.**

  a. Apply effective verbal communication skills in field.

  b. Apply effective written communication skills in field.

  c. Evaluate communication skills with client systems in field.

5. **Application of the planned change process with individuals, families, groups, organizations, and communities in field.**

  a. Identify phases of the planned change process in field.

  b. Engage individuals, families, groups, organizations, and communities in field.

  c. Conduct multidimensional assessment of client systems (individuals, families, groups, organizations, and communities) in field.

  d. Analyze multidimensional assessment of client systems (individuals, families, groups, organizations, and communities) in field.

  e. Develop multilevel plans with client systems in field.

  f. Implement interventions with client systems in field that are grounded in theories and knowledge.

  g. Terminate effectively with client systems in field.

  h. Evaluate practice in field with individuals, families, groups, organizations, and communities.

In Integrative Activity 1.1 you will have an opportunity to see how the preceding competencies relate to the core competencies and practice behaviors identified by CSWE in *EPAS* (2008). For instance, the field competency of "Develop skills for lifelong learning while in field" relates specifically to the core competency, "2.1.1 Identify as a professional social worker and conduct oneself accordingly" (*EPAS*, 2008, p. 3) and the specific practice behavior of "engage in career long learning" (*EPAS*, 2008, p. 3).

Hand-in-hand with identifying field competencies is identifying the tasks that you can engage in while in field to develop and demonstrate a particular competence. As you can see, Integrative Activity 1.1 also provides a list of possible tasks for you to consider engaging in while in field placement. For instance, in order to achieve the competence of developing as a lifelong learner, you might engage in ongoing training and education by attending community- or agency-based trainings, reading the literature, or viewing training videos. This task will assist you in meeting this competency in field and lay the foundation in your development as a lifelong learner once you are practicing as a social worker. As you complete various field tasks, you will develop and demonstrate the field competencies and ultimately demonstrate and achieve the necessary core competencies and practice behaviors of social work. Throughout the book you will notice "Helping Hands" icons in the margins; these icons help you connect the chapter content to the core competencies and recommended practice behaviors described in *EPAS* (2008). Each icon is labeled "EP" for "Educational Policy," followed by the number and letter of the recommended practice behavior. Last, at the end of each chapter, there will be a list of possible field tasks that you can engage in to develop and demonstrate competence in that related area of practice or professional development.

INTEGRATIVE ACTIVITY 1.1

Translating Core Competencies into Field Competencies and Tasks

Purpose: The purpose of this activity is to assist you in the process of developing your understanding of the *EPAS* (2008) Core Competencies and Practice Behaviors and how they relate to the field competencies outlined in the book, as well as identify the possible tasks you can engage in to demonstrate that competency in field. The first three columns outline the core competencies; characteristic knowledge, values, and skills; the resulting practice behaviors as identified in the *EPAS* (2008, pp. 3–7); the corresponding field competencies that are linked with that core competency; and the tasks you can engage in while in field in order to develop and demonstrate that you have met a particular core competency.

Directions: First, review the first four columns to familiarize yourself with the CSWE *EPAS* (2008) and the corresponding field competencies. Then review the tasks you can engage in while in field to develop and demonstrate each core competency and practice behaviors, and discuss with your field instructor in supervision.

Core Competency	Characteristic Knowledge, Values, and Skills	Resulting Practice Behaviors	Corresponding Field Competency	Field Tasks Note: The tasks are in no particular order of importance.
2.1.1— Identify as a professional social worker and conduct oneself accordingly.	*Social workers serve as representatives of the profession, its mission, and its core values. They know the profession's history. Social workers commit themselves to the profession's enhancement and to their own professional conduct and growth.*	*a. Advocate for client access to the services of social work;* *b. practice personal reflection and self-correction to assure continual professional development;* *c. attend to professional roles and boundaries;* *d. demonstrate professional demeanor in behavior, appearance, and communication;* *e. engage in career-long learning; and* *f. use supervision and consultation.*	1. Socialization and professional development as a social worker in field. a. Develop skills for lifelong learning while in field. b. Apply knowledge of organization, specifically relating history of the organization to history of the profession, to practice in field. d. Demonstrate understanding of the role and function of supervision in field. e. Use supervision effectively in field. f. Identify role of professional social worker and student in field. g. Appropriately utilize professional social work roles in field.	• Review related course work. • Engage in orientation and training. • Tour agency. • Introduce self to all staff. • Establish supervision time. • Attend and plan for supervision. • Use supervision appropriately. • Demonstrate understanding of agency. • Examine and analyze mission, goals and objectives, programs and services, history, funding, and organizational structure, and relate to history of profession and organizational theory. • Review and complete field and agency paperwork, time sheets, learning plan, safety assessment, evaluation, mileage reimbursement, incident reports, etc. • Determine title and role as a student. • Discuss culture of agency. • Identify backup when field instructor is not available. • Identify primary role and tasks. • Set up work space. • Obtain ID/computer/voice mail access. • Identify work schedule. • Discuss and follow dress code. • Function independently in agency. • Join social work club, a professional organization such as NASW, or community group. • Identify and engage in philanthropic, social action activities.

(Continued)

Core Competency	Characteristic Knowledge, Values, and Skills	Resulting Practice Behaviors	Corresponding Field Competency	Field Tasks Note: The tasks are in no particular order of importance.
				• Engage a mentor. • Attend agency-based, community, or campus trainings and events. • Engage in self-care activities, and monitor stress and burnout. • Explore professional development of self. • Identify key players and role of each according to the "learning triangle" (i.e., field instructor, field director, faculty field liaison). • Identify self as a student with client systems.
2.1.2—Apply social work ethical principles to guide professional practice.	Social workers have an obligation to conduct themselves ethically and to engage in ethical decision making. Social workers are knowledgeable about the value base of the profession, its ethical standards, and relevant law.	a. recognize and manage personal values in a way that allows professional values to guide practice; b. make ethical decisions by applying standards of the National Association of Social Workers Code of Ethics and, as applicable, of the International Federation of Social Workers/ International Association of Schools of Social Work Ethics in Social Work, Statement of Principles; c. tolerate ambiguity in resolving ethical conflicts; and d. apply strategies of ethical reasoning to arrive at principled decisions.	2. Ethical practice and consideration of diversity and social justice in field. a. Engage in ethical practice in field. b. Utilize an ethical decision-making process to resolve ethical dilemmas in field.	• Review related course work. • In supervision, identify and discuss personal values and distinguish personal and professional values. • Read and review NASW Code of Ethics and any agency-based code of ethics. • Discuss ethical principles and standards and any agency-based ethical standards. • Identify and discuss common ethical dilemmas in practice setting. • Conduct an agency audit regarding ethical practices. • Identify, analyze, and resolve ethical dilemmas using the NASW Code of Ethics standards as a guide.

(Continued)

Core Competency	Characteristic Knowledge, Values, and Skills	Resulting Practice Behaviors	Corresponding Field Competency	Field Tasks Note: The tasks are in no particular order of importance.
2.1.3—Apply critical thinking to inform and communicate professional judgments.	*Social workers are knowledgeable about the principles of logic, scientific inquiry, and reasoned discernment. They use criticl thinking augmented by creativity and curiosity. Critical thinking also requires the synthesis and communication of relevant information.*	*a. distinguish, appraise, and integrate multiple sources of knowledge, including research-based knowledge, and practice wisdom;* *b. analyze models of assessment, prevention, intervention, and evaluation; and* *c. demonstrate effective oral and written communication in working with individuals, families, groups, organizations, communities, and colleagues.*	1. Socialization and professional development as a social worker in field. h. Demonstrate ability to reflect on practice and professional development in field. 3. Integration of knowledge, values, and skills acquired in the classroom with the practice experiences of field. a. Demonstrate ability to link and utilize specific knowledge, values, and skills from courses with practice in field. b. Demonstrate ability to analyze field tasks using critical-thinking skills. c. Utilize understanding of the role of policy and policy development in practice at field agency. d. Apply analysis of client systems from the perspective of human development and the person and environment construct in field. e. Apply research findings to practice in field. 4. Effective communication skills in field. a. Apply effective verbal communication skills in field.	• Analyze field tasks. • Communicate with clients at the organizational level using verbal, nonverbal, and written skills. • Evaluate professional communication skills. • In supervision describe and explain practice tasks. • Present and analyze client system information. • Demonstrate ability to conceptualize practice. • Complete documentation, professional writing. • Use reflection to explore role, tasks, and experiences of field. • Articulate learning from tasks. • Explain knowledge, skills, and values developed as a result of field experiences.

(Continued)

Core Competency	Characteristic Knowledge, Values, and Skills	Resulting Practice Behaviors	Corresponding Field Competency	Field Tasks Note: The tasks are in no particular order of importance.
			b. Apply effective written communication skills in field. c. Evaluate communication skills with client systems in field.	
2.1.4— Engage diversity and difference in practice.	Social workers understand how diversity characterizes and shapes the human experience and is critical to the formation of identity. The dimensions of diversity are understood as the intersectionality of multiple factors including age, class, color, culture, disability, ethnicity, gender, gender identity and expression, immigration status, political ideology, race, religion, sex, and sexual orientation. Social workers appreciate that, as a consequence of difference, a person's life experiences may include oppression, poverty, marginalization, and alienation as well as privilege, power, and acclaim.	a. recognize the extent to which a culture's structures and values may oppress, marginalize, alienate, or create or enhance privilege and power; b. gain sufficient self-awareness to eliminate the influence of personal biases and values in working with diverse groups; c. recognize and communicate their understanding of the importance of difference in shaping life experiences; and d. view themselves as learners and engage those with whom they work as informants.	2. Ethical practice and consideration of diversity and social justice in field. c. Demonstrate an understanding of the impact of diversity and difference on clients. d. Develop culturally competent practice skills in field.	• Review related course work. • Identify diversity at the agency and client system level. • Increase knowledge of special population served by agency. • Identify value-based issues related to diversity. • Review standards of cultural competence as set forth by NASW. • Develop cultural competency skills in practice. • Design and implement culturally competent practice interventions.

(Continued)

Core Competency	Characteristic Knowledge, Values, and Skills	Resulting Practice Behaviors	Corresponding Field Competency	Field Tasks Note: The tasks are in no particular order of importance.
2.1.5— Advance human rights and social and economic justice.	*Each person, regardless of position in society, has basic human rights, such as freedom, safety, privacy, an adequate standard of living, health care, and education. Social workers recognize the global interconnections of oppression and are knowledgeable about theories of justice and strategies to promote human and civil rights. Social work incorporates social justice practices in organizations, institutions, and society to ensure that these basic human rights are distributed equitably and without prejudice.*	*a. understand the forms and mechanisms of oppression and discrimination;* *b. advocate for human rights and social and economic justice; and* *c. engage in practices that advance social and economic justice.*	2. Ethical practice and consideration of diversity and social justice in field. e. Demonstrate ability to advance social justice in field.	• Review related course work. • Identify and discuss issues of oppression and discrimination that directly impact clients in the agency at all levels. • Identify how the role of advocacy is utilized at the placement site to advance social and economic justice. • Design and implement interventions that target advocacy to address oppression and discrimination and issues of human rights and social and economic justice.
2.1.6— Engage in research-informed practice and practice-informed research.	*Social workers use practice experience to inform research, employ evidence-based interventions, evaluate their own practice, and use research findings to improve practice, policy, and social service delivery.*	*a. use practice experience to inform scientific inquiry; and* *b. use research evidence to inform practice.*	3. Integration of knowledge, values, and skills acquired in the classroom with the practice experiences of field. e. Apply research findings to practice in field.	• Review related course work. • Identify and discuss how research is used by agency to support activities of the organization. • Assist in agency's annual report, auditing, program evaluation, client satisfaction. • Identify at least one research question that relates to your placement setting. • Conduct literature review on practice area, identifying database searched and search parameters. • Read and discuss and present findings of research, and explain how it informs practice.

(Continued)

Core Competency	Characteristic Knowledge, Values, and Skills	Resulting Practice Behaviors	Corresponding Field Competency	Field Tasks Note: The tasks are in no particular order of importance.
	Social workers comprehend quantitative and qualitative research and understand scientific and ethical approaches to building knowledge.			
2.1.7—Apply knowledge of human behavior and the social environment.	*Social workers are knowledgeable about human behavior across the life course; the range of social systems in which people live; and the ways social systems promote or deter people in maintaining or achieving health and well-being. Social workers apply theories and knowledge from the liberal arts to understand biological, social, cultural, psychological, and spiritual development.*	a. *utilize conceptual frameworks to guide the processes of assessment, intervention, and evaluation; and* b. *critique and apply knowledge to understand person and environment.*	3. Integration of knowledge, values and skills acquired in the classroom with the practice experiences of field. d. Apply analysis of client systems from the perspective of human development and the person and environment construct in field.	• Review related course work. • Develop and conduct a multidimensional/multilevel assessment. • Utilize knowledge of development to understand client. • Demonstrate understanding of how behavior relates to and is impacted by social systems. • Demonstrate knowledge of theories by defining and explaining at least three theories that explain development and/or behavior.
2.1.8— Engage in policy practice to advance social and economic well-being and to deliver effective social work services.	*Social work practitioners understand that policy affects service delivery, and they actively engage in policy practice. Social workers know the history and current structures of*	a. analyze, formulate, and advocate for policies that advance social well-being; and b. collaborate with colleagues and clients for effective policy action.	3. Integration of knowledge, values, and skills acquired in the classroom with the practice experiences of field. c. Utilize understanding of the role of policy and policy development in practice at field agency.	• Review related course work. • Obtain and read agency policies and procedures. • Analyze current policy and impact on client system. • Engage in policy development. • Research legislative history of an existing or proposed policy. • Engage in advocacy at the legislative or bureaucratic level. • Prepare and present information in support of a policy or program reform.

(Continued)

Core Competency	Characteristic Knowledge, Values, and Skills	Resulting Practice Behaviors	Corresponding Field Competency	Field Tasks Note: The tasks are in no particular order of importance.
	social policies and services; the role of policy in service delivery; and the role of practice in policy development.		2. Ethical practice and consideration of diversity and social justice in field. e. Demonstrate ability to advance social justice in field.	
2.1.9— Respond to contexts that shape practice.	*Social workers are informed, resourceful, and proactive in responding to evolving organizational, community, and societal contexts at all levels of practice. Social workers recognize that the context of practice is dynamic, and use knowledge and skill to respond proactively.*	*a. continuously discover, appraise, and attend to changing locales, populations, scientific and technological developments, and emerging societal trends to provide relevant services; and* *b. provide leadership in promoting sustainable changes in service delivery and practice to improve the quality of social services.*	1. Socialization and professional development as a social worker in field. c. Apply understanding of how the organization impacts services and the profession, and in turn how the organization is impacted by societal issues.	• Review related course work. • Identify issues impacting agency practice at the organizational, community, and societal levels. • Respond to organizational, community, and societal contexts and impact practice in field.
2.1.10(a)– (d)—Engage, assess, intervene, and evaluate with individuals, families, groups, organizations, and communities.	*Professional practice involves the dynamic and interactive processes of engagement, assessment, intervention, and evaluation at multiple levels. Social workers have the knowledge and skills to practice with individuals, families, groups,*	*2.1.10(a)— Engagement Social workers a. substantively and affectively prepare for action with individuals, families, groups, organizations, and communities;* *b. use empathy and other interpersonal skills; and*	5. Application of the planned change process with individuals, families, groups, organizations, and communities in field. a. Identify phases of the planned change process in field. b. Engage individuals, families, groups, organizations, and communities in field.	• Review related course work. • Review phases of the planned change process in field. • Intake and engage individuals, families, groups—task and treatment, organizations, and communities via phone and in person. • Prepare for client system contacts. • Use empathy and effective interpersonal skills. • Identify client system goals. • Develop learning plan.

(Continued)

Core Competency	Characteristic Knowledge, Values, and Skills	Resulting Practice Behaviors	Corresponding Field Competency	Field Tasks Note: The tasks are in no particular order of importance.
	organizations, and communities. Practice knowledge includes identifying, analyzing, and implementing evidence-based interventions designed to achieve client goals; using research and technological advances; evaluating program outcomes and practice effectiveness; developing, analyzing, advocating, and providing leadership for policies and services; and promoting social and economic justice.	*c. develop a mutually agreed-on focus of work and desired outcomes.*		
	2.1.10(b)— Assessment Social workers *d. collect, organize, and interpret client data;* *e. assess client strengths and limitations;* *f. develop mutually agreed-on intervention goals and objectives; and* *g. select appropriate intervention strategies.*	c. Conduct multidimensional assessment of client systems (individuals, families, groups, organizations, and communities) in field. d. Analyze multidimensional assessment of client systems (individuals, families, groups, organizations, and communities) in field. e. Develop multilevel plans with client systems in field.	• Review related course work. • Gather information on client systems. • Identify assessments utilized by agency. • Conduct assessments (intakes, social history, ecomap, genogram, or other agency-based assessments) on client systems. • Develop and conduct a multidimensional/multilevel assessment. • Identify client system strengths and limitations. • Identify multilevel learning opportunities/objectives.

(Continued)

Core Competency	Characteristic Knowledge, Values, and Skills	Resulting Practice Behaviors	Corresponding Field Competency	Field Tasks Note: The tasks are in no particular order of importance.
		2.1.10(c)— *Intervention* *Social workers* *h. initiate actions to achieve organizational goals;* *i. implement prevention interventions that enhance client capacities;* *j. help clients resolve problems;* *k. negotiate, mediate, and advocate for clients; and* *l. facilitate transitions and endings.*	f. Implement plans to intervene with client systems in field that are grounded in theories and knowledge. g. Terminate effectively with client systems in field.	• Review related course work. • Identify multilevel plans that help client systems resolve problems. • Identify theories that direct intervention. • Engage in interventions (implement plans) that demonstrate the roles of negotiation, mediation, and advocacy. • Plan for and implement agency and client termination. • Discuss next steps after field with supervisor. • Identify tasks to achieve learning goals and objectives on learning plan.
		2.1.10(d)— *Evaluation* *Social workers* *m. critically analyze, monitor, and evaluate interventions.*	h. Evaluate practice in field with individuals, families, groups, organizations, and communities.	• Review related course work. • Monitor and evaluate practice strategies. • Engage in program level evaluation. • Evaluate progress in meeting goals and objectives of field and core competencies and practice behaviors.

REFLECTION QUESTION 1.2

As you review Interactive Activity 1.1, which field competencies are directly linked to EPAS (2008) core competencies and practice behaviors and which are indirectly linked? Next, review and identify the tasks that you will need to complete in order to demonstrate the field competencies. Are there any missing, or are there any additional tasks that you think will be necessary to engage in to demonstrate a competency? If so, jot those down to include on your learning plan.

THE WHO'S WHO OF FIELD EDUCATION

EP 2.1.1c

Now that you have laid the foundation for the big picture of field education, let's discuss and define the who's who of field education. The who's who refer to those individuals who are critical players in your field experience and their corresponding roles and responsibilities.

The Learning Triangle

Sherer and Peleg-Oren (2005) use the term *learning triangle* to conceptualize those involved in field education. They say, "Each side of the learning triangle—teachers, field instructors, and students—plays its own part in developing the professional social worker" (p. 316). This concept clearly identifies those involved in field education and reflects the notion that field is unique in that it requires multiple entities—the university, the student, and the agency—to come together and function as a whole. This can be depicted using a Venn diagram like the one in Figure 1.1.

The University

Role: Field Director and Faculty Field Liaison

Responsibilities: Develop program curriculum, including classroom and field education curriculum; develop field policies and procedures; identify sites; place students; train field instructors and students; evaluate and grade students, evaluate field instructors and sites; teach the integrated seminar; and, bring knowledge of social work and field education to bear on the field experience.

Field Education

The University/Agency/Student Shared Responsibilities: Develop a field education program that reflects the independent and interdependent nature of the roles and responsibilities of the University, Agency and Student, thus, realizing the vision of "signature pedagogy."

The Agency

Role: Field Instructor, Task Supervisor

Responsibilities: Provide orientation and training; assign multi-level field tasks and roles; facilitate weekly field supervision; assist in student's ability to integrate classroom and field; evaluate and grade student; and bring knowledge and practice experience to bear on the field experience.

The Student

Role: Student

Responsibilities: Learn; identify self as student; demonstrate beginning level professional behavior; attend and use supervision; apply generalist training in practice; integrate classroom and field; evaluate development as a social worker; and, bring life experience and education to bear on the field experience.

Figure 1.1 Learning Triangle

The use of a Venn diagram provides a visual representation of the distinct yet overlapping roles and responsibilities of each player and demonstrates that field is a unique part of social work education. As a student entering field, it is helpful to understand the following roles and responsibilities of each player.

The University

The first member of the learning triangle is the university and specifically the social work program within the university. Several roles within your program are important to define. First and foremost is the role of the field director or coordinator. This individual is responsible for overseeing the field program, which includes recruiting sites, placing students, establishing and defining all field paperwork and policies (most programs have a separate field manual), and training students and field instructors. The next important role is the faculty field liaison. The purpose of this role is to conduct site visits, engage in troubleshooting, and assign a final grade. The preceding roles may be fulfilled by one person or by many; thus it is important for you to familiarize yourself with your field office and the roles and requisite responsibilities of those in the field office, and print out or obtain a copy of your field manual.

Also, your program may offer an integrative seminar course as part of the curriculum. This course serves an important role. This course usually runs concurrent with field instruction and may be taught by a member of the social work department, the field faculty liaison, or field director. The purpose of the seminar course is to provide an opportunity for students to meet, usually weekly, and share their field experiences. Furthermore, it provides an additional opportunity to integrate classroom content with practice experiences through the completion of important academic assignments.

The Agency

The agency is the second member of the learning triangle and also provides a critical function. Without the agency, field education could not happen. It is the belief of field educators that some things that happen in field can happen only in field and are critically important to the development of social workers.

The field instructor is the most important person at the agency. This is the social work practitioner who has agreed to manage the field education experience, provide your orientation, develop your training plan, assign appropriate mulitlevel tasks, provide weekly supervision, and complete all required program paperwork so you can develop and demonstrate the competencies necessary to become a social worker. The field instructor brings practice experience and knowledge of the agency to field education. If you are in an agency that does not have a social worker on staff, your field instructor may be a person outside the agency or affiliated with the university.

You may have a task supervisor in addition to your field instructor. The task supervisor is a professional you work closely with, but the task supervisor is not the field instructor. This person may or may not be a social worker.

Last, you will work with and form relationships with many professional peers. Regardless of how much time has passed since being in school, most social workers report that they remember their field instructor and field experience. This reflects why field education is referred to as the capstone experience in social work education. It is where students integrate the knowledge, values, and skills they have learned or are learning in the classroom into their identity and practice as social workers. Kadushin (1991) states,

> There is general consensus that field instruction is the most significant, most productive, most memorable component of social work education. Within the general consensus, this conclusion is most vehemently and most enthusiastically supported by social work students—present and former. (p. 11)

The Student

You as the student have many roles and responsibilities to yourself, your program, and your agency. First and foremost, you are a student and your primary goal is to learn. Thus you have an ethical responsibility to always identify yourself as a student and to expect that your agency treat you as such. You also have a responsibility to remember that field education is an academic endeavor. This is often easier said than done. Many students struggle with this, identifying important activities of field as "boring"; saying they don't want to think about "that" (usually some required academic element of field), they just want to serve their clients; and not complete weekly reading or important field documents. I often have to remind students that the only reason they are at the agency is to learn and prepare to be a social worker, which can happen only by integrating the classroom curriculum with all the possible practice experiences at the agency. Therefore, it is absolutely necessary to consider the academic aspect of field while in field.

Most students enter field with volunteer service or paid work experience; however, regardless of your level of previous experience, it is important to remember that field is the first time you will have entered an agency as a social work student under the direct supervision of a social worker engaging in professional social work tasks.

Also, with all the competing demands you will face, you may be tempted to skim over or not even read this book or your field manual. I encourage you to carve out time to read everything assigned to you, because if you do not, you compromise your learning, training, and professional socialization. Incidentally, it is usually obvious to all involved in your training when you have not done your "homework." Thus I ask you to make a conscious commitment to your learning. I also ask you to trust those in the field office and your field instructor and realize that they have your educational best interest at heart and are not there to make your life difficult. While your field director's complete focus is on field education, your field instructor has multiple responsibilities and sometimes can overlook your academic needs as a student. Although this is understandable given the demands of practicing as a social worker and being a field instructor, it can place the burden of ensuring the academic focus of field on you the student. So if you are not prepared, have not read the manual or the chapter, or have not completed the integrative activity, you may miss an important opportunity to make or strengthen a new connection or increase your level of competence (not to mention your confidence). This book takes this into consideration and is grounded in an approach designed to empower you to assume the role of an active, engaged, and prepared learner.

Finally, it is important to realize that lifelong learning, which is central to being a professional social worker, is not tested nor graded in the traditional sense you are accustomed to, but it is nonetheless critical to the clients you will work with. Therefore, I encourage you to begin to embrace that now. A great deal of the reading and reflection will not be tested or graded in the way you are used to; however, you will be evaluated, and many of the competencies that you are expected to demonstrate cannot be met without reflection and academic integration.

REFLECTION QUESTION 1.3

Now that you have an introduction to field, reflect on and write about the following. First, reflect on the learning triangle and think about what you will need from each of the members, including from yourself, in order for field to be successful. Second, think about what you are hoping to get out of field. What are you most excited about as you think about field? And finally, what are you concerned about?

PROCESS AND CONTENT IN GENERALIST FIELD EDUCATION

The most exciting thing about field education is that it is both a process- and content-driven experience. In terms of the process, field has a beginning, middle, and an end. As students have reported and I have observed year after year, the first day of field is significantly different from the last. This process reflects a transformation of sorts or the unfolding of an experience that is equally important as the second part, which is the content of field. A competency-based education emphasizes requisite knowledge, values, and skills that are necessary for effective practice and lay the foundation of the student's ability to demonstrate competence in field. Thus you will simultaneously integrate educational content while going through an important process of socialization to the profession and professional development.

SOCIALIZATION TO THE PROFESSION

As stated earlier, one of the goals of field education is to assist you in your socialization to the profession and development as a social worker. This is accomplished through your ability to develop and demonstrate your professional identity as a social worker. Through a process of

EP 2.1.1d

- immersion in a professional organization,
- observation of professional social workers,
- role rehearsal, and
- reflection on current and past conceptualizations of social workers,

you will begin to develop your identity as a social worker. This means you will begin to conceptualize what it means to you to be a social worker and demonstrate that in your practice behaviors.

Field is exciting because you will have an opportunity to observe real-life professional social work practice in a social worker. This will be helpful as you will see behaviors you wish to emulate as well as behaviors you will feel are not a fit for who you are becoming as a professional social worker. In some settings, you will have interdisciplinary learning experiences in which you will observe other professionals such as nurses, teachers, administrators, and psychologists, to name a few. Observing and interacting with professionals from other professions provides an opportunity to compare and contrast them with social workers and thus define who social workers are and the role they play in the lives of clients.

Furthermore, field is an opportunity to determine if social work is the right fit for you as a profession. Many students tell me it is comforting to know that they have made the right choice. Field is also a safe opportunity to try on a particular role as a social worker. Just as many students tell me they could never work in their field setting again as do students who say their placement experience has confirmed that they have found the right professional practice area. Better yet, I have had students tell me that even though they did not see themselves working with the population they served in their field site, the significant knowledge, values, and skills they gained while working with that population in their field site will stay with them and contribute greatly in their development and practice as a social worker. All of the preceding socialization experiences form the foundation of how students begin to develop their own identities as social workers. These practice experiences are also important because they are real, and students often state that real-life practice experiences are handled very differently than the textbook case examples. Conversely, students have also told me that they have observed practice-based situations in their agencies that they could clearly point to and say, "I learned about that in class."

Your development as a professional social worker is a dynamic and ongoing process. The outcome of this process will be explored in greater detail toward the end of your field experience in Chapter 11. At this time, it is useful to consider the following reflection question as a way to begin to conceptualize professional development.

REFLECTION QUESTION 1.4

What does it mean to you to be a "professional"? What are the advantages of being a professional versus an employee, and are there any disadvantages? As you think about yourself as a professional social worker, what excites you or creates anxiety?

THE USE OF PORTFOLIOS IN FIELD

The generalist field education approach encourages you to be an active learner and to use reflection and various integrative activities in the learning process. To expand on the preceding, it is worth noting that faculty and students have found portfolios to be an effective tool in both the process of integrating curriculum and field, as well as professional development (Riser, 1999; Schatz and Simon, 1999). A portfolio can provide a concrete way to link curriculum to practice.

EP 2.1.3a

Schatz and Simon (1999) state that, "The use of a portfolio assignment supports students' learning through the creation of a tangible product that illustrates practice knowledge and skills" (p. 101). In addition they go on to say that, "A portfolio is a collection of selected materials that demonstrate one's knowledge, skills, and expertise amassed in a notebook or special type of binder" (p. 101). The purpose of a portfolio is to assist you in

1. better understanding and integrating the experiences of field with the curriculum of the classroom by linking various elements to the overarching areas of social work education,
2. improving supervision by providing concrete tangible products to discuss and review, and
3. displaying your professional development and accomplishments by including your résumé and samples of your work that may distinguish you from another social worker.

A portfolio can become a useful tool when applying for a job, graduate school, or your advanced field placement, or it can become a treasured keepsake of your field experience and education. Regardless of the outcome, developing a portfolio can be fun and educational. Integrative Activity 1.2: The Field Portfolio outlines the process of creating a portfolio and provides a list of possible elements to choose from to develop your portfolio.

INTEGRATIVE ACTIVITY 1.2

The Field Portfolio

Purpose: The purpose of the field portfolio is (1) it is an opportunity to create a tangible record of your work in field, (2) it will assist you in the integration of curriculum with the practice tasks of field, and (3) it will enable you to translate the specific elements of your site to the overarching aspects of generalist practice.

Directions: To create a portfolio, follow these steps:

1. Obtain a binder or accordion folder.
2. Create tabs for the sections; see outline for suggestions.
3. Identify and produce an element.
4. Place the element in the appropriate section.
5. Add elements to your portfolio over the course of your field education experience.

Suggested Elements: To assist in the process of selecting possible portfolio elements, a list has been provided. The items are grouped in sections that relate to aspects of the generalist field education approach. The items that make up the portfolio can come from two primary sources. First, an item may reflect a particular task that you do at your field site. For instance, if you conduct intakes, you could place a sample of an intake in the Intake subsection of the Planned Change Process section. Second, you can choose to do a particular task that is not a normal part of your agency role, such as, "write a comprehensive social history" or "complete an ecomap." Either of these items would be placed in the Assessment/Data Collection/Information Gathering subsection of the Planned Change Process section. Other items can flow directly from field such as integrative activities from the text and field paperwork such as your learning plan and field evaluation. Last, assignments from other courses can also be included.

The item itself and the process you go through to create your portfolio are useful in linking curriculum to practice. The portfolio becomes a record of your experiences and can be used to document your skills and accomplishments with prospective employers, graduate programs, or advanced practice field sites.

Field Portfolio Outline

I. Curriculum (foundation, concurrent, specialized)
   a. Course Syllabi
   b. Integrative Activity 2.3: Curriculum Review
   c. Training Certificates Related to Specialized Curriculum
   d. Significant Course Work
   e. Integrative Activity 13.1: Curriculum Analysis

II. The Organization
   a. Orientation Materials
   b. Integrative Activity 2.2: Agency Analysis
   c. Agency Brochure
   d. Integrative Activity 3.1: Identifying Multilevel Learning Tasks
   e. Integrative Activity 3.2: Identifying Foundational Roles of Social Work in Field

III. Field Supervision/Critical Thinking
   a. Integrative Activity 5.1: The Supervision Outline
   b. Integrative Activity 5.2: The Supervision Agenda
   c. Integrative Activity 5.3: Documenting Your Supervision Session
   d. Integrative Activity 9.1: Tasks Analysis

IV. Professional Communication Skills
  a. Verbal: Interviewing
    1. Integrative Activity 6.1: Assessing Interview Skills
    2. Integrative Activity 6.2: The Process Recording
    3. Audio/video transcript

  b. Written: Documentation/Professional Writing
    1. Integrative Activity 6.3: Writing a Case Note
    2. Group (task or treatment) note
    3. Program/Project Report
    4. Meeting Minutes
    5. Newsletter Article
    6. Agency Fliers
    7. Letter to the Editor

V. Foundational Roles
  a. Integrative Activity 3.2: Identifying Foundational Roles of Social Work in Field
    1. Broker
      a. Community Resources—Identify and describe three community resources you used as referrals
    2. Advocate
    3. Educator
    4. Facilitator
    5. Mediator
    6. Counselor

VI. Planned Change Process
  a. Integrative Activity 10.1: The Phases of the Planned Change Process in Field
  b. Integrative Activity 10.5: The Planned Change Case Analysis
  c. Phases of the Planned Change Process
    1. Intake and Engagement
      a. Intake
    2. Assessment/Data Collection/Information Gathering
      a. Multilevel Assessment Worksheet
      b. Integrative Activity 10.2: The Multidimensional/Multilevel Assessment
      c. Agency-based assessment tool (specify)
      d. Ecomap
      e. Genogram
      f. Community Assessment
      g. Social History
      h. Research
    3. Planning/Contracting
      a. Integrative Activity 10.4: Developing and Implementing Multilevel Plans
      b. Field Education Learning Plan
      c. Client Individualized Service Plan (ISP)
      d. Group (task or treatment) goals
      e. Program/project goals
    4. Implementation/Monitoring
      a. Integrative Activity 10.3: Identifying Theoretical Perspectives, Practice Models and Commonly Utilized Interventions in Field
      b. Integrative Activity 10.4: Developing and Implementing Multilevel Plans

5. Evaluation
    a. Individual Client Evaluation
    b. Group evaluation
    c. Program evaluation
    d. Client satisfaction survey
6. Termination
    a. Discharge summary
    b. Closing note
    c. Transfer summary
    d. Final report

VII. Policy
    a. Integrative Activity 8.4: Policy Analysis and Practice
    b. Copy(ies) of Agency/Local/State/Federal Policy(ies)

VIII. Research
    a. Research Paper
    b. Agency-based Research
    c. Integrative Activity 9.2: The Literature Review

IX. Professional Development
    a. Résumé
    b. Ethics analysis
    c. Ethical dilemma
    d. Membership
    e. Awards
    f. Integrative Activity 12.1: Professional Development of Self Capstone Paper

X. Other

Note: All elements in the portfolio must maintain confidentiality either through blacking out confidential information or creating elements without any identifying information. It is critically important to discuss this with your field instructor.

THE ROLE OF REFLECTION IN FIELD

To achieve both of the goals identified in the conceptualization of generalist field education—socialization to the profession and integration of the classroom content with the practice experiences of field—you will need to develop the skill of reflection.

    Canada and Furman (1999) emphasize being reflective as a critical part of both personal and professional growth and state that, "Personal engagement in learning is a transformative experience that requires reflectivity, the practice of introspective self-reflection about how one's inner life reflects on the outer world" (p. xxi). They relate reflection specifically to what they call, "reflective reading" and state that the prerequisite is ". . . silence—that is, quieting in order to know oneself, the inner stirrings of the heart, and the discerning wisdom of the intellect" (Canada & Furman, p. xxi). They go on to explain that reflective silence requires "a willingness to become introspective, to 'get centered,' and to pay gentle consistent attention to oneself and one's situation" (Canada & Furman, p. xxi).

    This useful concept when applied to field education is better called reflective experiencing (Larkin, 2010), which emphasizes the experiential nature of field education. Canada and Furman (1999) discuss the importance of building this skill through being

EP 2.1.1b

regular, consistent, and disciplined. It is important to set a time for reflection and keep to it by building it into your day or week.

Remember, the overall purpose of reflection and journal writing is to enable you to step back and take a longer, more integrated view of your field experiences. This is particularly important given that students are often practicing in hectic, chaotic, and high-paced settings where days can go by before they can "come up for air." In these types of situations, it is not uncommon for students to report that they don't even know what they did all week except that it was crazy. Or on the other hand, a student may find him- or herself engaged in what can seem to be a "boring" or mundane task and, by neglecting reflection, miss the learning opportunity present in the task. Making a commitment to regular and disciplined reflection becomes critically important to your development as a social worker. As Kiser (2008) states, "You might think of experience without reflection as being somewhat like an unread book sitting on a shelf, or perhaps a book that you have quickly scanned but not carefully read, understood, or thought about" (p. 70). My goal is to help you turn your field experiences into ones that resemble a well-read book, one that shows signs of study, with turned-down corners; fanned pages; items highlighted, underlined, and circled; and extensive notation in the margins. This is the point where field comes to life.

When writing field journals, it is important to go beyond the restating of events. Although setting the stage is helpful, your writing should be more than a blow-by-blow account of the day or a list of activities. The journal entry should express the thinking, feeling, and doing aspects of your field experiences. Reflection and journal writing are skills that do not come easy for all students; you may need to work on developing them. For help in getting started with your reflection and journal writing, see Integrative Activity 1.3: The Field Journal. This handout provides several categories you can select to reflect on.

INTEGRATIVE ACTIVITY   1.3

The Field Journal

Purpose: The purpose of this integrative activity is to provide some guidelines and suggested areas of reflection that will assist you in the development of your critical-thinking skills through the process of writing reflection journals. It is important to note that writing reflection journals is a skill; you need to determine how easily journal writing comes to you. The guidelines provided are structural in nature and may be all that you need. If that is not the case, consider the suggested areas of reflection that you can focus on in the context of a field experience, which can provide inspiration or a more structured approach when you write your reflection journals.

Directions: Read and follow these guidelines:

1. Find a quiet place and get comfortable.
2. Write legibly or type your journal entry.
3. Although the length is not as important as the time spent and the content, a general guideline is as follows: a minimum of 3–4 pages handwritten or 2–3 typed pages (standard font and margins).
4. The reflection journal is for you. It is a place to process your experiences, ask questions, and explore your thoughts and feelings about specific content areas, the field process, field experiences, and general questions concerning field.
5. If you hand in your journals and receive feedback, read the comments. One of the purposes of the feedback is to improve *your* journal writing skills so that *you* will get the most from this learning task.

Suggested Reflection Areas: Select one significant event or experience of field and explore it, addressing any, all, or one to two of the following specific areas that apply:

1. **Placement Experience:** Describe what happened; identify the significant events, including successes, concerns, and challenges.
2. **Self-Awareness:** What were you feeling, thinking, and doing about the situation?
3. **Diversity Issues:** What diversity issues, if any, were present in relation to this event, and how did you deal with them?
4. **Legal and Ethical Concerns:** What significant legal or ethical issues are there in relation to this situation, and what did you do regarding them?
5. **Organizational or Systemic Concerns:** What are the significant organizational or systems concerns or issues in relation to this event, and what did you do to address them? Include peer and coworker relationships and interactions.
6. **Supervision:** What was discussed in supervision about this experience? What did you think about how the supervisory meeting went? What did you do with the information?
7. **Learning:** What did you learn from this experience about yourself, agency, client, supervisor, etc.?
8. **Additional Observations:**

FINAL THOUGHTS ON THE IMPORTANCE OF FIELD

Field education is a significant learning experience because it is real life, or the living classroom. This means you will have the opportunity to get out of the classroom and work with real client systems in an agency under the supervision of a practicing social worker. Field education is also an opportunity to "do" while still being a student. Students are usually excited to have an opportunity to practice what they have learned or are still learning in the classroom. Furthermore, the role of a student has interesting qualities of its own.

As a student you have a unique opportunity to experience a practice setting in a way that you could never experience without being a student. That is, in many ways you are an insider and outsider at the same time. This provides a unique perspective that will give rise to many important observations. These important observations also often become tough questions about why something is the way that it is or why something is done a certain way. Do not be afraid to ask the tough questions, as they often lead to interesting tasks and accomplishments on the part of the student.

Suggested Field Tasks

- Identify key players and the role of each according to the learning triangle (i.e., field instructor, field director, faculty field liaison).
- Determine title and role as a student.
- Use reflection to explore role, tasks, and experiences of field.

Competency Notes

The following identifies where the CSWE *EPAS* (2008) Educational Policy (EP) and practice behaviors are discussed in the chapter.

EP 2.1.1–2.1.10 Social workers must be aware of the core competencies and practice behaviors necessary to function as a competent professional.

EP 2.1.1c Attend to professional roles and boundaries (p. 16): Social workers must develop an understanding of the professional roles and boundaries of professional social work practice.

EP 2.1.1d Demonstrate professional demeanor in behavior, appearance, and communication (p. 19): Social workers must develop an understanding of and demonstrate competence in professional behavior.

EP 2.1.3a Distinguish, appraise, and integrate multiple sources of knowledge, including research-based knowledge, and practice wisdom (p. 20): Social workers must develop the skills necessary to integrate multiple sources of information into their practice.

EP 2.1.1b Practice personal reflection and self-correction to assure continual professional development (p. 23): Social workers must develop the skill of reflection to analyze practice experiences and develop as a competent professional social worker.

References

Barretti, M. (2004). The professional socialization of undergraduate social work students. *The Journal of Baccalaureate Social Work, 9,* 10–30.

Bogo, M. (2010). *Achieving competence in social work through field education.* Toronto: University of Toronto Press.

Cochran, S., & Hanley, M. (1999). *Learning through field.* Boston: Allyn and Bacon.

Council on Social Work Education. (2008). *Educational policy and accreditation standards.* Alexandria, VA: Council on Social Work Education.

Canda, E. R., & Furman, L. D. (1999). *Spiritual diversity in social work practice: The heart of helping.* New York: The Free Press.

Cournoyer, B., & Stanley, M. (2002). *The social work portfolio: Planning, assessing and document-ing lifelong learning in a dynamic profession.* Pacific Grove, CA: Brooks/Cole.

DuBois, B., & Miley, K. (2005). *Social work: An empowering profession.* Boston: Allyn and Bacon.

Garner, J. (2006). Empowerment in social work field education: Examining triadic aspects of empowerment in the education process of the social work field student. *The Journal of Baccalaureate Social Work, 12*(1), 237–260.

Fortune, A. E. (1994). Field education. In F. J. Reamer(Ed.), *The foundations of social work Knowledge* (pp. 151–194). New York: Columbia University Press.

Jenkins, L. E., & Sheafor, B. W. (1982). An overview of social work field instruction. In B. W. Sheafor, & L. E. Jenkins (Eds.), *Quality field instruction in social work.* White Plains, NY: Longman.

Johnson, L., & Yanca, S. (2007). *Social work practice: A generalist approach.* Boston: Allyn and Bacon.

Kadushin, A. (1991). Introduction. In Dean Schneck, Bart Grossman, & Urania Glassman (Eds.), *Field education in social work: Contemporary issues and trends.* Iowa: Kendall/Hunt Publish-ing Co.

Kirst-Ashman, K., & Hull Jr., G (2006). *Understanding generalist practice* (4th ed.) Pacific Grove, CA: Brooks/Cole.

Kiser, P. (2008). *The human services internship: getting the most from your experience* (2nd ed.) Belmont, CA: Thomson Brooks/Cole.

Larkin, S. (2010). Spiritually sensitive professional development of self: A curricular module for field education. *Social Work and Christianity, 37*(4), 446–466.

Leighninger, L. (2000). *Creating a new profession: The beginnings of social work education in the United States.* Alexandria, VA: Council on Social Work Education, Inc.

Miley, K., O'Melia, M., & DuBois, B. (2007). *Generalist social work practice: An empowering approach.* Boston: Allyn and Bacon.

Reamer, F. (1994). *The foundations of social work knowledge.* New York: Columbia University Press.

Riser, E. (1999). Student practice portfolios: Integrating diversity and learning in the field experience. *Arete, 23*(1), 89–96.

Schatz, M. S., Jenkins, L. E., & Sheafor, B. W. (1990). Milford refined: A model of initial and advanced generalist social work. *Journal of Social Work Education, 26*(3), 217.

Schatz, M. S., & Simon, S. (1999). The portfolio approach for generalist social work practice: A successful tool for students in field education. *The Journal of Baccalaureate Social Work, 5*(1), 99.

Schneck, D., Grossman, B., & Glassman, U. (eds). (1991). *Field education in social work: Contemporary issues and trends.* Iowa: Kendall/Hunt Publishing Co.

Sherer, M., & Peleg-Oren, N. (2005). Differences of teachers', field instructors', and students' views on job analysis of social work students. *Journal of Social Work Education, 41*(2), 315.

Valentine, D. P. (2004). Field education: Exploring the future, expanding the vision. *Journal of Social Work Education, 40*(1), 3.

Wayne, J., Bogo, M., & Raskin, M. (2006). The need for radical change in field education. *Journal of Social Work Education, 42*(1), 161.

Wolk, J. L., & Wertheimer, M. R. (1999). Generalist practice vs. case management: An accreditation contradiction. *Journal of Social Work Education, 35*(1), 101.

CHAPTER 2

The Organization: Orientation and Training

The first few days at your organization are very important because many critical things need to happen for you to maximize your opportunities and have a successful field education experience. The purpose of this chapter is to provide you with the necessary resources to begin your field placement successfully. In this chapter, you will focus on two important topics: first, the organization and its impact on your learning, and second, your orientation and training plan, with specific emphasis on the role of curriculum in orientation and training.

THE ORGANIZATION

The organization you have selected to serve as your field site is a very important and often underemphasized aspect of your learning experience in two ways. First, your professional socialization to the profession depends on affiliation with an agency, your field instructor, agency peers, and other professional organizations you interact with. Second, your individual development as a social worker absolutely will be impacted by the agency, meaning the type of services, culture, and practices of your agency will contribute to who you become as a social worker. So it is helpful to consider the type and culture of your placement agency and the impact those factors can have on your learning, your experience of social work as a profession, and the type of social work practiced in the agency.

Student-in-Organization

Person-in-environment is a long-held foundational concept of social work practice that considers the reciprocal nature and interplay of people and their environments and "sets social work apart from other helping professions" (Sheafor and Horejsi, 2008, p. 8). This concept is useful when applied to your field education experience and requires you to adopt a student-in-organization perspective.

The student-in-organization perspective considers the reciprocal nature and interplay of you the student with your organization. The perspective suggests that your interaction with the organization will shape your field education experience and that in turn, you likely will impact your organization.

The significance of the student-in-organization perspective can best be understood by considering various aspects of an organization. For instance, the type of agency you selected may be significant. For example, if you selected a large bureaucracy, there may be multiple layers of authority and a complex decision-making process. There may also be extensive paperwork, and your role as the social work student may have firm boundaries. The experience of a student in a large, bureaucratic organization will be much different than that of a colleague whose agency is small, has only one or two levels of authority and decision making, and where the student may be able to be fully integrated not only at the service provision level but also in decision making. One is not necessarily preferable over the other, but it is important to consider the potential impact of the organization on your learning. Furthermore, the culture, role of the social worker, services, and even the leadership style of the director can impact you and your learning.

EP 2.1.9a

What I have found fascinating about working with the same agencies and field instructors year after year is how much the organization can impact a student. For instance, one year I had a student placed at an agency who began to struggle with completing the necessary tasks and started questioning the work of the agency. Things became so difficult for the student that he even questioned whether social work was the right profession for him. After a long and involved process, which included working directly with the student and the field instructor, it was mutually agreed that the student would switch placements.

In the second setting, the student thrived. It became clear that the student needed a more structured setting with clearly defined roles and tasks, which had not been present in the first setting due to the nature of the agency's work. It was fascinating to observe the same student in two very different agencies doing very different work and hear his account of how he felt each agency positively and negatively impacted his ability to learn. It is important to note that the first setting was an excellent setting with a highly competent field instructor and where previous students had been successful. I remember discussing this observation with both the student and the field instructor. Each of us realized that the interplay between the agency, the role and services, and the student definitely impacts the learning and in this case, impacted the student's ability to demonstrate specific social work skills.

Thus it will be important for you to explore your initial observations and reaction to your agency and reflect on the impact the agency may have on you and your learning, as well as the impact you can have on your agency. To prepare for this reflection, spend your first day or two observing your organization. Pay attention to everything: notice the flow of the day; the interaction between the workers, supervisors and peers, and the workers and clients; hang out in the break room and listen to what the staff are saying and the tone; and last, pay attention to how you feel in the setting itself. Once you have engaged in this observation, consider Reflection Question 2.1.

REFLECTION QUESTION 2.1

Given your initial impressions of the agency based on your observation day(s) and reflecting on the student-in-organization perspective, what did you notice? How would you describe the agency? What impact do you think the agency will have on you, your learning, and your development as a social worker? Similarly, reflect on what impact you think you may have on your agency?

Once you have had a chance to get acquainted with your agency, the next step in orientation and training is to develop your orientation plan. In the following section, you will be introduced to and shown how to develop a multilevel orientation plan to help you gain your bearings in your new agency.

MULTILEVEL ORIENTATION

The first step is to discuss the plan for your orientation with your field instructor. To develop a successful orientation plan, it is recommended to take a multilevel approach that considers orientation at the individual, agency, and larger system levels. Integrative Activity 2.1: Orientation and Training provides an excellent overview of orientation that you can follow as you move through the orientation process. This overview identifies several broad areas to consider, along with useful questions to discuss with your field instructor.

Individual Level

At the individual level, consider those things you need to discuss and negotiate with your field instructor. For instance, one of the first things is to get to know each other. This discussion is a type of introduction. Although you most likely interviewed with your field instructor during the placement process, it is important to begin to develop a strong working relationship now that you are in the field. The relationship with your field instructor is especially important given that he or she is the person you will be working closely with and who will be evaluating you throughout your field experience at the agency. In preparation for this discussion, review Integrative Activity 2.1 to assemble a list of useful questions.

First of all, interview your field instructor and ask that individual to share his or her background. This is a wonderful opportunity to learn about your field instructor's journey to the profession. This can include asking the field instructor where he or she went to school; what he or she liked and disliked about the education, specifically focusing on the field experience; and why the individual wanted to be a field instructor. Next, share your background. This can include what brought you to social work, your interest in the agency, and the experiences you bring to the agency.

Next, discuss your learning style and field instructor's teaching style. This is important to determine the fit between the two. If you are a "doer" for instance, and your field instructor thinks you need to go through a structured learning process that includes reading and verbal discussion prior to "doing," this might be frustrating. On the flip side, perhaps you like to read, discuss, practice, and prepare before you "do," but your field instructor believes that it is best for you to "get out there," complete a task, and then interweave the training into the discussion of the task. Either of these conflicting styles could become frustrating and even create problems for you and your field instructor. That being said, there may be times when there is not a perfect match between your learning style and your field instructor's teaching style.

For example, I had a student who was very hands-on and described her learning style as that of a "doer." This student was in a placement site where the field instructor felt there needed to be a comprehensive orientation and training plan that covered several topic areas and insisted this be completed prior to beginning work as a case manager.

After discussing the situation with both the student and field instructor, it became clear that they had not discussed their learning and teaching styles and that the mismatch was becoming problematic.

I encouraged them to discuss what was going on. The student could explain that the best plan needed to include "doing" as a part of orientation and training, and the field instructor could explain that the fast-paced nature of the setting and the complex needs of the clients meant that "doing" should come after a comprehensive orientation and training plan that would improve the student's overall experience. So they negotiated a plan that increased the pace and included more direct observation. Once the orientation and training plan was completed, the student could begin working as a case manager, and it became clear to both that the modified plan worked well. The student realized she could provide a more effective service as a case manager due to being well oriented and trained. And the field instructor realized that for this student, having some experience was necessary to give the content a context. What became a situation that needed intervention could have been avoided had the student and field instructor discussed and negotiated the training plan early in the placement. As you can see, it is important to discuss your learning style and learn about your field instructor's teaching style prior to beginning the work of field.

Agency Level

At the agency level, orientation activities are focused on the organization. This starts with the five Ws: *who, what, where, when,* and *why.* The Who involves meeting everyone and getting to know each member of the staff. Ask your field instructor the easiest way to meet everyone. The introductions can be done at a staff meeting or more informally by walking around the office. Also, ask for the organizational chart. Familiarizing yourself with the organizational chart is part of integrative activity 2.2 Agency Analysis, which will be discussed in more detail later and will help you begin to organize your understanding of who is who. Obviously, you and your field instructor need to consider the size of your agency and determine what is needed. If you are in a very large agency's program, you may not need to know everyone within the entire organization. So focus your initial introductions on those at your program. If you are in a small agency, you may be able to meet everyone on your first day.

The What focuses on several different things that are important for you to know. First and foremost, what is the agency's mission? What is the history of the agency? What does the agency do? What are the agency's funding sources? What do each of the staff members you met during the Who phase do at the agency? It is important to note that the organizational chart will also help you with this. What are the overarching policies and procedures of the agency? What will be your role and primary task(s)? What are your field instructor's expectations of you? What should you wear? Last, what are you hoping to accomplish? All of these questions will help you develop competence in two important areas: (1) understanding your role and (2) understanding the context of your agency such as the agency's history and mission and how they impact practice.

EP 2.1.1c, d
EP 2.1.9a

The Where involves where everything is and goes. This can include the bathroom, client records, office supplies, and kitchen. Also find out where your office will be and where you can keep academic- and agency-based work. Last, make sure to discuss any policies and procedures that go along with the Where.

The When includes the timing of the work tasks. This might involve important training activities, such as completing an agency-based orientation or being trained on a particular client documentation program prior to working with clients. This may also involve the timing of paperwork. For instance, if you will be required to write case notes, the agency may have a policy that all case notes need to be completed within 24 hours of the delivery of the service. Thus you and your field instructor will need to build in time to discuss the process and provide you with sufficient training to meet this expectation. Also, find out when important regularly scheduled agency-based meetings occur, such as the staff meeting. Finally and most important, ask when you will have your supervision session.

The last thing to consider as you begin your field placement is the Why. I have found that this is an important and often missed aspect of orientation. It has been my experience that the more a student understands why things at the agency are done the way they are, the easier it is for the student to manage the demands of field and thus improve overall learning. So don't be afraid to ask questions. Also, remember that your field instructor may have been doing a certain procedure for a long time and most likely it has become second nature. Therefore, the field instructor may not even think about why he or she does it the way that they do. So make sure you ask the important and even seemingly mundane questions.

EP 2.1.3a

I know many students who have asked important questions and as a result challenged the agency to see their services or practices in a new light. For example, I recall a student who had to complete three different forms at intake that all gathered similar information. During a staff meeting, the student asked why there wasn't just one central form that could gather all the needed information at one time. The social workers in the agency considered this and asked the student to work on a mock-up of such a form. The student was happy to engage in this macro-level task, particularly since he had brought this up in the first place. As a result, the forms were condensed into one, which met all the various funders' needs and was more client friendly. This positive change came as the result of a simple question.

Larger System Level

The last area of the multilevel orientation is to consider the larger system. First, this involves understanding the overall agency in which your program exists. For instance, one of the sites I work with is a program within an agency that has over 20 programs; so it is important to understand the larger agency as a whole. By understanding your agency as a whole, you can better identify potential learning opportunities to include in your learning plan, which will be discussed in detail in Chapter 6.

EP 2.1.9a

Another important area to explore is the social service system your agency may be intricately connected to. For instance, if you are doing your placement at the local prosecutor's office as a guardian ad litem, it is critically important to understand the relationship between the prosecutor's office and the county department of children's protective services as well as the larger child welfare system. This may also include understanding any policy or legislation that directly impacts your services, such as the Child Abuse Prevention and Treatment Act, which specifies various child welfare services.

Last, reflect on the community or neighborhood in which your agency resides and/or serves. You may need to understand important things about the community to be effective in your placement site.

By completing Integrative Activity 2.1: Orientation and Training, you will have the opportunity to conduct a comprehensive, multilevel orientation. The outcome should be that you will feel grounded in your agency and better positioned to reap all the possible benefits from your placement site.

INTEGRATIVE ACTIVITY 2.1

Orientation and Training

Purpose: The purpose of this integrative activity is to provide a foundation for developing a multilevel orientation and training plan. The following framework includes general things for you to consider as well as specific questions to discuss with your field instructor.

Directions: First consider the general areas as you plan your orientation, and then discuss the specific questions offered.

Multilevel Orientation: In order to have a successful field experience, it is important to plan a comprehensive and successful orientation and training plan. Thus first consider the following large overarching areas and then review each specific area with your field instructor.
- Develop a comprehensive orientation plan.
- Engage your field instructor, and develop the supervisory relationship.
- Meet and join with staff.
- Engage clients.
- Develop a comprehensive training plan.
- Identify role and primary tasks.
- Review agency policies and procedures.
- Review safety.
- Discuss the limits of your role as a social work student and any limits to tasks.

Individual Level

1. Get to know your field instructor.
   a. What attracted you to social work?
   b. Where did you go to school?
   c. What did you like and dislike about your education, particularly your field experience?
   d. Why did you want to be a field instructor?
   e. What is your teaching style?
2. Share your background with your field instructor, and answer all questions 1a–1d that apply. For 1e, focus on your learning style.

Agency Level

1. Does the agency have a structured orientation program?
   a. If so, can I attend?
   b. If not, what do I need to know and how will my orientation be handled?
2. Discuss the five Ws: *who, what, where, when,* and *why.*
   Who—meet everyone
   What—review the mission and history, all services and programs offered by agency, funding, roles, tasks of student, policies and procedures, what everyone does, expectations, dress, what you the student want to accomplish
   Where—discuss the location of the bathroom, copier, break room, copy paper, client files, student office, student belongings, etc.
   When—timelines for tasks, paperwork, supervision session, important agency meetings, especially staff meeting
   Why—discuss anything you don't understand, rationale for things, why things are done the way they are, etc.; may need to be revisited overtime, particularly as you develop more skills and engage in more complex tasks

Larger System Level

Learn about:

1. Overall agency
2. Interaction of agency with social service system
3. Policies and legislation that are important to agency services
4. Community or neighborhood issues that impact agency

Training: To have a successful placement, it is critical that you are trained on the tasks you will be performing in your agency. Develop a training plan using the following guidelines:

1. Review the five-step training plan.
2. Identify the specific training needs.
3. Develop plan for training; include observation, doing while under observation, and independent work in plan.
4. Engage in and discuss training.
5. Revisit training needs through the placement.

AGENCY ANALYSIS

EP 2.1.1a, c, d
EP 2.1.3a
EP 2.1.9a

An interesting learning task to engage in at the completion of your multilevel orientation is to conduct an agency analysis. Integrative Activity 2.2 will help you conduct your agency analysis. First, however, it is worth discussing why doing your own agency analysis is essential to your work in field.

Conducting an agency analysis will help you develop and demonstrate the competence of critical thinking through your ability to integrate and apply what you have learned about organizations, such as organizational theory, to an analysis of your agency. Second, it relates to the competence of developing the ability to function within your agency, because the better informed you are about your agency, the better you can represent your agency. Third, it enables you to consider the contexts that shape practice by reflecting on the impact your agency has on the larger system and the impact the larger system has on your agency. Last, the more you know and understand about your agency, the better you can serve your clients and advocate client access to services. Thus Integrative Activity 2.2: Agency Analysis will enable you to synthesize the information you gathered during orientation and develop a comprehensive understanding of your agency.

INTEGRATIVE ACTIVITY 2.2

Agency Analysis

Purpose: The purpose of this integrative activity is to assist you in the process of learning about and analyzing your field agency. It is very important to have a complete understanding of your agency, including the programs and services, funding, and history. This knowledge will enable you to function more successfully as a member of the organization and better serve your clients. In addition, it is helpful to think critically about the purpose, structure, and function of your organization and answer the fundamental question: Is this agency meeting its mission?

Directions: Gather information about each area, and once you have gathered all information, discuss your analysis of your agency in supervision with your field instructor. You may need to contact others in your agency to gather the needed information.

1. Gather the following information about your agency:
   - Mission, goals, and objectives
   - History
   - Philosophy, values, and culture
   - Type of organization
   - Programs and services offered
   - Funding base, including a budget
   - Organizational structure (obtain or create an organizational chart and locate self on chart)
   - Supervision function and structure for staff
   - Relationship of agency to larger social service system
   - Current issues impacting the agency
   - Future direction of agency
   - Oversight or accrediting bodies, and impact on services
   - Impact of policy(ies) on agency
   - Cultural competence of agency and staff
2. Overall reflection and analysis (answer the questions)
   - Is the agency meeting its mission?
   - What do think about the agency? What surprised you?
   - How does the agency's history relate to the history of the profession?
   - Based on your knowledge of organizational theory, how would you conceptualize how your organization functions?
   - What are the agency's strengths?
   - What are the agency's blind spots?
   - If you were in charge, is there anything you would do differently? If no, why? If yes, what and how?

THE ROLE OF CURRICULUM IN ORIENTATION

An important part of the orientation process is orientating to the academic goals of field education in the context of your particular field agency. The most important is the integration of theory and practice. This is accomplished by first developing the ability to link the classroom curriculum to the practice tasks of the agency, and then demonstrating the core competencies and practice behaviors identified by your program in your field agency.

Generalist field education is grounded in, integrates, and impacts curriculum. On the one hand, this is obvious: students in a social work program take various classes and engage in field education to complete their degree, making both the classroom and field curriculum critical components of social work education. However, there can be a gap between the front loading of theories taught in the classroom and the practice experiences of field that typically but not always come later (Lam, 2004), meaning students can struggle with applying their classroom learning in field. This same gap can also occur in programs where field and classroom courses run concurrently. The linkage of the classroom content to the field and the field to the classroom is often not as clear as you might have first imagined.

Therefore, to address this issue and increase the ability of students to link classroom content to field, discuss and review your curriculum with your field instructor. Integrative Activity 2.3: Curriculum Review, is one way to ground you and your field instructor in your program's curriculum and the content you are learning. In social work education, a particular program's course work is the curriculum, and reflects the values and specific culture of that school.

EP 2.1.1e;
EP 2.1.3a

Three types of curriculum are important to discuss. The first is foundation curriculum, which are the courses, including content and outcomes, taken prior to entering field. The second is concurrent curriculum, which refers to the courses, including content and outcomes, taken while in field. The third type is specialized curriculum, which is knowledge, values, and skills that are specific to your practice setting. The specialized curriculum that you identify may not have been a part of your program's curriculum and will need to be acquired during the field experience. Integrative Activity 2.3: Curriculum Review provides an opportunity to plan with your field instructor how that information will be learned. For example, content may be presented in the supervision session or by attending agency- or community-based trainings, reading books, conducting a literature review, and last, by watching training videos. Identifying and planning for developing specialized knowledge will be the first step in developing your ability to engage in career-long learning and an important part of being a professional social worker.

A useful resource in the curriculum review process is to look over your course syllabi. The syllabi will provide useful information such as course objectives and accreditation standards, and it may even outline specific core competencies and practice behaviors targeted by that course. Also, as a part of the accreditation process, many programs develop curricular maps, which provide a comprehensive understanding of the course and the course objectives, as well as the core competencies and practice behaviors targeted by each course. Ask your field director if your program has such a resource for you to review and offer in your discussion with your field instructor.

The review of curriculum will ground you and your field instructor and provide an opportunity to identify the course content and outcomes that will serve as the foundation to your field experience. This activity will also identify any gaps in your learning and provide an opportunity to develop a plan for learning specialized curriculum. Without you and your field instructor being firmly grounded in your curriculum, it will be more difficult to apply the curriculum to the tasks of field. The curriculum review also organizes what can be overwhelming and often lost prior to entering field. As students enter field, they are often simultaneously overwhelmed with curricular content and anxious about their ability to enter field and practice. Yet they are equally anxious to "get to work" and often resistant to more "classroom" learning. This challenging set of dynamics requires a clear vision for how to approach the field experience to achieve the goals of field education.

The curriculum review task also serves an important role in the engagement process between you and your field instructor. Having the opportunity to inform your field instructor about something you know, your course work, learning, and thoughts about how that course work can be integrated into the setting, provides an opportunity for you to share your expertise. This comes at a time when you may understandably feel in over your head. One question I love to have students ask their field instructor during this process is, "What course(s) did you enjoy the most and why"? Also ask in what, if any, content areas the field instructor felt he or she wasn't prepared enough in and how he or she dealt with that in field practice.

This discussion is also helpful for your field instructor who may have been out of the classroom for some time and may work with several schools that have different course offerings. This will help your field instructor become grounded in an area that is critically important to his or her ability to assist you in linking curriculum and practice.

As you can see, this part of orientation becomes a win-win because this task can help alleviate the initial anxiety you may feel in the beginning of the field experience as well as the anxiety your field instructor may feel about how to help you meet the goal of linking curriculum to practice.

INTEGRATIVE ACTIVITY **2.3**

Curriculum Review

Purpose: The purpose of this integrative activity is twofold: (1) to ground you and your field instructor in your program's curriculum by identifying courses in the areas of foundation and concurrent as well as identifying the specialized knowledge needs and plan for achieving that knowledge, and (2) to provide a foundation for later task analysis.

Directions: First, in the areas of foundation curriculum and concurrent curriculum, review your program's social work courses, and identify the learning outcomes of those courses. Then identify how those learning outcomes can be directly applied to your practice at your field agency. Second, in the area of specialized learning, identify the plan for how you will develop the knowledge, values, and skills specific to your practice in field. Note: specialized curriculum tasks can be included on your learning plan.

1. **Foundation Curriculum**—Social work courses taken prior to entering field

Courses Taken:	Learning Outcomes:	Application to Field:

2. **Concurrent Curriculum**—Social work courses to be taken during field

Courses to Be Taken:	Projected Learning Outcome:	Application to Field:

3. **Specialized Curriculum**—Content specific to field site

Content to Be Learned at Field Site:	Projected Learning Outcome:	Plan/Application to Field:

THE TRAINING PLAN

EP 2.1.1c

Once you have begun your orientation process, you need to consider the plan for your training. Refer back to Integrative Activity 2.1: Orientation and Training, which provides a section on training to guide your discussion with your field instructor. This is an equally important discussion because your training is the best introduction to what social work practice entails at your agency and more specifically your role within the agency. The lack of effective training can become a barrier to your learning in one of two ways. First, it can prevent you from being able to perform an important practice task, and second, it can compromise your ability to learn from the task.

For instance, if you are in a placement setting where you provide group treatment but have not been adequately trained to cofacilitate or independently run a group, you may not be able to develop or demonstrate competence as a group facilitator. Furthermore, you may even end up feeling overwhelmed, be unclear about what you are doing, and worse, lose your confidence. All of this can prevent you from achieving the necessary competencies related to this task. Thus it is important to discuss the plan for your

Step 1	**Identify Tasks**
Step 2	**Assess Baseline Competence** Using a 5-point scale with 1 = Not at all Competent and 5 = Completely Competent, assess your level of competence for all tasks identified by the field instructor that require training. This rating will be based on past work, volunteer experience, and degree of specialization of task.
Step 3	**Observe Task** Shadow field instructor and agency peers engaging in identified tasks.
Step 4	**Do Task under Direct Observation**
Step 5	**Do Task Independently** Reassess level of competence, report in supervision, and revisit any necessary steps throughout the placement.

Figure 2.1 Five-Step Training Plan

training as a group facilitator. Also, discuss with your field instructor the expectations for your level of competence. For instance, if you have never attended or facilitated a treatment or task group, it would be unrealistic to expect that you could independently run an effective group right away. The expectation should be to observe, cofacilitate, develop, and demonstrate a foundational understanding of group work, and last, facilitate a group session on your own under observation. This entire training process would then culminate in you facilitating group sessions on your own.

That being said, the pace and process of this training plan should be discussed and negotiated with your field instructor and be very clear to you. This will enable you to accomplish an important task and demonstrate the corresponding practice behaviors. Far too often, I see students being thrown into tasks with no discussion about the plan for training, which results in the learning being compromised. To assist you in this process, I recommend following a Five-Step Training Plan like the one outlined in Figure 2.1. If your agency has a different training plan in place, be sure to ask questions until you understand and feel comfortable with it.

Monitoring your training is an ongoing process as you move from task to task and as your skill and ability level develops over time in your agency. I encourage you to discuss your training needs during the first few days each semester in conjunction with putting your learning plan together, which will be discussed in Chapter 3.

Suggested Field Tasks

- Review related course work (complete Integrative Activity: 2.1 Curriculum Review).
- Engage in orientation and training.
- Tour agency.
- Introduce self to all staff.
- Examine and analyze mission, goals and objectives, programs and services, history, funding, and organizational structure and relate to history of profession and organizational theory.
- Determine title.
- Discuss culture of agency.
- Identify backup when FI is not available.
- Set up work space.

- Obtain ID/computer/voice mail access.
- Identify work schedule.
- Discuss and follow dress code.
- Demonstrate ability to conceptualize practice.
- Identify issues impacting agency practice at the organizational, community, and societal levels.
- Attend agency-based, community, or campus trainings and events.

Competency Notes

The following identifies where the CSWE *EPAS* (2008) Educational Policy (EP) and practice behaviors are discussed in the chapter.

EP 2.1.1a Advocate for client access to the services of social work (p. 34): Social workers must be able to analyze an agency and develop an understanding of that agency and how it works within a broader context. This is important in competently providing clients with access to services.

EP 2.1.1c Attend to professional roles and boundaries (pp. 31, 34, 38): By developing an understanding of the services and role(s) of the social worker in an agency, you will develop an understanding of the professional roles social workers provide within an agency and thus competently provide those roles.

EP 2.1.1d Demonstrate professional demeanor in behavior, appearance, and communication (pp. 31, 34): Social workers need to develop an understanding of the expectations held by an agency for professional behavior in order to be able to demonstrate competence and function as professionals in an agency.

EP2.1.1e Engage in career-long learning (p. 35): Social workers need to develop an understanding of the role of lifelong learning in the development of a competent professional social worker by identifying learning needs specific to the agency and developing a plan for developing competence in the identified knowledge, values, and skills.

EP 2.1.3a Distinguish, appraise, and integrate multiple sources of knowledge, including research-based knowledge and practice wisdom (pp. 32, 34, 35): Social workers need to develop the ability to integrate knowledge acquired in the classroom with knowledge developed as a result of practice.

EP 2.1.9a Continuously discover, appraise, and attend to changing locales, populations, scientific and technological development, and emerging societal trends to provide relevant services (pp. 29, 31, 32, 34): Social workers need to develop an understanding of an agency within the context of its environment and the larger social system and how the agency is impacted by what is going on within and around it, and thus provide services that respond to this context.

References

Cochrane, S. F., & Hanley, M. M. (1999). *Learning through field: A developmental approach.* Needham Heights, MA: Allyn and Bacon.

Lam, D. (2004). Problem based-learning: An integration of theory and field. *Journal of Social Work Education, 40*(3), 371.

Sheafor, B., & Horejsi, C. (2008). *Techniques and guidelines for social work practice.* Boston: Pearson Education, Inc.

CHAPTER 3

The Plan and Pace of Learning in Field

This chapter will explore the plan for and pace of your learning in field. Establishing a plan for your learning is important and begins with drawing up your learning plan. The pace of your learning refers to how slowly or quickly you will move from orientation and training to independent practice and requires that you consider several key concepts and steps.

THE LEARNING PLAN

The learning plan is an important document in several ways. First, the learning plan provides a sense of direction for your learning that ensures you have an effective field experience and ultimately accomplish what you need to by the conclusion of field. Second, the learning plan helps you pace your learning, meaning it will specifically reference tasks that reflect your process as you move from orientation and training to independent practice. For instance, the learning plan will include tasks that reference shadowing, cofacilitating, and ultimately conducting. The language of the task provides a built-in pacing for you to follow. Third, the learning plan assists in the fulfillment of the overall purpose of field, which is threefold:

1. to integrate classroom and field,
2. to become socialized to the profession, and
3. to develop as a generalist ready to practice or apply your generalist training to your advanced practice field experience.

It is important to note that constructing your learning plan is a useful learning experience in its own right because it mirrors the engagement, planning and contracting, and evaluation phases of the planned change process that you will use with your clients. By developing your learning plan you are using and integrating what you have learned in the classroom with an important activity of field. Furthermore, writing a learning plan requires competence in professional writing: you need to be able to develop agreed-upon goals and

EP 2.1.10c
EP 2.1.3c

41

objectives, determine appropriate tasks to meet the goals and objectives, implement strategies identified in the plan, and last, monitor and evaluate your plan, all of which are important skills for a social worker.

This chapter will provide an overview of the information you need to develop your learning plan and instructions for using your learning plan as an educational tool during field. The chapter covers the elements of a learning plan, including writing learning objectives, selecting the tasks and roles you will engage in to meet your objectives, and developing a plan for evaluation. In addition to this, the chapter will discuss how the learning plan can be like a road map throughout field, with opportunities to consider the pace of learning and monitor progress.

Elements of the Learning Plan

As mentioned earlier, certain elements need to go into a learning plan to make it an effective and useful document. A well-constructed learning plan should include

1. the goals and objectives of field,
2. the tasks and roles you will engage in at your site to meet the goals and objectives,
3. a plan for evaluation,
4. demographic information such as your and your field instructor's names, the agency's name, dates of the plan, and perhaps your title, and role, and
5. signatures to document agreement by all involved parties.

To familiarize yourself with your learning plan and identify the preceding elements, review the learning plan required by your program. In all likelihood this document can be found online or in your program's field manual.

Goals and Objectives

EP 2.1.3c
EP 2.1.10c

The first step in developing a learning plan is to identify your goals and objectives for field. The ability to identify goals and objectives is grounded in your knowledge of what goals and objectives are and your skill level in writing them. Knowledge about goals and objectives would fall within the curricular area of practice, specifically the planned change process phase of planning and contracting.

In social work practice, a goal is defined as a, ". . . specific statement of intended outcomes. Goal statements should be clear, meaningful, and attainable. Whenever possible, they should reflect the client's priorities and be stated in the client's own language" (Kagel and Kopels, 2008, p. 69). Obviously, you are not a client, but the ideas reflected in the preceding definition hold true for you in field. That is, the goals you set for field should reflect the intended outcomes of field education. Your goals should be "clear, meaningful, and attainable" (Kagel and Kopels, 2008, p. 69) in your own words and reflect your personal goals and interests. Furthermore, goals are the end result: as you are writing your learning plan, ask yourself what you need and hope to accomplish as a result of field.

Although the terms *goals* and *objectives* are often used interchangeably, they are different. Goals tend to be broad, sweeping statements, where an objective, "is more specific and written in a manner that allows and facilitates measurement and evaluation" (Sheafor and Horejsi, 2008, p. 332). As Sheafor and Horejsi (2008) state, "A properly written objective will answer a five-part question: (1) who . . . (2) will do what . . . (3) to what extent . . . (4) under what conditions . . . (5) by when" (p. 332).

In the context of field, your goals will reflect large overarching outcomes of field education and most often include the use of action-oriented verbs like *to know, to learn, to develop,* and *to demonstrate.* Given that goals tend to be broad and sweeping in their scope, once you have determined the global outcomes of field education, you will then want to break those into smaller, attainable objectives. Objectives, like stepping stones, will help you meet the larger goal, like getting across the river. An objective tends to be smaller in its scope, specific, well defined, concrete, and measurable. To lend each objective concreteness, you need to indicate what you will be doing, how you will do it, and by when. The type of language that is helpful when writing objectives is language that reflects behavior, meaning what you will do. Examples of good action words could include but are not limited to *attend, schedule, participate in, cofacilitate, conduct,* and *write.* Horejsi and Garthwait (1999) state that "a learning objective brings together in a single outcome statement a goal, a description of learning activities, and evaluation criteria" (p. 22). Using this definition as a foundation, look at a possible learning objective for a student:

1. "A goal,"—To learn about the cycle of violence . . .
2. ". . . a description of learning activities"—. . . by reading an article and viewing a video,
3. ". . . and evaluation criteria"— . . . and demonstrate knowledge by presenting content in supervision by end of September and apply knowledge to at least one case by the end of October.

Such a learning objective becomes useful to you and your field instructor in that it is specific and clearly identifies the intended outcome, what you will do to achieve the objective, and provides clarity for how you and your field instructor will evaluate whether or not you met the objective. You and your field instructor can easily measure if you read the article and watched the training video by your ability to present the content and apply the knowledge to a specific case in supervision. Thus having clearly worded objectives takes the mystery out of evaluation in that it enables you and your field instructor to determine that an objective was met or not met.

Now that we have defined goals and objectives and reviewed the components of an objective of learning, the next step is to consider your learning tasks.

Multilevel Learning Tasks

The tasks that a social worker engages in to assist clients in meeting their goals and objectives are critically important to social work practice. Sheafor and Horejsi (2008) define a task as,

> some specified and observable problem-solving action or step that can be evaluated in terms of whether it was achieved or completed. Preferably, a task is an action that can be accomplished in a matter of days or at the most a couple of weeks. A task can be viewed as one of the many steps or short-term activities that must be completed to achieve an objective. (p. 333)

This definition is applicable to field in that you, your field instructor, and field director will all be participating in identifying what you will be doing at the agency to achieve the objectives of learning. The learning tasks will come from a variety of sources. The first source for identifying learning tasks will come from the agency. You need to consider the activities that relate to what the social worker does in the agency. You can determine many of the expected activities by reviewing the current job description of the position with which your role is most closely aligned. By reviewing the job description you will obtain useful information to translate into your learning plan. Additional sources for researching and identifying your learning tasks will come from activities related to the population served and activities that reflect the issues addressed by the agency.

Second, you should consider your own personal interests related to your development as a social worker. Again, reflect on what you would like to get out of the field experience and identify tasks aligned to the work you might do.

Third, you should consult with your field instructor for ideas for possible tasks that may not be readily apparent. For instance, perhaps you can get involved with a special project or current issue that the agency is experiencing, such as research or program evaluation.

Last, look to your program, field director, faculty field liaison, or department faculty for suggested and possibly required learning tasks as well. For instance, many programs require that students complete process recording. The purpose of gathering options from all these sources is to ensure that you are engaging in a comprehensive array of learning tasks.

In addition to identifying the specific learning tasks that you will engage in at your agency, you also need to consider the scope of the learning tasks that you needed to develop as a competent generalist practitioner ready to practice or apply your generalist training to advanced field instruction. As you will recall from Chapter 1, the Generalist Field Education Approach requires students to engage in multilevel tasks. By including multilevel tasks in your learning plan, you ensure that you develop the skills necessary to practice at multiple levels. This is important to prepare you to assume a variety of different types of positions and job responsibilities after you complete your education.

Multilevel tasks fall within four primary levels or areas of practice. The primary levels are micro- (individuals and families), mezzo- (groups, treatment and task), and macro- (organizations, communities, and neighborhoods in addition to large societal and political systems). In addition, given field education's emphasis on socialization and professional development, the last level or area of tasks would be those that contribute to your professional socialization.

Sometimes it is hard to see multilevel tasks for what they are and even harder to take advantage of them if you are not mindful during your field experience. In my experience, this most often occurred when students conducted mezzo, macro, or professional socialization tasks, such as attending staff meetings, engaging in administrative tasks, reading training materials, conducting research, and completing documentation. However, when the task was clearly defined and linked to generalist practice, the same students could see the role the task played in their development as a social worker. As a result, the student developed a better understanding of the depth and breadth of social work practice at all of the multiple levels.

So far, the importance of having multilevel practice experiences has been established; however, in all likelihood, your tasks will be clustered in one or two levels that reflect the services and role of the social worker in the agency, meaning you may have more tasks in one area than the other areas. This is understandable because you probably selected the agency in part due to the services and role of the social worker and had a desire to learn to practice in that particular area. Yet your development and socialization as a generalist practitioner may be hampered if you don't have opportunities to complete tasks at other levels as well.

For example, I had a student at an agency doing primarily micro-level case management services. The student loved the agency and services and was receiving an excellent learning experience. However, the experiences were heavily focused on micro-individual work. As a result of the need to engage in multilevel tasks, the student could identify two mezzo-level learning tasks: (1) cofacilitate a group and (2) conduct educational presentations in the community. These particular services were done by another group of social workers in the agency, so the field instructor had to connect the student with the other social workers. Fortunately it ended up being a fairly easy process to set up the learning tasks. As a result, the student could add two mezzo practice tasks to the learning plan, and to everyone's satisfaction the student reported that the work not only complemented the micro-level case management services, but also helped develop important mezzo practice skills. By the completion of the field experience, the student felt better prepared for what was to come after field.

To facilitate the process of identifying the multilevel learning tasks that you will engage in at your field site, complete Integrative Activity 3.1: Identifying Multilevel Learning Tasks. Once you have identified your multilevel tasks, include them in your learning plan. The list came from several sources, namely; agencies, the literature (Riebschleger and Grettenberger, 2006; Plionis, Bailey-Etta, and Manning, 2002; Hendricks, Finch, and Franks, 2005; Birkenmaier and Berg-Weger, 2007), and input from students, faculty, and field instructors. The list is not exhaustive; you can engage in a task that is not on this list as long as it is a social work task and can be linked to a goal statement.

INTEGRATIVE ACTIVITY   **3.1**

Identifying Multilevel Learning Tasks

Directions: Identify the tasks that you will engage in at your agency by placing a check mark in the box next to each. You must select tasks from all four areas.

Professional Socialization	• Attend supervision. ❑
	• Set supervision session time. ❑
	• Develop and use an agenda. ❑
	• Keep supervision session notes. ❑
	• Orient to agency and field education. ❑
	• Tour agency. ❑
	• Introduce self to all staff. ❑
	• Conduct an agency analysis. ❑
	• Examine mission, goals, and objectives. ❑
	• Learn about programs and services. ❑
	• Learn about funding and review a budget. ❑
	• Review the organizational structure; put self on organizational chart. ❑
	• Obtain and read agency policies and procedures. ❑
	• Review and complete agency paperwork. ❑
	• Complete professional paperwork, such as mileage reimbursement or incident reports. ❑
	• Review client files. ❑
	• Complete case notes. ❑
	• Write reports. ❑
	• Identify title. ❑
	• Identify primary tasks. ❑
	• Set up work space; obtain computer/voice mail access. ❑
	• Identify work schedule. ❑
	• Discuss dress code. ❑

(Continued)

	• Engage in ethical behavior. ❏
	  • Read NASW Code of Ethics and any agency ethical standards. ❏
	  • Identify common ethical dilemmas in practice setting. ❏
	  • Identify and analyze ethical dilemmas using the NASW Code of Ethics. ❏
	  • Conduct ethics analysis of agency practices. ❏
	
	• Develop professional identity. ❏
	  • Join social work club or professional organization, i.e., NASW, community group. ❏
	  • Identify philanthropic activities. ❏
	  • Engage a mentor. ❏
	  • Attend any agency/community/campus trainings/events. ❏
	
	• Engage in self-care activities, and monitor stress and burnout. ❏
	• Complete field paperwork. ❏

Micro—Individuals/Families	• Practice with individuals. ❏
	  • Outreach to clients by telephone or in writing to set up appointments for interviews. ❏
	  • Prep for first contacts, reviewing records. ❏
	  • Conduct intake interviews. ❏
	  • Conduct assessments: ❏
	    • social history ❏
	    • ecomap ❏
	    • genogram ❏
	  • Engage in casework/case management. ❏
	    • Establish a caseload. ❏
	  • Contract with client to develop service plan. ❏
	  • Develop and implement interventions, plans. ❏
	  • Complete documentation. ❏
	  • Make referrals—broker on behalf of clients. ❏
	  • Analyze communication skills. ❏
	    • Complete interview checklist. ❏
	    • Complete process recording. ❏

Mid-/Mezzo—Groups/ Task/ Treatment	• Practice in treatment group settings. ❏
	  • Observe a group/conduct group analysis. ❏
	  • Cofacilitate a support group/conduct group analysis of coleaders. ❏
	  • Gather information to determine client interest in a group—needs assessments. ❏
	  • Develop outline for planning a group. ❏
	  • Develop curriculum/group session activities. ❏
	  • Complete documentation. ❏
	  • Increase knowledge of types of groups/research group skills. ❏
	  • Facilitate group sessions. ❏
	
	• Practice in task group. ❏
	  • Attend TX meeting, interdisciplinary TX meeting. ❏
	  • Attend a task group/join a committee. ❏
	  • Cofacilitate a task group meeting-develop agenda, write minutes, learn *Robert's Rules of Order—Parliamentary Procedure.* ❏
	  • Complete documentation. ❏
	  • Facilitate a task group. ❏

(Continued)

Macro—Organizational Practice/Community Organizing/Policy/Political-Legislative/Research	• Engage in organizational practice. ❑
	  • Participate in fund-raising activities. ❑
	    • Engage in grant writing. ❑
	  • Engage in research activities to support activities of the organization; assist in agency's annual report, auditing. ❑
	  • Explore/participate in program evaluation. ❑
	  • Write flyers, brochures, newsletters regarding agency services or programs. ❑
	  • Attend board meeting. ❑
	  • Analyze one social/agency policy. ❑
	  • Write a policy. ❑
	  • Develop and implement a program. ❑
	
	• Engage in community organizing. ❑
	  • Conduct community needs assessment. ❑
	  • Participate in a community action/coalition group/task force. ❑
	  • Develop agreement to work with another agency, including establishing funding. ❑
	
	• Engage in policy development. ❑
	  • Research legislative history of an existing or proposed program. ❑
	  • Engage in advocacy at the legislative/bureaucratic level. ❑
	  • Prepare and present testimony in support of a policy or program reform. ❑
	
	• Engage in political practice. ❑
	  • Participate in voter registration. ❑
	  • Organize and disseminate information regarding a levy or important issue. ❑
	  • Participate in a campaign. ❑
	    • Canvassing, tabling, phone banking. ❑

This task list was developed using several sources from the literature *Learning to Teach, Teaching to Learn,* by Hendricks, Finch, and Franks, 2005; *The Practicum Companion for Social Work,* by Julie Birkenmaier and Marla Berg-Weger, 2007; and the "Generalist Practice Scale," developed by Riebschleger and Grettenberger, 2006.

If you are asked to complete a task that is not on the list, you will want to determine if it is an appropriate task. To determine if a task is appropriate, explore two things. First, find out if the task is normally completed by the social workers at the agency. If that is the case, then it is fine for you to engage in that task. For example, suppose you were asked to provide child care for the parents in a substance-abuse group meeting. In doing so, you learned that all the social workers in the agency rotate through the role because attendance at group is better if child care is offered. In this case, taking on the task might fit the criterion of being part of a multilevel learning experience. That being said, the student still needs to consider how the task relates to the larger goals and objectives. Assisting in child care could be linked to diversity and cultural competence if working with the children increases the student's understanding of child development, or it could be linked to professional development in the area of fulfilling the role of the social worker in the agency. However, the student also wants to consider the appropriateness of the task in the context of the time available and as compared to other task opportunities. In other words, a student may not want to spend time each week engaging in child care when other learning options are available. Therefore, a thorough discussion with the field instructor to evaluate all of the preceding possibilities is necessary.

On the other hand, if the agency doesn't normally provide child care and you are asked to do that, or if other non-social-work staff provides child care most of the time, this might not be an appropriate task for you. For instance, suppose that a student is asked to watch the children while the social worker meets with the child's mom to discuss the case. If child care is usually provided by a non-social-work staff member and providing child care is not normally what the social worker would be doing, then attending to the child probably is not an appropriate learning task. Taking care of the child, while undoubtedly important to the work, may actually be taking away from your learning because you would otherwise be observing the social worker working with the mom. Again, the student and field instructor need to discuss and determine the purpose of a task and how the task is linked to the achievement of the student's goals and objectives.

Second, it is important to determine if a particular task has merit and will contribute significantly to your learning, the latter being the most important. However, making a determination about the value of a particular task is not always cut-and-dried. For instance, suppose you are asked to cover the phones because there is a crisis in the agency and all the staff is pulled into a meeting. Answering the phones at the front desk is not the job of the social worker, but you can help out as all professionals do from time and time, and the task actually becomes a great learning experience in that the student can speak to clients firsthand and get a sense of the types of calls the agency gets and what to do with the callers. At the end of the day, this particular task proves to be beneficial even though it was clearly situation specific; that is, you will not answer the phones on a regular basis, but on that day doing something that wasn't the social worker's job ended up being productive.

One last example is the opposite of the preceding scenario. At an agency where a student of mine was placed, a staff member of the agency asked the student to do a task not normally done by the social worker. It involved performing physical care activities with the client. At the time, the student thought it might not be an appropriate task, but the field instructor was not at the agency and the student did not feel comfortable saying no. The student completed the task, but was very upset about being asked in the first place. Fortunately, the student could complete the task without any harm being done to the student or the client, and the student even reported some benefit. However, later in a discussion with the student about the situation, it became clear that the task could have put the student at risk and the student reported being extremely uncomfortable. So the student was informed to discuss the situation with the field instructor and establish a plan for determining appropriate tasks and how to handle situations that may come up when the field instructor is not at the agency. This is an example of a situation where a student is asked to do something that is not appropriate and not productive and even created anxiety for the student.

EP 2.1.1c

As shown from all the examples offered, it is extremely important that you determine your primary tasks, ensure that everyone in the agency knows your role and primary tasks, and feel empowered to evaluate the requests that will come up from time to time in your agency. The best way to provide clarity with regard to your tasks is to

1. create a well constructed and comprehensive learning plan,
2. identify the tasks and roles you will regularly engage in on the learning plan,
3. ask your field instructor to let others in the agency know your role and primary tasks, and
4. when and if you are asked to do something outside of your learning plan, pause and reflect on the appropriateness of the task and if necessary ask the purpose and goal of the task. If you are still unsure consult with your field director or faculty field liaison.

The goal is for you to join the agency fully as a team member; this may require flexibility on your part from time to time, while at the same time ensuring that you are not asked to do things that are clearly not related to your development as a social worker.

Now that you are familiar with multilevel learning tasks, the next thing to think about as you are putting your learning plan together is the foundational roles of social work that you may use in conjunction with a task.

Foundational Roles of Social Work Practice in Field

The generalist field education approach outlined in chapter 1 requires that students in field engage in the foundational roles of social work. This is due to the fact that from a generalist perspective, the foundational roles that the professional social worker uses are critically important to effective practice, as can be seen in its inclusion, implicitly or explicitly, in various definitions of generalist practice. I often hear students use the terms *case manager, advocate, facilitate,* and *educate,* but the students do not usually identify them as foundational roles of social work practice. Instead students use them in more general ways or understand that a particular role just happens to be the name of a particular job, as is the case with the term *case manager.* On the converse, students rarely state, "I brokered today" but regularly talk about referring a client to a service which is the function of the role of the broker. Thus, it is important to increase your understanding of the foundational social work roles and how those roles are referred to in your agency, and ensure that you have opportunities to use the roles in your practice in field. This will in part be accomplished by including various foundational roles in your learning task as well as increasing your knowledge and understanding of the roles you are providing in the context of your position at the agency. For instance, if your agency identifies the primary role of the social worker as a case manager and you will be fulfilling that role as a student, ask yourself, what does that mean to be a case manager? What is the role of a case manager? And, how do I manage a case? As a result of this focused examination and answering these questions, you will become more fully grounded in that particular role. Last, the more familiar you are with the foundational roles used by the social worker(s) in your agency, the better you will be able to develop competence in attending to your professional roles and boundaries, a practice behavior associated with identifying and conducting yourself as a professional social worker.

Kirst-Ashman and Hull (2009) identify eight foundational roles of social work: counselor, educator, broker, case manager, mobilizer, mediator, facilitator, and advocate (pp. 25–26). With regard to the use of the foundational roles of social work practice, Dubois and Miley (2005) state that,

EP 2.1.1c

> Rather than the social worker's starting with the roles or strategies and then determining the plans of action, the nature of the situation should drive the selection of roles and strategies. Client systems' challenges, rather than the preferred methods of practitioners, generate strategies. (p. 229)

The notion of fitting the role to the need versus providing the role because that is what the social worker or agency does is a critically important concept for you to grasp in your practice in field and one that can be complicated by your overarching role within the agency.

To assist you in the process of delineating your overarching role within the agency as a social work student from the foundational roles that social workers use to assist clients, as well as identify the overlap, review and discuss Integrative Activity 3.2: Identifying Foundational Roles of Social Work in Field with your field instructor. The first thing this activity asks you to do is to discuss and clarify your role. To guide you in this discussion,

1. review the agency job description to determine your role,
2. review the professional roles of social work practice, and consider the opportunities for using the various roles in the agency, and
3. link the various roles to your multilevel learning tasks.

INTEGRATIVE ACTIVITY 3.2

Identifying Foundational Roles of Social Work in Field

Purpose: The purpose of this activity is twofold. First, it will assist you in identifying your role in the agency. This is accomplished by you and your field instructor (1) reviewing the agency job description of the social worker and (2) deciding together, based on the opportunities, learning objectives, and your interests, what your primary role will look like. Second, the activity will provide you an opportunity to review the foundational roles of social work practice with your field instructor and identify tasks in which you will be able to integrate the role and thus develop competence.

Role of Social Worker in Agency	Primary Role as Student
(Review job description and describe.)	(Identify and describe.)

Role	Role Defined	Field Task Identify the field tasks and targeted client systems that will enable you to fulfill the identified role.	Processing and Evaluation Identify how your ability to perform the role will be processed and evaluated.
Counselor	This role is fulfilled by the student when the student provides support, encouragement, and suggestions and assists the client in the planned change process. For example, a student might listen to, support, and explore options for how a mother might handle her child's problems in school.		
Educator	This role is fulfilled by the student when he or she provides information and teaches the client system. For example, a student will provide information to the client system about anger management in the context of a group for urban youth.		
Broker	This role is fulfilled when the student links a client system with a needed resource. For instance, the student might refer the client to an AA or NA group.		

(Continued)

Case Manager	This role is fulfilled by the student when he or she coordinates needed services provided by different community agencies. For instance, the student might coordinate the services for a client who is being discharged from the hospital.		
Mobilizer	This role is fulfilled by the student when he or she convenes community people and resources to identify needs. For example, a student might encourage community residents to address crime that is not being addressed through a community policing program.		
Mediator	This role is fulfilled by the student when he or she resolves disputes and conflicts between system members. For instance, the student might work as a go-between for members of a neighborhood and local developers.		
Facilitator	This role is fulfilled by the student when he or she leads groups. For instance, a student might run a group for girls in a community youth program.		
Advocate	This is fulfilled by the student who stands up for and represents the needs or interests of a client so that the client receives resources. For instance, the student may contact the landlord on behalf of the client requesting an extension on an eviction notice.		
Other:			

One role that you as a student in field can target is that of brokering or linking clients with needed resources. This is an important and satisfying role and can be accomplished by first researching and updating community resources and then linking your clients to a needed resource. Other common roles that students will practice while in field are advocate, counselor, facilitator, and educator.

In terms of your professional socialization and development, it is important for you to have opportunities to explain your role to clients, staff in the agency, students in seminar, and faculty. Thus it may be useful for you to develop a student job description.

Once you have reviewed the eight foundational roles, integrate a role in the learning task when possible. For example, going back to the student who was able to add the two mezzo practice tasks, both tasks included a foundational role of social work practice in the task: (1) facilitate a support group and (2) educate clients by conducting community-based presentations. As you can see, both *facilitate* and *educate* were included in the learning task and specifically reference a foundational social work role. By writing your learning task in a way that includes a role, when possible, you will become grounded in the roles themselves and ensure you are having opportunities to use the foundational roles. One last thing that is important to mention is that some learning tasks will not include a foundational role. This may be due to the fact that the task is very straightforward, as in the example of reading an article and viewing a video to develop knowledge. In fact, many of the orientation and training-related learning tasks may not involve a role. It is when the student moves from orientation and training to practicing that the roles become more clear.

Now that you have reviewed multilevel learning tasks and how to integrate the foundational roles of social work into a learning task, the last part of the learning objective is the plan for evaluation.

The Plan for Evaluation

EP 2.1.10m

If you refer back to the guiding definition of a "learning objective," you will recall a well-constructed learning objective also includes a plan for evaluation. It enables you and your field instructor to determine if the learning task was completed and the corresponding goal and objective met. A well-constructed learning objective includes information that identifies how the objective will be evaluated, or the evaluation plan. This ultimately sets the stage for the final field evaluation process.

The evaluation plan includes information such as due dates, number of times something is done, and the activities or resources used to measure an objective for learning and goal. Referring back to the sample learning objective, notice that several things are identified to assist in evaluating that learning objective. For instance, you and your field instructor can readily determine if a specific due date when something is to be completed was met and an activity, such as discussing in supervision and applying content learned to a case, has been completed. Obviously, meeting a due date or completing an activity will not be the only standard by which an objective is evaluated, particularly in the context of the final field evaluation, but starting with a well-constructed objective will set the stage.

The final field evaluation will most likely take place at the end of each semester or quarter and weighs heavily in the grade you receive for field. A well-constructed final evaluation will reflect the learning plan and relate directly to the goals and objectives set forth. The evaluation process should involve both you and your field instructor along with any other critical players in the agency reviewing your progress and determining

OBJECTIVE FOR LEARNING		
1. Goal Statement	2. Learning Task(s) (with Integrated Role)	3. Plan for Evaluation
Sample Goal Statement:		

Figure 3.1 Developing Objectives for Learning

an overall evaluation of your performance. You should conduct a self-assessment and be ready to discuss your assessment, as well as hear your field instructor's assessment of your performance. If you have any concerns or questions about the outcome of your evaluation, discuss those with your field instructor first, as he or she may be able to resolve them. If that discussion does not sufficiently address your concerns, take them to your faculty field liaison or field director.

Figure 3.1 offers a way of thinking about and practice developing learning objectives for field that integrates all of the areas discussed earlier, namely, a goal statement, learning tasks with integrated role, and plan for evaluation.

As you can see, an Objective for learning consists of a goal statement, learning task(s) and possible integrated role and plan for evaluation. This format is in keeping with Horejsi and Garthwait's (1999) definition of "learning objectives," but instead of the objective being one multifaceted sentence, the Objective for Learning is broken down into three parts: (1) a goal statement, (2) learning task(s) with integrated role, and (3) plan for evaluation, which makes it easier to write and evaluate. Using Figure 3.1, construct one sample Objective for Learning.

REFLECTION QUESTION 3.1

Now that you have had a chance to review the elements of the learning plan, specifically focusing on goals and objectives, tasks and roles, and a plan for evaluation, the first thing to think about is, what you are hoping to accomplish? In your answer, jot down goal statements. Next, consider expectations for field as identified by your program, field instructor, and the agency. Then start thinking about the kinds of multilevel tasks and roles you can engage in, as well as those that you want to engage in. Last, identify ways in which your tasks, objectives, and goals can be evaluated.

Developing Your Learning Plan

To develop a well-constructed learning plan that includes all the information discussed previously, complete Integrative Activity 3.3: Constructing the Field Learning Plan. This activity will give you all the necessary information to draft your program's learning plan as well as develop your skill in writing learning objectives.

INTEGRATIVE ACTIVITY 3.3

Constructing the Field Learning Plan

Purpose: The purpose of this activity is to assist you in gathering the information you will need to complete your program's learning plan, as well as develop your skill in writing objectives for learning.

Direction: In each section, jot down the requested information.

1. **Primary role within agency:** (see Integrative Activity 3.2)

2. **Primary tasks:** (see Integrative Activities 3.1 and 3.2)

Micro:

Mezzo:

Macro:

Professional socialization:

3. Identifying learning objectives:

List all of the goals and objectives you are hoping to accomplish as a result of your field experience. To gather this list, consider the goals of the social worker(s) at the agency; your personal interests, goals, and objectives as a professional social worker; goals and objectives that relate to the population served or services offered; special projects or issues impacting the agency; and goals and objectives for field as outlined by your university field director, faculty field liaison, and course work.

In each of the five overarching areas of field competence (see Chapter 1), practice writing learning objectives, including multilevel learning tasks integrating the foundational roles of social work and the evaluation plan. Refer back to the list you developed earlier and link to the five overarching goal areas.

Goal Area 1: Socialization and professional development as a social worker in field.

Learning Objective:	Learning Tasks with Roles:	Evaluation Plan:

Goal Area 2: Ethical practice and consideration of diversity and social justice.

Learning Objective:	Learning Tasks with Roles:	Evaluation Plan:

Goal Area 3: Integration of knowledge, values, and skills acquired in the classroom with the practice experiences of field.

Learning Objective:	Learning Tasks with Roles:	Evaluation Plan:

Goal Area 4: Effective communication skills in field.

Learning Objective:	Learning Tasks with Roles:	Evaluation Plan:

Goal Area 5: Application of the planned change process with individuals, families, groups, organizations, and communities in field.

Learning Objective:	Learning Tasks with Roles:	Evaluation Plan:

Other: Competence specific to field site and program

Learning Objective:	Learning Tasks with Roles:	Evaluation Plan:

Once you have completed this activity, draft your program's learning plan and obtain any needed signatures.

Effective Use of the Learning Plan

As discussed at the beginning of this chapter, the learning plan provides direction and assists you in achieving what you hope to accomplish in field. You need to consider how best to use the document as a tool in your learning and development as a competent social worker.

The first and most obvious use is to keep a copy of the learning plan and periodically review it on your own and in supervision with your field instructor. Students have asked me countless times for a copy of their learning plan so they and their field instructor could complete the final field evaluation. I am usually surprised and concerned that neither the student nor the field instructor had a copy to begin with, and I question their ability to have effectively monitored their progress in field without having referenced their learning plan.

Second, if issues come up with regard to your tasks, such as being asked to engage in a task that is not on your learning plan or not having an opportunity to complete a task that is on the learning plan, use the learning plan as a way to resolve the issue. For instance, I had a student who had a task on the learning plan that the student was not getting to due to spending too much time each day completing another task. By reviewing the learning plan and discussing the agreed-upon tasks with the field instructor and identifying the issue as the fact that the student wasn't getting to a particular task because the other task was taking up so much time, the student could renegotiate the days at field, which then allowed enough time to complete all the agreed-upon tasks. When you have your learning plan and refer to it, you often can avoid issues in the first place and more swiftly resolve an issue if one does come up.

Last, use the learning plan to monitor your progress. This helps develop your confidence as you cross off tasks that you have accomplished, as well as help you refocus your time to complete those tasks that may have fallen through the cracks and have yet to be accomplished. Remember, the number of hours spent per week in field will seem like a lot at first, but once you are working, the time goes very quickly. So it is important to stay on top of your time and use it in the most productive ways possible.

The Pace of Learning

Now that you have completed your learning plan, it is important to think about how the learning plan can facilitate the pace of your learning. This refers to how quickly or slowly you move from orientation and training to independently practicing as a social work student. The learning plan should include tasks that reflect the pace, with some involving shadowing and cofacilitating, to others reflecting independence. The first thing to discuss related to the pace of your learning is your transition from shadowing to independent practice.

From Shadowing to Independent Practice

The transition you will make from shadowing to practicing independently as a social work student is similar to the steps involved in training (see Chapter 2) with an important step in your training plan being shadowing. However, how you move from that first day when you shadowed the social worker doing a home visit as part of your training to conducting home visits with your own cases as an independently practicing social work student is an important process to consider. There is no hard-and-fast rule; a lot of this process will be individualized to the style of your field instructor, the training process at your agency, the needs of your role, and your skill level as the student. However, you can do a few things to facilitate this transition.

EC 2.1.1c

First, make sure you have opportunities to shadow and observe many different social workers doing a variety of tasks and roles. Observing other social workers is an excellent learning experience for three reasons:

1. you are exposed to a lot of different styles of social workers,
2. you meet a variety of clients experiencing a variety of issues, and
3. you begin to reflect on how you will handle a similar situation when you are practicing.

All of this becomes important as you move from shadowing to independent practice.

As a part of your shadowing experience, make sure you can observe your field instructor providing various tasks and roles whenever possible. Observing your field instructor will give you a sense of who that person is as a social worker and an opportunity to see a more experienced worker. This contributes to your development and often helps you identify more targeted goals or markers of competent practice.

For instance, I had a student who was able to observe the field instructor conducting intakes. As a result, the student identified the skill level of the field instructor who was interviewing, specifically the instructor's ability to seamlessly engage the client and gather the needed information. The student noted that the style was very conversational. As a result, the student stated wanting to be able to do that. The ability of the student to target a skill as something the student hoped to accomplish became very useful with regard to establishing the pace and steps involved in meeting that goal.

Next, begin to perform a task while under direct observation. As nerve-racking as this can be, it is an important part of the process. Year after year, at the end of field, students tell me they wish they had had more opportunities to be observed and given specific feedback. To bridge this gap, I encourage you to do a few tasks under direct observation. The reason this is such a helpful task is because it is the best way to get feedback. Also, in terms of the learning process, you can engage in a task without having to know everything or be expected to handle every eventuality, because your field instructor or agency designee is there with you. Once you get over the nerves, you will notice that it is actually comforting to have someone there who will be completing the task with you.

The last step is to do learning tasks independently. You have defined your role within the agency, have been orientated and trained, and have clearly identified your learning tasks in the learning plan, and now it is time to engage in those tasks independently. Let's discuss what this might look like. In most agencies it will be very straightforward: you will be assigned a caseload, project, or task that you will complete independently. However, in some agencies, independent work will need to be defined and perhaps even negotiated.

For instance, in some agencies, a student cannot have official case ownership, meaning the student cannot be identified as the primary social worker on the case. However, it is important for a student to have some version of a caseload and role on the cases; so even if the student cannot be the official "caseworker," he or she can still learn the cases and work as independently on the cases as possible. Another way to think about independent practice as a social work student is to describe what something should *not* look like: for instance, a student who comes to field every day and is randomly assigned to workers, cases, and tasks. Or when a student comes to field each day and has to find work to do. Both situations can happen, and they tend to create a hectic learning environment that is not effective.

How casework should look is as follows: the student is assigned certain cases to work and coworks those cases with the agency social worker. *Coworking* refers to the student and social worker working in tandem, with the student leading sessions or visits, asking questions to gather needed information, and completing any documentation, which is then reviewed and signed off on by the agency social worker. Another example is in the case of a student who is in an agency where official and legal reports are completed and presented. In this case, the student can work on the report and write a rough draft; based on that, the social worker completes the final version and presents to the recipient, such as in a court hearing, with the student present. The primary goal of all field tasks, regardless of how the task has to be structured for a student, is to give the student a sense of continuity through case assignment and the ability to practice as independently as possible.

Other students will be in a setting that easily translates to independent practice, thus the preceding situations will not be an issue. Either way, it is important that the learning plan reflect the plan for your eventual independent practice and that you discuss this process with your field instructor during the first few weeks of field.

As a final thought, it is interesting to note that macro-level tasks tend to lend themselves nicely to independent practice. Take, for example, a student who will be developing a new policy for the agency. Once the student and field instructor determine the plan for how best to approach this task, the student will have a great deal of control over completing this task independently.

REFLECTION QUESTION 3.2

As you think about practicing independently, what does that look like in your agency? What are you excited about, and what are your concerns? What do you need from yourself, your field instructor, and field director or faculty field liaison to become independent at your field site?

Troubleshooting—Discussing the Pace of Learning

From time to time throughout your field experience, the pace of your learning may ebb and flow. This can be due to a number of variables and may require troubleshooting. During various points in the process of going from shadowing to independent practice, issues can arise such as a student feeling that he or she is endlessly shadowing and not having opportunities to begin coworking. Or a student feels he or she has no real opportunity for independent practice; or conversely, a student is thrown into running a group the second week of field and has no idea what he or she is doing. Last, a student might be avoiding independent practice because the student is unsure he or she can be effective.

All of the preceding situations can happen, and in fact, they are more common than not. So it is important to discuss the pace of your learning in supervision. For some, this conversation will flow easily and naturally, but for others it may be more difficult. This is one of the reasons why attending and using supervision is a professional socialization task, but sometimes it is not easy to develop this relationship and use it to discuss your learning process. Once again, this is where your learning plan can be an effective tool, but only if it clearly identifies the tasks that will assist you as you move from shadowing to independent practice.

If you are having issues with the pace of your learning, bring the learning plan to supervision and discuss your progress on various tasks. Also, your field director, faculty field liaison, and site visit can be effective resources to use to address any concerns you are having with regard to the pace of your learning. The bottom line is to ensure that you, the university, and the agency are all doing their part to create the best learning environment and experience possible.

Suggested Field Tasks

- Review and complete field paperwork, learning plan, and field evaluation.
- Identify primary role and tasks.
- Review social worker's job description.
- Identify learning opportunities and objectives.
- Develop learning plan.
- Identify multilevel tasks to achieve learning goals and objectives identified on learning plan.

- Evaluate progress in meeting goals and objectives of field and core competencies and practice behaviors.
- Discuss pace of learning.

Competency Notes

The following identifies where the CSWE *EPAS* (2008) Educational Policy (EP) and practice behaviors are discussed in the chapter.

EP 2.1.1c Attend to professional roles and boundaries (pp. 48, 49, 58): Social workers need to develop an understanding of the role of the social worker in an agency in order to competently function as a professional.

EP 2.1.3c Demonstrate effective oral and written communication in working with individuals, families, groups, organizations, communities, and colleagues (pp. 41, 42): Social workers need to develop competence in writing goals and objectives.

EP 2.1.10c Develop a mutually agreed-on focus of work and desired outcomes (pp. 41, 42): Social workers need to develop competence in developing a plan.

EP 2.1.10m Social workers critically analyze, monitor, and evaluate interventions (p. 52): Social workers need to be able to competently consider evaluation and evaluate all aspects of practice.

References

Birkenmaier, J., & Berg-Weger, M. (2007). *The practicum companion for social work: Integrating class and field work*. Boston: Pearson Education , Inc.

Cochran, S., & Hanley, M. (1999). *Learning through field*. Boston: Allyn and Bacon.

DuBois, B., & Miley, K. (2005). *Social work: An empowering profession*. Boston: Allyn and Bacon.

Hendricks, C., Finch, J., & Franks, C. (2005). *Learning to teach, teaching to learn: A guide for social work field education*. Alexandria, VA: CSWE Press.

Horejsi, C., & Garthwait, C. (1999). *The social work practicum: A guide and workbook for students*. Boston: Allyn and Bacon.

Johnson, L., & Yanca, S. (2007). *Social work practice: A generalist approach*. Boston: Allyn and Bacon.

Kagel, J., & Kopels, S. (2008). *Social work records*. Long Grove, IL: Waveland Press, Inc.

Kirst-Ashman, K., & Hull, Jr., G. (2009). *Understanding generalist practice* (5th ed.). Belmont, CA: Brooks/Cole.

Pilonis, E., Bailey-Etta, B., & Manning, M. (2002). Implementing the generalist model in practice: Implications for curriculum and best practices. *Journal of Teaching in Social Work, 22*(3/4), 103–119.

Riebschleger, J., & Grettenberger, S. (2006). Assessing graduating BSW field students' preparation for generalist practice. *The Journal of Baccalaureate Social Work, 12*(1), 184.

Schatz, M. S., Jenkins, L. E., & Sheafor, B. W. (1990). Milford refined: A model of initial and advanced generalist social work. *Journal of Social Work Education, 26*(3), 217.

Sheafor, B., and Horejsi, C. (2008). *Techniques and guidelines for social work practice*. Boston: Pearson Education, Inc.

Sherer, M., & Peleg-Oren, N. (2005). Differences of teachers', field instructors', and students' views on job analysis of social work students. *Journal of Social Work Education, 41*(2), 315.

Wolk, J. L., & Wertheimer, M. R. (1999). Generalist practice vs. case management: An accreditation contradiction. *Journal of Social Work Education, 35*(1), 101.

CHAPTER 4

Safety in Field

As students leave the classroom and enter the agency, safety in field education becomes an important issue that students often don't fully consider. Two studies in particular, Ellison (1996) and Tully, Kropf, and Price (1993) point to this fact. As a field director, I consider your safety a top priority. With regard to violence encountered by students in field, either verbal or physical, according to Ellison's 1996 national study of BSW and MSW field programs, "out of a total of 17,650 students in field (N = 11,557 MSW, 6,093 BSW) a relatively small number of students experienced any type of violence while in field" (p. 86). Ellison (1996) goes on to report, "The bad news is that 77 students experienced some type of violence while in their field program" (p. 86). Although this study (Ellison, 1996) indicates that the vast majority of students will not experience an issue related to violence, the author encourages caution because the study looked specifically at reported or known instances and may not have captured all instances of violence that students may have experienced.

Tully, Kropf, and Price (1993) surveyed both social work students and field instructors to identify safety issues and found that undergraduate and graduate students as well as field instructors experienced instances of violence, physical and verbal. Interestingly enough, the incidence of violence (verbal and physical) was higher for field instructors than students. The authors concluded that this may be due to the fact that student status protects students more from potential harm. Students in this study (Tully, Kropf, and Price , 1993) also reported safety concerns related to their agency, such as having to work with potentially dangerous clients, working in neighborhoods that have high rates of violence, and being exposed to various communicable diseases. This is important because it expands the discussion beyond violence to the need to consider safety more broadly. Last, Fogel, Ellison, and Morrow (2001) found that sexual harassment occurred in field placement settings. Thus it is important to increase your understanding of potential safety issues.

Tully, Kropf, and Price (1993) looked at what agencies are doing in terms of policies and training and found two important things. First, most of the students in the study reported that their agencies did not have policies regarding violence or they were not made aware of them if the agencies did. Second, few students received any training

S-elf	- Carry liability insurance.
	- Identify yourself as a student.
	- Communicate your whereabouts.
	- Employ physical safety measures.
A-gency	- Know safety policies and procedures.
	- Consider client population served.
	- Ensure professional well-being.
	- Attend supervision.
	- Practice within your role as a student.
	- Know legal liability.
	- Review mandated reporting, duty to warn/prevent harm.
F-eelings	- Trust your gut.
	- Ensure psychological well-being.
	- Engage in self-care, oxygen mask metaphor.
	- Manage stress and potential burnout.
	- Educate self and be aware of vicarious trauma.
E-nvironment	- Assess internal and external agency environment—lighting, parking.
	- Assess type, location, and time of day of service, i.e., in-office, in-home, or community based.

Figure 4.1 SAFE Field Education

on safety at their agency. Interestingly, there was a gap between the field instructors' reports that their agencies had safety policies and the students' reports that they knew the policies. This begs the question, what do you need to know to reduce your risk in field? DiGiulio (2001) indicated that universities have a responsibility to consider safety and "acknowledge potential risks associated with field education and to minimize those risks by providing knowledge and preparation in safety procedures" (p. 69). The need to equip you with the resources to ensure your safety becomes extremely important.

SAFETY IN FIELD

As you think about safety in field education, it is useful to take a holistic approach. As shown in Figure 4.1, SAFE Field Education, there are several things to consider when addressing safety in field. To organize your thinking, I have identified three overarching areas of safety. They are physical, psychological, and professional well-being. As part of your safety planning, complete Integrative Activity 4.1: Field Safety Assessment at the end of this chapter with your field instructor to develop your and your field instructor's awareness of safety at your field site.

THREE AREAS OF WELL-BEING

Physical Well-Being

The first area of safety in field education to consider is physical well-being. This specifically addresses your bodily well-being when coming to and leaving your field site and while in your day-to-day activities at your agency, and targets physical violence.

The first thing you want to consider is your primary mode of transportation to and from your field site. For example, if you are driving, identify where you will be parking. If you are taking the bus or train, how far do you need to walk to the stop from home or the university and to your agency? During the winter months and if you are working in the evening, consider your safety needs at night. Are the stops well lit and public, or are they dark and remote? In addition, consider the lighting of the building itself and the parking lot. If you do not consider your travel in the evenings to be safe, discuss this concern with your field instructor. If you are traveling to and from home visits or working in neighborhoods and in the community, you will want to make sure you know where you are going and whether there are any safety issues related to the neighborhood where you will be working. If you are driving, make sure you have a full tank of gas and that your car is in good working order. Also, always make sure you know where you are going, have a charged cell phone, and are aware of your environment.

While working one-on-one with clients or in a group setting, always consider the population you are working with to determine if there are any client-population-based physical safety issues. Make sure to discuss this with your supervisor, as some agencies have safety measures that they use in their day-to-day practice. For instance, an agency may have a panic button that a social worker can take along to an individual or group session, or a code word to be used over the phone system should the social worker need assistance. So review and know your agency's safety policies and procedures.

You also can consider other things to ensure your physical safety when in the office, at a client's home, or in the community, such as how to position yourself in a room with a client. To increase your physical safety, make sure the client does not block the doorway and you have a clear exit. Last, you always want to be aware of your client's behavior and any change in behavior, as well as in your surroundings. By all means, trust your gut. If something seems wrong or different, make sure to ask for assistance. I always tell my students that it is OK to abandon a task if they do not feel safe for whatever reason.

When coming and going throughout your workday, it is very important that someone knows where you are at all times. This is best handled in agencies that have In/Out boards so staff can get a clear visual of who is out and who has not returned. If your agency does not have a structured In/Out system, establish an informal system with your field instructor or agency secretary. The goal of this system is that if you do not return, someone will look for you. Additional safety measures can entail using the locator device on your cell phone if your phone has one. This will send out a GPS signal if someone tries to locate the phone. Make sure your field instructor has emergency contacts should something happen and you need assistance. Last, when going out into the community, have some form of identification on your person at all times. The best form of ID is if you can get an ID badge from the agency with your picture, name, title as social work student, and agency name. Most ID badges also include on the back a number to contact in the event of an emergency. If your agency does not have photo ID badges for students, use your university photo ID and carry a card in your wallet with your agency name, number, and field instructor contact information.

Last, be aware of the potential for health risks through exposure to serious communicable diseases such as tuberculosis and other bothersome issues such as lice, scabies, bedbugs, and standard viruses that can cause colds and flues. The best prevention is, first of all, to be educated with regard to the potential risks specific to your work, and second, to employ the number one precautionary practice: regular hand washing. In specified settings with specific populations, you may need to employ more targeted and elaborate health safety measures. If this is the case, discuss health safety measures, policies, and best practices with your field instructor.

Psychological Well-Being

The next area of safety in field for you to consider is psychological well-being. This relates specifically to the thoughts and feelings you will experience as a result of your work and how you manage them. The concepts of vicarious trauma, stress management, burn-out, and self-care are important to discuss. Vicarious trauma can occur after a worker or student is exposed to trauma experienced by a client, ". . . social workers and other helpers may develop symptoms of trauma themselves, such as intrusive thoughts and images, sleeplessness, bystander guilt, and feelings of vulnerability, helplessness, self-doubt, and rage" (Sheafor and Horrejsi, 2008, p. 571). This can happen as the result of being exposed to traumatic client situations, unusual case experiences, photos, and client records.

I remember early on in my practice at a mental health crisis agency, I had a client come in for short-term crisis counseling. During the first session, the client, a young woman, recounted in graphic detail her rape by a family member and the current symptoms, including flashbacks that were triggered when she was in a room that reminded her of where the rape took place. Needless to say, I was stunned and could not get the details out of my head. The client never returned. That was more than 20 years ago, and I can still recall the entire session in vivid detail: what the client looked like, what the room looked like, and the story. I continued to notice difficulties I was having working at the crisis center with clients who were experiencing domestic violence, incest, and suicide, and realized, after disclosing my difficulties sleeping and various intrusive thoughts to my supervisor, that I was experiencing vicarious trauma. After processing this issue and engaging in deliberate self-care, I was able to combat the effects of working in a crisis center. Fortunately with increased practice experience, I was able to develop the skills necessary to process difficult client situations in a variety of settings that included a child welfare setting that again challenged me with experiences of vicarious trauma. I think my practice experiences have made me increasingly sensitive to the experiences of my students and the need to prepare them for managing what they will experience in field.

I have had students develop symptoms of vicarious trauma and have reassured them that this is normal. I have worked with them and their field instructor to address their needs. One critically important tool in managing vicarious trauma is discussing the issue and the feelings you are experiencing in supervision. Students must build a strong relationship with their field instructor and peers at the agency so that when they experience difficult cases they can freely discuss their concerns. One agency I worked with handled issues of vicarious trauma extremely well by first normalizing the experience, and second engaging in a debriefing session to assist the student and field instructor in processing the difficult details of the case.

Some of the warning signs of vicarious trauma can be loss of energy, lack of self-care, disconnecting from others, increased sensitivity to fear or threat, change in worldview, and a feeling of hopelessness or despair. It is important to regularly check in with your field instructor during your supervision session about how you are feeling and what you are noticing about yourself as you are experiencing field. Dane (2002) states that, "Personal life events can influence the work and induce vulnerability for the student who is a survivor of trauma. It is important for new social workers to monitor their reactions and responses" (p. 9).

If you are not getting what you need at your agency or if for whatever reason you cannot discuss your concerns with your field instructor, it is critically important to contact your field director or faculty field liaison. That person will be able to assist you in the process of identifying the vicarious trauma, notifying your placement site, and working with you and your field instructor to develop a plan to address the issue. Last, if your program has an integrated field seminar course, you as a student can also go there to share your reactions to the work you are doing and gain support from students who may be experiencing similar issues.

Intricately woven with vicarious trauma are stress management and burnout. These refer to the difficulties you may experience associated with field education in general and your particular work at your agency. For instance, I tell my students that field is stressful. As you recall, the introduction to this book discussed the challenges associated with field in general. Similarly, your unique situation (course load, outside work and family demands, field schedule), and field site setting (challenging population, chaotic work environment, tough cases), may create sources of stress for you as well. As a part of your personal well-being, it is important to continuously monitor your level of stress and be aware of the potential for burnout while in field. "The concept of burnout has been used to understand workers' reactions to the demands of the work environment" (Dane, 2002, p. 5). Dane (2002) goes on the say, "Burnout is perceived as a negative experience, and can appear as physical and emotional exhaustion, negativity about accomplishments, and depersonalization" (p. 5).

It is very important that you employ good stress management and self-care techniques so that the cumulative stress of the field placement does not lead to burnout. I like to use the metaphor of the oxygen mask to explain why it is so important to engage in self-care. When you fly on an airplane, the flight attendant will instruct you that in the event of a drop in cabin pressure you should put on your oxygen mask. They go on to say that if you are traveling with young children or people who may need assistance, it is critical to put your oxygen mask on first and then assist the other person.

REFLECTION QUESTION 4.1

Why do you think the airline personnel instruct people flying to put their oxygen mask on first before assisting others, and how do you think this relates to field education?

The most obvious reason is that as a social worker, you will be assisting individuals who are in need and they need to know that you are there, at your best, ready and able to assist them. The better off you are, the better you will be able to serve your clients. Interestingly enough, good self-care will also protect you better from overall stress and burnout. Self-care will be discussed in more detail in Chapter 12 when we discuss professional development of self.

Professional Well-Being

EP 2.1.2a

The last area of consideration related to safety in field education is professional well-being. I consider professional well-being to be analogous to issues of ethical practice and professional liability or malpractice. With regard to ethical practice, as a student, you are bound by the ethical conduct standards of the agency and the profession as outlined in the NASW Code of Ethics. Ethical practice and dealing with ethical dilemmas will be discussed in more detail in Chapter 7. With regard to issues of professional liability and malpractice, Lynch and Versen (2003) state that, "Professional liability or professional malpractice is defined as a form of negligence on the part of practitioners" (p. 58). Consideration of liability in field will develop your understanding of your current and future liability concerns as a student and practicing social worker.

It is critical to realize that all members of the field education endeavor, the university (field director/faculty liaison), the student, and the agency (field instructor) share in liability (Zakutansky, 1993). Lynch and Versen (2003) state that, "Prudent practice of social work today requires that social workers at all levels and settings have an awareness of malpractice liability issues and risk management strategies" (p. 58). The need to be aware of liability issues extends to you the student. In fact, your field instructor experiences what is referred to as vicarious liability. This means that your field instructor is ultimately responsible for what you do. In fact, Lynch and Versen (2003) reported that students and their field instructors have been named in lawsuits. So it is important that as you enter your agency in the capacity of a social work student under supervision of a social worker, you first know the professional responsibilities that relate to issues of legal liability, and second meet these responsibilities through best practice. Your ability to reduce your and your field instructor's level of risk will directly impact your placement and possibly your future as a professional social worker. A few best practices will reduce your level of risk and increase your overall professional well-being.

First and foremost, as you enter your field agency as a social work student under the supervision of a professional social worker, it is critically important that you carry malpractice or liability insurance. Most programs offer this through the university, and the student or university pays the cost. If your agency wants a copy, either request one from your field director or your university bill may have an actual line item that says liability insurance. The purpose of liability insurance is to protect you, the university, the agency, and the client should something happen that results in you being sued. If your university does not offer malpractice insurance, you can obtain it through the National Association of Social Workers (NASW) or other private insurance companies. Some students even carry their own personal liability insurance in addition to the coverage offered through the school.

The next thing to do to ensure your professional well-being is to inform all the clients you come in contact with that you are a student. Your field instructor is responsible, according to the NASW Code of Ethics, to ensure that this happens. Interestingly enough, year after year I have seen students enter agencies, be given tasks, but never be introduced properly to their clients. In fact, one of my students was observing a treatment group but was never introduced by the social worker nor did the student introduce herself. As a result, the student was mistaken for being a member of the group. It became very awkward for the student to run the group later. Therefore, it is very important to discuss this ahead of time with your field instructor and determine who will be introducing you. Furthermore, if you ever find yourself in a professional situation where you have not been properly introduced, go ahead and introduce yourself. This is an excellent way for you to show assertiveness and the ability to be proactive, as well as ensure that you are meeting this important ethical standard.

EP 2.1.1c

Another way to ensure your professional well-being is to attend supervision regularly. It is critically important that you and your field instructor be very clear about your tasks and the plan for your work. I encourage you to keep notes on your supervision sessions so that if something happens with a client you would be able to reference your notes on the supervision session in which you discussed the case. Notes are also a wonderful way to document your progress on a case, as well as write down questions you have for future supervision sessions. If you are taking notes, make sure not to write down any identifying information so as not to breach confidentiality and keep your supervision notes at the agency.

EP 2.1.1f

If supervision is not happening for whatever reason, it is important to notify your field director or faculty field liaison so that the issue can be discussed and a plan of action implemented to address the situation. I am fascinated by these occurrences, given the vicarious liability that field instructors incur when they agree to supervise a student. That being said, as a field instructor who was also providing direct service and functioning as a supervisor, there were times when a crisis occurred and I had to cancel a student's supervision session. If this happens to you, it is very important that you reschedule immediately, and sometimes you will be the one approaching your field instructor and requesting that you reschedule. The previous scenario is different from a chronic pattern of not having supervision; that is a much more serious issue, particularly in light of professional well-being and it must be addressed. The inability of the field instructor and agency to resolve this could necessitate your having to secure a different placement.

EP 2.1.1c

The next best practice area is to know your role as the social work student and practice only within the boundaries of that role. As social workers we have an ethical responsibility to practice only within our area of expertise. If you encounter a client situation that is beyond your training or role, it is critical that you obtain supervision and assistance for the client.

Unfortunately practicing beyond your level of expertise or role can happen in an agency more easily than you would think. Remember the example from chapter 3 where the student was asked to complete a task that was not on her learning plan, this is also an excellent example of when a student is asked to practice out side the scope of his or her role. As you will recall the student was asked to make a home visit and check on the client's well-being. The visit entailed tasks in the area of daily living activities such as toileting and bathing. The student was not trained to fulfill these tasks and by agreeing to make the home visit, put herself at risk should something have happened to the client during the visit. After discussing the situation, the student determined that she should have declined the request and stated that she can only perform tasks that are within her role and area of expertise.

The last and perhaps most important areas of risk reduction involve mandated reporting, duty to warn and preventing harm. These are extremely serious issues, so much so that I recommend you have a specific discussion addressing these potential practice situations with your field instructor, field director, and field faculty liaison. If you are ever in a situation in which you suspect abuse or neglect or a client is expressing homicidal or suicidal ideation, notify your field instructor immediately. Of course, if you are experiencing an emergency, contact the police and emergency personnel first and then your field instructor and field director.

I always tell my students to watch out when your field instructor or agency task supervisor asks you to do a task that is routine or involves a case that is "easy," because you never know what will come up. Last, make sure you have the names and numbers of your field instructor's supervisor and other agency personnel should your attempts to contact your field instructor fail.

In short, it is always important to be prepared. The following example from a student I was supervising when I practiced illustrates just how important it is to be prepared for anything, even during a routine task. I asked the student to go on the home visit and obtain the client's signature on the needed release-of-information form. I told the student that this case was going well, the client was pleasant, and that it would be fine to touch base with the client and see how things were going. I was sitting at my desk about half an hour after the student left when I received a frantic call. The student was on the phone and told me that the client had disclosed suicide ideation, and the student didn't know what to do next. I told the student to stay with the client and that I would be there shortly to provide the student supervision to deal with the crisis. Needless to say, the student did the right thing to contact me, the field instructor, given the risk associated with the situation. The student and I were able to get the client to agree to a psychiatric assessment at a local hospital's psychiatric emergency services. The client was ultimately admitted and referred for a psychiatric consult.

REFLECTION QUESTION 4.2

Now that you have had a chance to review the three areas of physical, psychological, and professional well-being, how do you think these areas relate to your field site? What, if anything, are you aware of now related to your safety needs in your field agency.

Assessing Safety in Field

Now that you have had a chance to review and consider the three areas of physical, psychological and professional well-being, complete and discuss Integrative Activity 4.1: Field Safety Assessment with your field instructor.

EP 2.1.3a

INTEGRATIVE ACTIVITY 4.1

Field Safety Assessment

Purpose: The purpose of this integrative activity is to help you and your field instructor assess your safety at your field site in three primary areas: physical, psychological, and professional. It will also help you increase your understanding of your level of safety and identify issues that can impact safety.

Directions: Review and discuss this assessment with your field instructor, and identify any areas that need specific attention to reduce the level of risk. Circle the appropriate answer, simply put the acronym "NA" if any items do not apply to your field agency, and write in any written answers. Once you have answered all questions, assess the agency's level of safety and your ability to address your safety needs. Last, identify any plan or plans to address safety overall and in the three specific areas of physical, psychological, and professional well-being.

I. Orientation
a. Does the agency have safety policies? — Yes No
b. Does the agency offer safety training as part of the orientation? — Yes No
c. Are you familiar with the safety policies? — Yes No
d. Have you participated in safety orientation or training? — Yes No
e. Have you and your field instructor reviewed your university's safety guidelines? — Yes No
f. Will you be receiving any special training related to safety? — Yes No
   If so, please specify.

II. Physical Well-Being
A. Getting to and from Agency
1. What is your mode of transportation to and from your placement site: (circle answer)
   Car   Bus   Train   Walking   Bicycle
2. How accessible is your primary mode of transportation to the agency?
   Will you be walking far to get to the agency?

3. Does your agency offer an escort service to your mode of transportation? — Yes No
4. Does the area neighborhood present increased risks? — Yes No
5. How do you assess the physical surrounds of your agency? — Safe Unsafe
6. Is the agency well lit, both inside and out? — Yes No
7. Are there fire procedures in place? — Yes No
8. Is the parking lot well lit? — Yes No

B. Working Outside the Office

1. What is the procedure for traveling to home visits and outreach activities?

2. If you drive your own vehicle to your placement site, are you expected to use your own vehicle for these visits?   Yes   No

3. What is the insurance plan for using your vehicle during the field day?

4. Have you discussed your program's policy regarding use of your personal vehicle while conducting field work and transporting clients?   Yes   No

5. Does your agency have any specific safety procedures regarding home visits and outreach activities, such as:

Sign-in/Sign-out procedure	Yes	No
Call-in procedure	Yes	No
Buddy system	Yes	No
Escorts	Yes	No

If other procedures are used, please explain:

6. If none, what is the plan you have developed to address your safety while conducting home visits or outreach work?

7. Do you have an identification badge?   Yes   No

8. Does someone know where you are at all times?   Yes   No

9. What is the plan if you find yourself in a situation with a potentially violent or threatening person?

10. How are high-risk neighborhoods or areas identified? What is the plan for maintaining your safety when working in high-risk neighborhoods or areas?

11. Will you be doing any after-hours or evening work?   Yes   No
12. If yes, what safety practices are recommended?   Yes   No
13. Does your field instructor have your emergency contact information?   Yes   No

C. Health

1. Are there health risks in this agency setting, such as risks for communicable diseases?   Yes   No

2. If yes, what are those risks and what precautions are you taking?

3. Have you been trained on precautionary procedures and prevention, particularly from communicable disease or infections, as well as parasites such as lice, scabies, and bedbugs?   Yes   No

4. If not, what is the plan for training in this area?

III. Psychological Well-Being
A. Vicarious Trauma

1. Does the population or issues of practice present a risk for vicarious trauma?   Yes   No

2. If yes, what have you discussed with your field instructor about how you will be preventing and managing risks related to vicarious trauma? Please describe.

B. Stress Management and Burnout

1. Have you discussed your level or risk for burnout and reviewed stress-management techniques?   Yes   No

2. What are ways you manage your stress at your placement?

C. Self-Care
1. What are your primary self-care techniques? (List below.)

IV. Professional Well-Being

A. Liability Insurance

1. Do you currently have liability insurance?	Yes	No
2. Have you discussed and reviewed issues of ethical practice in supervision with your field instructor?	Yes	No

B. Supervision

1. Do you have a set time for supervision?	Yes	No
2. Are you attending regular supervision?	Yes	No

C. Role and Training

1. Do you know your role?	Yes	No
2. Have you been trained to fulfill your primary role?	Yes	No
3. Are you practicing within your role?	Yes	No

D. Crisis Management

1. Have you discussed mandated reporting and duty to warn and prevent harm in supervision?	Yes	No
2. Do you know who to contact if there is a crisis?	Yes	No
3. Do you know who to contact if you can't reach your field instructor?	Yes	No

V. Overview Safety Assessment

1. Overall, how safe would you rate the agency?

   Safe   Somewhat Safe   Unsafe

2. How would you rate your own preparedness at this time to participate safely in your field experience?

   Well Prepared   Somewhat Prepared   Not at all Prepared

3. Have you discussed the results of this safety assessment with your field instructor?   Yes   No

4. What, if any, specific plan(s) of action will you implement as a result of this assessment in order to address your overall safety in field? And what plan(s) of action will you implement in the following specific areas?
   a. Overall
   b. Physical
   c. Psychological
   d. Professional

5. Have you discussed the results of this assessment with your field director or faculty field liaison?   Yes   No

Now that you have considered all the information addressed in the assessment and determined the overall level of safety at your agency, discuss with both your field instructor and field director or faculty field liaison anything that needs to be done to increase safety.

Suggested Field Tasks

- Complete Safety Assessment.
- Attend and plan for supervision.
- Use supervision appropriately.

- Determine title and role as student.
- Engage in self-care activities and monitor stress and burnout.
- Identify self as a student with client systems.
- Discuss ethical principles and standards and any agency-based ethical standards.

Competency Notes

The following identifies where the CSWE *EPAS* (2008) Educational Policy (EP) and practice behaviors are discussed in the chapter.

EP 2.1.1c Attend to professional roles and boundaries (p. 67, 68): Social workers need to competently identify and work within the defined roles for their position in an agency and understand how practicing within that role ensures their and the clients' professional well-being.

EP 2.1.1f Use supervision and consultation (p. 67): Social workers need to develop and maintain a strong relationship with their supervisor and discuss their work with clients to ensure they are providing sanctioned services and thus ensure that they and their clients remain safe. In addition, supervision provides an opportunity to address potential fatigue, burnout, and vicarious trauma, which can potentially threaten both physical and psychological well-being if not addressed.

EP 2.1.2a Recognize and manage personal values in a way that allows professional values to guide practice (p. 66): Social workers need to develop an understanding of the values and ethical principles and standards outlined in the NASW Code of Ethics as well as their own values and how those values interact in practice to ensure that their practice remains ethical and thus provides for their professional well-being.

EP 2.1.3a Distinguish, appraise, and integrate multiple sources of knowledge, including research-based knowledge and practice wisdom (p. 69): Social workers need to develop a comprehensive understanding of professional well-being and the role of safety in competent professional practice.

References

Dane, B. (2002). Duty to inform: Preparing social work students to understand vicarious traumatization. *Journal of Teaching in Social Work, 22*(3/4), 3–19.

DiGiulio, J. F. (2001). The power of collaboration: developing a safety training program for student interns. *The Journal of Baccalaureate Social Work, 7*(1), 69–77.

Ellison, M. (1996). Field can be hazardous to your well-being: Fact or fiction? *The Journal of Baccalaureate Social Work, 2*(1), 79–89.

Fogel, S. J., Ellison, M.E., and Morrow, D. F. (2001). Baccalaureate social work graduates respond: Is sexual harassment a problem in field placements? *The Journal of Baccalaureate Social Work, 7*(1), 79–93.

Gelman, S. R. (1997). Liability issues in social work education. *Journal of Social Work Education, 32*(3), 351–361.

Lynch, J. G., & Versen, G. R. (2003). Social work supervisor liability: Risk factors and strategies for risk reduction. *Administration in Social Work, 27*(2), 57–72.

Tully, C. T., Kropf, N. P., & Price, J. L. (1993). Is field a hard hat area? A study of violence in field placements. *Journal of Social Work Education, 29*, 191–199.

Zakutansky, T. J. (1993). Ethical and legal issues in field education: Shared responsibility and risk. *Journal of Social Work Education, 29*(3), 338–347.

Field Supervision

This chapter will review both the functions and the structure or logistics of field supervision, as well as provide the resources necessary to develop a successful supervisory relationship. In addition, the chapter will provide the information necessary for you to use the supervision session effectively, thus empowering you to co-create a supervision environment that enables you to meet the goals of field education.

FIELD SUPERVISION

Critical to effective field education is the supervision you receive from your field instructor at your field agency. Field supervision is multifaceted; that is, it has several different functions and structural or logistical aspects. There is much in the literature that documents the importance and complex nature of field supervision (Abramson and Fortune, 1990; Barretti, 2004; Bennett and Deal, 2009; Ellison, 1994; Fortune and Abramson, 1993; Knight 1996; Knight, 2001; Okundaye, Gray, C., and Gray, L., 1999; Webb, 1988). According to Fortune and Abramson (1993), "Students were more satisfied if they discussed learning needs in depth, had supervision scheduled regularly, and discussed evaluations prior to getting a formal document" (p. 103). Fortune and Abramson (1993) also found ". . . that the critical aspect of a satisfying placement is a balanced approach in which the student may engage in self-directed learning while also having sufficient structure and conceptual challenge" (p. 108). So as you enter field it is critical that you focus on,

1. defining the functions of supervision, and
2. establishing the structure or logistics of the supervision.

EP 2.1.1f

FUNCTIONS OF FIELD SUPERVISION

Kadushin (1991) states that, "While both field instructors and agency supervisors engage in the three principal cluster functions of supervision—administrative, educational and supportive—their effective implementation is even more difficult for field instructors than it is for agency supervisors" (p. 11–12). In her study on the anxiety that students felt entering field, Gelman (2004) found that 28% of the students surveyed were concerned about the quality of the supervision they would receive. Of the concerns related to supervision, Gelman (2004) found that students were most concerned about the content and time of supervision as well as the ability of the field supervisor to evaluate the student fairly. Developing effective field supervision is a challenge for both students and field instructors. To combat this challenge and alleviate the anxiety that you may feel as you enter field, we will discuss each function specifically.

Administrative Function of Field Supervision

Field supervision has several administrative functions. First and foremost the field instructor is responsible for the overall management of your placement. This means your field instructor is responsible for your orientation, training, and task assignment, as well as setting and monitoring your schedule. Second, your field instructor is responsible to assist you in the completion of all necessary agency and university-based paperwork. In terms of the agency, this may include fingerprinting, background checks, and mandatory orientation meetings. With regard to the university-based paperwork, the field instructor is responsible to complete the initial paperwork, affiliation and cooperative agreements, time sheets, learning plans, and final field evaluations.

The field instructor is also responsible to evaluate your performance while in field. The evaluation the field instructor provides will take many different forms, both formal and informal. In terms of the informal evaluation provided, it will be in the form of ongoing feedback throughout the placement experience about your performance in any given task. In terms of the formal evaluation, it will be in the form of the final field evaluation, which will also include a recommended grade. It is important to note that you will be intricately involved in this process through the process of self-evaluation as well as having an opportunity to provide feedback with regard to the final evaluation and grade. In terms of a midterm evaluation, that will either be formal or informal depending on your program's requirements. Even if your program does not require a midterm evaluation, I recommend you touch base with your field instructor and ask for feedback on how you are doing. During this meeting, I also recommend that you share your thoughts about how you think the placement and your learning process is going. Last, the field instructor will also be involved in reviewing and evaluating your agency-based work, such as reviewing case notes, observing you providing various professional tasks, and processing your casework. Last, the field instructor may also review and evaluate important academic work such as process recordings and assist in various academic assignments.

Educational Function of Field Supervision

In terms of the educational function, the main purpose of field supervision is to assist you in the learning process. The difference between field supervision and employee-based supervision is that the focus of field supervision is on education and learning. By placing the emphasis of the supervision session on learning and not just on training, this will address the challenges you may face as you sit down for a supervision session. Students report that often when they meet with their field instructor, they briefly check in, run through the work tasks, identify any training needs, and are done fifteen minutes later. Based on this description, the student is missing important opportunities for learning in a variety of areas. Furthermore, students often report that they don't know what is supposed to happen in the field supervision session, so when the session is missed they don't necessarily think it is a problem. Or because they work closely with their field instructor and discuss things all day, they see no need for formal supervision. Thus by focusing the session on education, this can open the door for a variety of effective learning tasks. One educational activity of supervision that can be added to the weekly supervision session is to deliberately target the integration of curriculum into practice at field. An example of this is to review, each week in the supervision session, one of the ethical standards from the NASW Code of Ethics and apply that standard directly to practice situations at the agency. This learning activity is different in many ways from your previous classroom-based learning on ethics in that the exploration of the code of ethics and the various standards is now specifically applied to client-based situations in the agency, thus providing you with the opportunity to apply the code to real case situations as apposed to cases in your book. Your supervision session truly becomes field-based learning through this process of targeted integration of curriculum with practice.

Supportive Function of Field Supervision

The last function of supervision is supportive. For you, support can look and feel like many different things. One, it is being made to feel that you matter and are welcomed into the agency. Two, you will see your field instructor making time for you and engaging in activities in which you can get to know one another. Third, your field instructor will advocate for your learning needs and explain your role and presence in the agency to the other staff. Last, when you have concerns or problems, your field instructor will listen and assist you in a problem-solving process. As you can see, the relationship you build with your field instructor is critical to meeting this function, not only for your learning but also to contribute to the quality of your field experience and socialization as a professional. Barretti (2004) in her study on the professional socialization of undergraduate social work students states that, ". . . positive relationships and identifications with their role models were reported as helping students become better people, better listeners, and more whole, functional, happy, confident, and self-aware" (p. 20). Ensuring that this function can occur becomes critical to your success in field and is often challenging due to multiple factors. First of all, your field instructor will have multiple demands that can take precedence over your supervision; your agency at times may be chaotic and crisis oriented, which can result in you not being able to plan for the day; and last, your anxieties about what the relationship with the supervisor will entail. All of the preceding can present barriers to the development of the supervisory relationship, and without developing a supportive relationship, it may be more difficult for the other functions to be achieved.

We have discussed the three primary functions of field supervision, all of which are important. That being said, getting the weekly supervision session to happen on a consistent and set basis is the first hurdle to overcome, and it is necessary to ensure that the functions discussed previously can be realized. Knight (1996) found that of 12 schools surveyed, ". . . more than 20%" (p. 411) were not meeting the one hour a week of required supervision. Unless supervision occurs on a regular basis, none of the functions of supervision can be met. It is important to focus on the structure and logistics of supervision; this has to do with the when, where, and what, and ensuring supervision's consistent presence in your field experience.

THE STRUCTURE AND LOGISTICS OF SUPERVISION

It is important that you and your field instructor discuss the structure and logistics of field supervision. Several elements to the supervision session are necessary to consider to maximize its effectiveness in your learning. They are,

1. timing,
2. content, and
3. tools.

Timing

The first thing to consider is timing; this refers to the day of the week, time of day, and length of the session. The best way to address the timing of supervision is to establish a regular and consistent time, write it in your calendar, and by all means stick to it. This should be the first thing you do during your first week of field. For instance, some students like to start the week off in supervision, so they meet at 9:00 a.m. on their first day of the week. Other students like to end the week with supervision, so they meet at 4:00 p.m. on the last day of their week. It really doesn't matter when you meet as long as you have a set time and stick to it. In terms of the length of the session, most programs identify the amount of time; check with your program to ensure that you are meeting the requirement. An hour a week is a fairly standard guideline.

Having a set time is particularly important in the beginning of field because this will socialize you to attending supervision and will assist in your ability to develop competence in the use of supervision. It is also helpful to have a set time because you can learn what can wait until supervision and what needs to be answered immediately. Finally, day-to-day life in an agency can become very hectic, and days and even weeks can slip by; so it is important to know you have your supervision time well established.

In some settings, the student may work side-by-side with the field instructor. This can be a wonderful experience and can often result in immediate ongoing supervision. But it is important to realize that there is critical learning that may not occur in those types of contact and that will, in fact, occur only during uninterrupted structured supervision sessions. In other settings, students may not see their field instructor on a daily basis, so it is important to have that supervision time set aside in both the student's and field instructor's schedules. It is also important to note that attending the supervision session is a task that falls in the "professional socialization" category of the multilevel field tasks discussed in Chapter 3. Last, an important outcome of using supervision appropriately is the ability to determine what can wait and what cannot. That is, what do you need to ask or tell your field instructor or task supervisor immediately and what can wait until your scheduled supervision session. This skill will not be readily developed if you do not have a set time. A set time allows you to plan for the session and determine what needs to be addressed when.

Content

The content of a supervision session refers to what will be discussed. The two primary areas of discussion will be agency-based content and education-based content. Agency-based content will focus on the agency, such as your orientation, training, task assignment, role, clients served, services, and policies and procedures. Education-based content will focus primarily on two overarching goals of field education: your socialization and development as a social worker and the integration of the classroom and field.

A way to help you identify potential content for the supervision session is to complete Integrative Activity 5.1: The Supervision Outline. The supervision outline will assist you and your field instructor in designing the layout of the supervision sessions over the course of a semester or quarter and is similar to designing a curriculum for a course or a group.

There are three columns. The first column is the week; it includes 16. You may want to add in your actual supervision date and time or any other dates that are important. The second column is for content. This is where you will identify the agency- or university-based content you want to talk about during the supervision session. For instance, during the first few weeks, you may want to include orientation and training, a discussion of your learning plan, and safety. The third column includes any supervision tools you may need for that session, such as your learning plan or a case note. A few template items are also included that most students will discuss; however, if the placement of these doesn't fit your program or agency, simply cross them out and move them to the appropriate week.

The purpose of this activity is to help you plan ahead for the entire semester or quarter in terms of identifying important due dates and content that needs to be discussed that is time sensitive, and to ensure that you and your field instructor have considered the big picture of supervision. For instance, on the outline you may include the need to discuss the learning plan and final field evaluations as well as their due dates to ensure that you can meet them. You may also include a discussion of important trainings that are time sensitive, such as a documentation training that you must attend before you can input case notes into the computer system. You may also want to identify midterm and a plan to discuss your progress to date. Furthermore, refer back to Integrative Activity 2.3: Curriculum Review for the specialized content identified, determine when and how that will be obtained, and place that on your outline. Last, for other ideas, look to your course work or ask your field instructor for ideas of content-related items that can be included in the outline. Both you and your field instructor should keep a copy of the outline with the designated time, location, and content of the session.

INTEGRATIVE ACTIVITY 5.1

The Supervision Outline

Purpose: The purpose of this outline is for you and your field instructor to develop a curriculum for field supervision. This will include the content you and your field instructor want to discuss in each supervision session as well as any materials you need to bring to supervision session.

Directions: In the first column, **Week**, include the specific date and time of your supervision session and any other dates that are important. In the second column, **Agency-Based Content**, write in the content you and your field instructor need to discuss that relates to the agency; this could be important training and orientation material. In the next column, include **Field-Education-Based Content** that needs to be discussed; for information, look at your course syllabi and field manual. Last, in the **Supervision Tools** column, identify any materials, including any paperwork, handouts, and worksheets, that you will need to go over or interactive activities you want to engage in with your field instructor during the session.

Note: You will want to use this for more than one semester, so make a copy or pencil in entries that can be erased later.

Week	Agency-Based Content	Field-Education-Based Content	Supervision Tools
1 Date: Time:			
2 Date: Time:			
3 Date: Time:			
4 Date: Time:			
5 Date: Time:			
6 Date: Time:			
7 Date: Time:			
8 Date: Time:			
9 Date: Time:			
10 Date: Time:			
11 Date: Time:			
12 Date: Time:			
13 Date: Time:			
14 Date: Time:			
15 Date: Time:			
16 Date: Time:			

Having an outline of the supervision sessions will allow you and your field instructor to plan ahead and thus better use your supervision time. When the weekly sessions are designed like a syllabus or curriculum for a course or group, the individual supervision sessions will have more focus and be better integrated with the goals of field education.

Now that you have considered the big picture of your supervision needs over an entire semester or quarter, the next step is to begin to think about how you want to structure the flow of content of a specific session. Integrative Activity 5.2: The Supervision Agenda will assist you in this process by encouraging you to jot down agenda items for discussion in a session in several categories;

1. agency-based content,
2. education-based content, and
3. other.

By completing this activity and identifying the content to be discussed prior to the start of each session, you will ensure that you are equally focusing on all areas as well as demonstrating leadership for the development of the content of a particular session.

INTEGRATIVE ACTIVITY 5.2

The Supervision Agenda

Purpose: The purpose of this activity is to help you develop an agenda for your supervision session.

Directions: In each of the following areas, list items that you want to discuss in your next supervision session that correspond with each area. For subsequent supervision sessions, refer back to this activity to organize your thinking and identify content for discussion.

---

1. Agency-Based Content:

2. Education-Based Content:

3. Other:

4. Questions:

At the onset of your field experience, you will look to your field instructor to lead the supervision session because much of the focus will be on orientation and training and establishing the critical tasks of field. However, as you move toward more independent practice, it is important for you to begin to demonstrate leadership in the use of the supervision session. Many of the integrative activities already discussed in this book assisted you in the process of structuring the supervision session. For instance, engaging in a discussion about your curriculum, as a result of completing Integrative Activity 2.3: Curriculum Review, you were sharing in the development of the content for that session. Your shared leadership, in the use of the supervision session, will increase throughout the year as you focus more on your client system tasks, and you will be able to demonstrate your competence in your use of supervision.

EP 2.1.1f

As you take on more leadership in determining the agenda, you are also developing and demonstrating your professional communication.

Interestingly enough, communication in the supervision session is an area in which students express some anxiety and often state they don't know what to say. By planning out and even practicing what you want to discuss or share in the supervision session, you will be better prepared to demonstrate competence in this important area.

EP 2.1.1d

The last thing to consider with regard to the content of the supervision session is to keep supervision notes. Writing supervision notes supports the development of your competence in professional writing and also provides a record of the specific plans developed for client system work and your learning process.

Integrative Activity 5.3: Documenting Your Supervision Session suggests you keep a record of your supervision session by documenting the date, the content discussed, and the plan of action or next steps.

EP 2.1.3c

INTEGRATIVE ACTIVITY 5.3

Documenting Your Supervision Session

Purpose: The purpose of this activity is to assist you in the development of your note taking skills as well as provide a record of your supervision session.

Directions: Select a supervision session, and in each of the following areas, document the content discussed.

Session Date:

1. Agency- and Education-Based Content Discussed:

2. Next Steps/Plan of Action:

3. Strength Areas:

4. Areas Needing to Be Worked On:

The Tools of Supervision

Last, it is important for you to discuss the tools of supervision that you may use while in field. The tools of supervision refer to specific concrete and tangible items that may be brought to the supervision session to augment a discussion or even may be specific interactive activities that you engage in with your field instructor. For instance, a concrete tangible item that can be used as a tool in supervision could be a written document such as a case note, an assessment, an outline of a program you are working on developing, an integrative activity, or an academic assignment such as a process recording. The concrete item, brought to and used in the supervision session, provides an opportunity for learning that is specific. By reviewing a case note that you wrote on a specific client contact, you will end up having a more directed learning experience than if you were to just discuss case noting in general. Examples of an interactive supervision tool could be to watch a video or listen to an audio recording of a client session, coworking a session with a client, or receiving training information in the supervision session. It is important to note that an interactive supervision tool may happen in the supervision session or outside the session. For those tools that happen outside the session, it is important to process them right after the activity or in the next session. Similar to the outcome of the use of a concrete tangible tool, the use of an interactive tool in supervision maximizes your learning and increases the likelihood that supervision will be more than a quick review of your tasks or setting the plan for the week.

Identifying the learning tools that will be used in the supervision session is important in that it will ensure that all possible activities that can assist in the learning process are being used. These tools may be incorporated in the learning plan and thus contribute to the evaluation process. Year after year, the students with whom I work give me feedback that they want more concrete learning opportunities in and outside of the supervision session, such as going over their case notes, observing their field instructor and discussing their observations, and being directly observed. This discussion will hopefully identify all the possible tools for learning and negotiating their use.

REFLECTION QUESTION 5.1

Now that you have had an opportunity to consider the functions and logistics of field supervision, what are you hoping to get out supervision? What do you need from your field instructor for supervision to be a productive and helpful activity? What are your concerns, if any, about field supervision? What do you need to do to benefit from supervision? What specific tools are you hoping to use in and outside your supervision session?

Suggested Field Tasks

- Establish supervision time.
- Attend and plan for supervision.
- Use supervision appropriately.
- In supervision describe and explain practice tasks.
- Complete documentation, professional writing.

Competency Notes

The following identifies where the CSWE *EPAS* (2008) Educational Policy (EP) and practice behaviors are discussed in the chapter.

EP 2.1.1d Demonstrate professional demeanor in behavior, appearance, and communication (p. 80): By attending supervision social workers develop and demonstrate competent professional behavior.

EP 2.1.1f Use supervision and consultation (pp. 73, 80): Social workers need to develop an understanding of how to use supervision and consultation to function as a competent professional.

EP 2.1.3c Demonstrate effective oral and written communication in working with individuals, families, groups, organizations, communities, and colleagues (p. 80): Social workers develop and demonstrate competence in communicating orally and in writing about their practice with individuals, families, groups, the agency, communities, and colleagues in the supervision session.

References

Abramson, J. S. & Fortune, A. E. (1990). Improving field instruction: An evaluation of a seminar for new field instructors. *Journal of Social Work Education, 26*(3), 273–286.

Bennett, S. & Deal, K. H. (2009). Beginnings and endings in social work supervision: The interaction between attachment and developmental processes. *Journal of Teaching in Social Work, 29,* 101–117.

Barretti, M. (2004). The professional socialization of undergraduate social work students. *The Journal of Baccalaureate Social Work, 9,* 10–30.

Bogo, M., & Vayda, E. (1998). *The practice of field instruction in social work: Theory and process* (2nd ed.). New York: Columbia University Press.

Cavazos, A. (1996). Measuring BSW student learning in field instruction. *Journal of Social work Education, 32*(3), 389–398.

Cochran, S., & Hanley, M. (1999). *Learning through field.* Boston: Allyn and Bacon.

Council on Social Work Education. (2008). *Educational policy and accreditation standards.* Alexandria, VA: Council on Social Work Education.

Dettlaff, A. (2003). *From mission to evaluation: A field instructor training program.* Alexandria, VA: Council on Social Work Education.

Ellison, M. (1994). Critical field instruction behaviors: Student and field instructor views. *Arete, 18*(2), 12–21.

Fortune, A. E., & Abramson, J. S. (1993). Predictors of satisfaction with field practicum among social work students. *The Clinical Supervisor, 11*(1), 95–110.

Gelman, C. (2004). Special section: Field education in social work anxiety experienced by foundation-year MSW students entering field placement: Implications for admission, curriculum, and field education. *Journal of Social Work Education, 40*(1). 39–54.

Kadushin, A. (1991) Introduction. In Dean Schneck, Bart Grossman, & Urania Glassman (eds.), *Field education in social work: Contemporary issues and trends.* Iowa: Kendall/Hunt Publishing Co.

Knight, C. (1996). A study of MSW and BSW student's perceptions of their field instructors. *Journal of Social Work Education, 32*(3), 399–414.

Knight, C. (2001). The process of field instruction: BSW and MSW students' views of effective field supervision. *Journal of Social Work Education, 37*(2), 357–379.

Okundaye, J.N., Gray, C., & Gray, L. B. (1999). Reimaging field instruction from a spiritually sensitive perspective: An alternative approach. *Social Work, 44*(4), 371–383.

Reid, W. J., Bailey-Dempsey, C., & Viggiani, P. (1996). Evaluating student field education: An empirical study. *Journal of Social Work Education, 32*(1), 45.

Skolnik, L., & Papell, C. P. (1994). Holistic designs for field instruction in the contemporary social work curriculum. *Journal of Social Work Education, 30*(1), 90.

Webb, N. (1988). The role of the field instructor in the socialization of students. *Social Casework, 69*(1), 35–40.

CHAPTER 6

Effective Communication Skills for Field

Central to competent practice in field is developing and demonstrating effective communication skills. Communication can be defined as ". . . a process in which one individual conveys information—either intentionally or unintentionally—to another" (Sheafor and Horejsi, 2008, p. 134). This chapter will lay the foundation for you to both develop and demonstrate competence in your oral and written communication with individuals, families, groups, organizations, communities, and colleagues and provide resources for you to assess and analyze your communication skills.

COMMUNICATION SKILLS FOR GENERALIST PRACTICE

EP 2.1.3c

The first thing to consider is how you will adapt the communication skills you have learned in your course work to the multilevel tasks you will be engaging in at field. As you begin to think about this, you may realize that some of the skills will be used in the same way regardless of the task, while others will need to be adapted. To help you develop an understanding of the multifaceted nature of communication in field, let's review multilevel communication.

First and foremost, most social work students consider their micro-level communication with individuals and families to be foundational to being a social worker. When working with individuals and families, you focus on developing and demonstrating active listening, reflecting back, question asking, and summarizing. The next level is communicating at the mezzo level, which focuses on how you use your communication skills when working in treatment or task groups. When working in groups, you continue to practice the skill of active listening but may use reflecting back in a different way than you might with an individual client. For instance, with one-on-one contacts, the communication is directed specifically to the individual client. However, when running a group, you may be reflecting back what an individual member has said, but direct the reflection to the entire group and adapt what you say to apply more generally to the group as a whole as opposed to just the individual who first made the comment. This is done intentionally and reflects the goals and structure of group work versus individual work. As a result of your reflecting-back statement, another member of the group may respond, showing that reflecting back may look different depending on the task. Similarly, when facilitating and or participating in a task group, how you use your foundational communication skills will vary depending on the composition of the group and the goals. For instance, if you are cochairing the fund-raising committee of your agency, your communication may be informal. But if you are presenting material you have researched to the program and services subcommittee of the board, your communication may need to be more formal and professional.

Last, consider your communication at the macro-level within your organization and in the community. This involves communication within the agency and on behalf of the organization in the community and encompasses a variety of skills. For instance, how you communicate in the break room with the other social workers, at the annual agency retreat, or in the community at a meeting where you are representing your agency will all differ and require varying skills. Communication at the macro-level will reflect both formal and informal styles of communication as well as your ability to discern the appropriate type of communication depending on the practice situation. You will pick up on the formal and informal communication patterns as you become more comfortable at the agency. One example is the joking around that may take place during lunch versus the serious and more professional communication style of a staff meeting that is looking at a funding crisis. The ability to recognize these variations when communicating at different levels is important for communicating effectively in field.

REFLECTION QUESTION 6.1

Now that you have had a chance to review multilevel communication, identify the primary multilevel communication you will be engaging in at your site. What types of communication, oral and written, will you engage in with individuals, families, groups, organizations, and communities at your agency? What, if any, concerns do you have about multilevel communication at your agency? Where do you see your current strengths related to communication, and what will you need to work on while in field?

ORAL COMMUNICATION SKILLS

At the heart of effective oral communication are the following core interpersonal qualities:

1. warmth,
2. empathy,
3. respect, and
4. genuineness (Chang, Scott, and Decker, 2009, and Sheafor and Horejsi, 2008).

Your ability to demonstrate these qualities when communicating orally in field will lay the foundation for your interactions with individuals, families, groups, organizations, communities and with colleagues. In addition to the core qualities that ground your contacts with clients, you will also need to develop and demonstrate several basic communication skills such as,

EP 2.1.10b

- active listening,
- expressing understanding through the use of reflecting back,

- using questions to gather information,
- information giving,
- reframing,
- summarizing,
- seeking clarification,
- using positive confrontation,
- establishing goals,
- planning, and
- evaluating (Chang, Scott and Decker, 2009; Sidell and Smiley, 2008).

These communication skills lay the foundation for effective communication in field. The most useful task to engage in at field to apply and develop these foundational oral communication skills is interviewing.

Interviewing

Interviewing is an excellent task because an interview provides you with the structure necessary to practice many important skills. The first thing you need to do is identify the opportunities you will have in field to engage in interviewing. Interviewing is defined as the opportunity to engage a client system in a purposeful conversation that allows for exploration of an issue. It is very important to have an opportunity to sit down with a client system and engage in a conversation.

When interviewing, you will be able to practice,

1. introducing yourself as a student,
2. explaining your role,
3. reviewing and discussing the purpose and plan for the interview,
4. discussing confidentiality and the limits of confidentiality,
5. engaging your client in a conversation that is directed to a goal, and
6. last, ending the interview, which usually includes summarizing, identifying who will do what, and planning for the next contact if applicable.

These structural and functional aspects of an interview create a rich learning experience for you to practice your oral communication skills. Furthermore, more often than not, you will be able to plan for the contact ahead of time as well as discuss and process the interview in supervision.

Interviewing can look very different depending on your agency and role. For instance, the interviewing you do may consist of onetime contacts, as in the example of the student who is working at a local social services agency that offers a food pantry, or may involve ongoing contacts, as in the case of an agency that provides medical case management services for individuals who are (human immunodeficiency virus) HIV positive. Regardless of the type of service, you need to develop and demonstrate your ability to open an interview, use active listening, ask questions—open and closed ended, reflect back, summarize, and close an interview.

An important part of developing your communication skills is the ability to reflect on and analyze an interview. A helpful way to think about an interview is to visualize a tree. Just as a tree is made up of roots, a trunk and many branches, the conversation between you and your client, which is the interview, can also be broken down into the three main parts which reflect the parts of the tree. The roots represent the issues that are bringing the client to your attention. Some of the issues maybe evident to the client such as the need for housing. While other issues such as an underlying mental health or substance abuse condition or the impact of childhood abuse or neglect maybe not be as evident. The trunk can embody the overall foundation or purpose of the interview. This takes into consideration the referral, agency and services, your role, and purpose of the meeting. Once the conversation starts, the interview moves up to the branches, with each branch representing a possible direction the conversation can take, based on what the client says to you and what you say or don't say back to your client. You want to be able to think about the direction the conversation takes and develop your skill in directing that conversation as well as having an idea of where the conversation is headed.

Integrative Activity 6.1: Assessing Interviewing Skills offers a way to develop your skill in assessing and analyzing your oral communication skills, as well as demonstrating competence in this important practice behavior. The interview assessment is a quick way to determine if you are meeting the structural aspects of an interview. After an interview with an individual, complete the checklist to determine if you hit the main structural aspects of an interview.

This activity can be used in two different ways: (1) you can use it to self-assess your skill development, or (2) you can conduct an interview under the direct observation of your field instructor or an agency designee you feel comfortable with and have that person provide you with feedback. The latter can provide valuable information to assess your competence in communication skills.

INTEGRATIVE ACTIVITY 6.1

Assessing Interviewing Skills

Purpose: The purpose of this activity is to assist you in developing and assessing your interviewing skills.

Directions: After an interview, review each skill and blind spot and indicate if you demonstrated that or not. Once you have completed the checklist, reflect on your strengths and weaknesses and use this assessment to build your skills. This may also be used by your field instructor or agency designee to obtain outside feedback while you are under direct observation.

Communication Skill	Demonstrated	Not Demonstrated	Comments
Opening			
1. Greeted client	❑	❑	
2. Introduced self as student	❑	❑	
3. Explained purpose, duration of interview	❑	❑	
4. Explained role	❑	❑	
5. Explained confidentiality and limits	❑	❑	
6. Invited client to talk	❑	❑	
7. Reviewed any necessary paperwork	❑	❑	
Questioning			
1. Asked closed-ended questions	❑	❑	
2. Asked open-ended questions	❑	❑	
3. Listened to answers	❑	❑	
4. Balanced talking with listening	❑	❑	
5. Answered client's questions	❑	❑	
6. Allowed for silence	❑	❑	

Communication Skill	Demonstrated	Not Demonstrated	Comments
Expressing Understanding			
1. Displayed warmth and empathy	❏	❏	
2. Reflected back content	❏	❏	
3. Reflected back feelings	❏	❏	
4. Summarized content and feelings	❏	❏	
5. Expressed understanding of meaning	❏	❏	
6. Managed client's affect	❏	❏	
Seeking Clarification			
1. Used positive confrontation to increase understanding	❏	❏	
2. Provided information, instructions, directions or feedback	❏	❏	
3. Used reframing to change perspective of situation	❏	❏	
Nonverbal Communication			
1. Maintained eye contact	❏	❏	
2. Used a warm tone of voice	❏	❏	
3. Displayed a relaxed facial expression	❏	❏	
4. Demonstrated interest in what client was saying	❏	❏	
5. Displayed a relaxed posture	❏	❏	
6. Demonstrated congruence between verbal and nonverbal	❏	❏	
7. Demonstrated distracting body movements	❏	❏	
Structure of Interview			
1. Nice pace	❏	❏	
2. Good transitions between questions	❏	❏	
3. A clear beginning, middle, and end to the interview	❏	❏	
Common Interview Blind Spots			
1. Gave advice	❏	❏	
2. Talked too much	❏	❏	
3. Demonstrated disconnect, moved from topic to topic	❏	❏	
4. Missed opportunities for expressing understanding	❏	❏	
5. Interrupted client	❏	❏	
6. Jumped to reassure client	❏	❏	
7. Abruptly ended the interview	❏	❏	
8. Jumped to problem solving	❏	❏	
9. Asked leading questions	❏	❏	
Closing			
1. Indicated interview was ending	❏	❏	
2. Summarized interview	❏	❏	
3. Reviewed agreed-upon plan	❏	❏	
4. Saw if client had any questions	❏	❏	
5. Indicated plan for future meetings if applicable	❏	❏	

Integrative Activity 6.2: The Process Recording provides a deeper way of analyzing and evaluating the flow and direction an interview takes and determining what you as the social work student and the client did or did not do to advance the conversation. The process recording is a useful tool that provides a more intensive exploration of an interview as opposed to the interview assessment, which offers a quick structural assessment of the interview (Graybeal, 1995; Mullin & Canning, 2007; and Neuman, 1997). Following an interview, prepare a process recording. Once you have completed the process recording, ask your field instructor for feedback. Once your field instructor has reviewed it, discuss the interview in supervision. The feedback can focus on your strengths and growth areas as well as on what the field instructor might have done differently. The feedback you get from both your self-assessment and your field instructor's assessment is invaluable to your learning.

INTEGRATIVE ACTIVITY 6.2

The Process Recording

Purpose: The purpose of completing a process recording is to assist you in the development and assessment of your communication skills, as well as provide a structured opportunity for demonstrating competence.

Directions: Select a client, and using the following form, provide a detailed account of an interview. The process recording should include:

1. who was present, when and where the interview took place;
2. the purpose of the interview;
3. what phase of the helping process you are in, and what you are hoping to accomplish;
4. your role and activities, and what you did (interventions);
5. a detailed description of the interview, including what you said and what the client said, specific dialogue, back-and-forth (like a script);
6. a detailed description of your thoughts and reactions during the interview, addressing what you were thinking and trying to accomplish;
7. your analysis of how you did, and what you would do the same or differently;
8. your analysis of the clients situation, needs, issues, affect, strengths, etc., based on the interview;
9. your analysis of the outcome of the interventions used in the interview, incorporating feedback from field instructor, and
10. plan for the next interaction or contact, if any.

Process Recording Format: First, provide a description of the background of the interview addressing the first three areas from the preceding list. Then document the specific dialogue of the interaction; that is, write out what you said and what the client said back in a script form. In the second column, provide your analysis, addressing what was going on for you, what you were thinking at the time, and what you were trying to accomplish. Once you have completed writing the process recording, review and discuss it in supervision with your field instructor. Ask your field instructor to provide comments in the third column.

Note: The process recording is not limited to one page. This is just the format; use additional pages if necessary to document the client system contact.

Note: Format adapted from *Human Service Agencies An Orientation to Fieldwork*, by Alle-Corliss & Alle-Corliss, 1998, p. 240

Interview Background
(# 1–4 from the preceding directions)

Interview Dialogue (# 5 from the preceding directions)	Student Analysis During Interview (#6 from the preceding directions)	Field Instructor Feedback

(Continued)

Overall Analysis of Interview
(# 7–10 from the preceding directions)

Although both of the preceding integrative activities (6.1 and 6.2) are best done with individual clients, they can also be done with a treatment or task group session as a way to evaluate your communication skills at the mezzo level.

Last, the most real-life and ultimately most effective tool for evaluating your communication skills is audio or video recording an interview. If you have this opportunity at your agency, take it. There is nothing like seeing yourself working with clients in person.

Nonverbal Communication

So far we have focused primarily on oral communication. However, the nonverbal communication that accompanies all oral communication is an important part of oral communication worth noting. In fact research indicates that two thirds of all communication is nonverbal (Beall, 2004).

Some of the nonverbal communications that a client may display and that you will want to pay attention to are,

- eye contact,
- facial expressions,
- body positioning and posture,
- tone of voice,
- dress and appearance,
- movement, and
- whether what a client is communicating nonverbally matches what they are saying orally (Sheafor & Horesji, 2008; and Sidell & Smiley, 2008).

It is also important to develop your awareness of nonverbal communication because a change in a client's nonverbal communication can signify a change in the client. Last, it is important to remember that any communication is two-way, meaning that you, too, are communicating nonverbally. It is equally important to be attuned to what you may be saying to a client during an interview.

Telephone Communication

The last and often most challenging oral communication for students is the communication conducted over the phone. Interestingly enough, many students tell me they are most anxious about this form of communication. However, social workers spend much time on the phone with and on behalf of clients. Interestingly, phone work is verbal communication without the corresponding nonverbal communication cues; that is, you do not have the advantage of seeing the client or person you are talking with, so you do not have that important information to aid you in your work. Phone work can involve working on a hotline, calling clients to schedule appointments and gather information, and contacting other professionals to discuss client needs and progress. The latter is often referred to as collateral contacts and can make up much of your work; thus it is important to become comfortable with this type of communication.

REFLECTION QUESTION 6.2

Now that you have had a chance to consider oral communication, particularly related to interviewing, nonverbal, and phone-based communication in field, what are your thoughts about your ability to effectively demonstrate and use your communication skills and engage in the tasks of interviewing and telephone contact? What are your concerns, if any?

Written Communication Skills

The next area of communication to consider in field is written communication. The written communication you will use requires a wide range of skills. The written documents that you produce will vary depending on your agency and tasks, as well as on whether or not you primarily work with individuals, families, groups, organizations, or communities.

At the micro-level, the work you do with individuals and families needs to be documented. This most likely consists of writing various documents that are contained in client records. The first step in familiarizing yourself with the written documents you need to produce at the micro-level is to review the client record. Client records are the official documents amassed in a binder or maintained electronically by the agency. These may include but are not limited to intake, consent to treat, releases of information, case notes, assessments, incident reports, call logs, service plans, discharge reports, and transfer summaries. A client record may also contain copies of documents created by other agencies that are used when serving the client. As a student, you are responsible to document the work you do with clients. By maintaining accurate records, you are protecting the clients in case something happens to you and another worker needs to take over the case. Similarly, you protect yourself and your field instructor by documenting your actions on a case.

Once you have reviewed the client record, you want to discuss with your field instructor the plan for you to write your own documents. At the micro-level, the most common form of documentation to develop your written communication skills is the case note. A case note includes written text that documents what was said during the contact, your assessment and plan, as well as when the contact started and ended, the date, and type of contact.

There are several different formats for a case note. For instance, the SOAP note:

S = Subjective information, which includes what the client feels about or perceives and is based on self-report;
O = Objective information, which is content obtained by direct observation;
A = Assessment, which refers to the conclusions drawn by the social worker, and last,
P = Plan, which is what the social worker will be doing (Sheafor & Horesji, 2008).

Another format is the SOAIGP:

S = Supplemental information provided by the client,
O = Observations by the social worker,
A = Activities that will be done on behalf of the client,
I = Impressions and the social worker's assessment,
G = Goals, and last,
P = Plan of action (Kagel and Kopels, 2008).

The format that I used when I first practiced at a crisis intervention agency that provided a suicide prevention hotline was CAP:

C = Complaint,
A = Assessment, and
P = Plan.

This format was a succinct way to document client hotline calls.

Regardless of the format of your case notes, note taking while interviewing is an important skill that is integral in your ability to write accurate case notes. In all likelihood, you will not be able to memorize all that is said during an interview, so you will want to take notes. This challenging task requires skill in that you will need to be able to simultaneously,

- ask questions,
- jot down responses, and
- respond using your interviewing skills.

The best way to develop this skill is to follow these steps. First, before you begin your interview, create an outline of the questions and information you need and leave space for the client's answers. This will not only provide an easy way to keep track of your client's responses but will also keep you on track while interviewing. Second, inform your client that you need to jot down a few things while you are talking so that you don't miss anything important. By letting your client know what you need, both you and your client will be more comfortable during the interview. Last, if a form needs to be completed, bring the form with you so you can go over it with the client.

One thing to remember is that paperwork may be overwhelming to clients for a variety of reasons. It is important to be aware of this while you are working with your clients. I once had a client who needed to complete several forms, so I handed them to the client. As soon as I handed the documents to the client, the client looked at the forms and then back at me and became visibly upset. So much so that the client decided it wasn't a good time to meet. It occurred to me that perhaps the client could not read the forms, so I quickly interjected and said something about the fact that I, too, found the paperwork confusing and asked if the client would like us to go over it together. The client immediately relaxed and said yes. As a result of this experience, I have always made it a practice to ask my clients if they would like us to go over the paperwork together or if they would like to go over it for themselves. This way, a client can defer to me and not be made to feel uncomfortable about paperwork.

In addition to writing case notes, you also need to be skilled at writing assessments or social histories, discharge reports, and transfer summaries. It is important to determine the plan for you to be able to engage in these tasks and create these documents.

At the mezzo-level, you need to document treatment group sessions. This type of note should indicate who attended the group and what the group covered. You may also need to document your work on task groups. The documentation for a task group would include who attended the meeting, what was discussed, and any tasks that group members agreed to do before the next meeting.

At the macro-level, written communication may be in the form of formal reports, such as annual reports, newsletters, an article for the local paper, a manual, agency policies and procedures, forms, and any materials for various services of the agency, such as group materials. To develop and demonstrate competence in documenting client contact, complete Integrative Activity 6.3: Writing a Case Note.

INTEGRATIVE ACTIVITY 6.3

Writing a Case Note

Purpose: The purpose of this activity is to develop and demonstrate your skill in documentation.

Directions: Following a client contact, write a case note documenting the contact. This can be done with your agency's format or you may select one of the following formats. Once you have written your case note documenting a client contact, submit the case note to your field instructor for review and discussion.

The CAP Method:

C (Complaint):

A (Assessment):

P (Plan):

The SOAP Note Method:

S (Subjective Content):

O (Objective Content):

A (Assessment):

P (Plan):

COMMUNICATION AND TECHNOLOGY

As you are well aware, we currently live in the information age, and the use of technology in social work practice has expanded greatly. In fact, while reading this chapter, you very likely have already checked your e-mail a few times, glanced at your Facebook page, and became distracted by the multiple notifications of your current text messages. For me the story of technology and social work practice began in the early 1990s. In fact, I have a vivid memory of the day the agency I was working at installed voice mail, and I thought to myself how terrible it was that a client would get a recorded message instead of speaking to a person. Now many of my professional tasks are solely completed via e-mail and teleconferencing. I have developed strong professional relationships and completed important tasks with individuals I have not even met in person. With the rise in the use of technology in social work practice, it is important to identify the role and use of technology in your agency, as well as your agency's expectations of your ability to effectively use technology in your practice in the agency.

Internet and E-Mail Use in Agencies

Ishizuki and Cotter (2008) found that the use of Internet and e-mail communication is increasing and that they are important tools for social workers. Communicating via these tools can take many forms. For instance, your agency and field instructor may use e-mail when communicating with the staff. It is important to determine whether you will have an agency-based e-mail account and how often you need to be checking your account. If you will not have an e-mail account at the agency, discuss how you will receive agency information communicated via e-mail. If you will be using your personal e-mail account, first and foremost make sure your e-mail address is appropriate. If not, as in the case of an address that is a personal reference or was picked for fun, you may want to consider revising it to a more standard format. With regard to using e-mail to communicate with clients, it is very important to discuss this with your field instructor and determine the agency policy before you give a client your e-mail address. Finn and Krysik (2007) in their study regarding UE (unsolicited e-mail) found that social workers are receiving unsolicited e-mails from clients, and the growth in the use of electronic communication will necessitate, "agency policies and infrastructure that promote e-mail safety and confidentiality" (p. 35). Should you receive an unsolicited e-mail from a current or potential client or anyone in the community requesting information, notify your field instructor and discuss how to handle the situation. In addition to email use, the use of the internet to facilitate social work practice is well recognized. For instance, social workers may conduct searches for information and to locate and learn about community resources. Students can also log on to their university's library via the internet and search for articles that can advance their and other social workers' practice in the agency. However, some agencies may monitor internet searches and may not want employees, volunteers, and students using agency computers to do their online shopping, banking, updating their personal Facebook status, or accessing sites that the agency considers inappropriate. Other agencies may feel that it is fine when someone is on their lunch break to do the above. That is why it is so important to discuss this with your field instructor and know and follow the agency's policies and procedures that govern use of the internet at work.

Cell Phone Usage

In addition, you also want to discuss the use of cell phones and determine if you will have access to a cell phone when at the agency. The use of cell phones in social work practice has many important advantages. For instance, the field instructors I work with tell me they are increasingly using cell phones to text their clients, as many of their clients have unlimited texting and do not even have a landline. Texting the client has become a practice that not only protects the client's limited resources but also is efficient. Furthermore, cell phones can be useful when in field for communicating with a supervisor or being notified of changing appointments or crises. However, once you are engaged with a client system it is critically important that your cell phone be on silent and not checked until you are done with the contact. In the event you are waiting for an important client related call, let your client know that if the call comes in you will need to take it. A common question students have about cell phone use while in field is whether they can use their own personal phone. This is an important discussion to have with your field director and field instructor; for more on this specific question, see Chapter 11.

Social Networking

With regard to social networking, more and more agencies are turning to Facebook as an effective means to communicate their mission and educate others about their services. Interestingly, for one agency, their use of Facebook resulted from the director getting a "friend" request from a client on the director's personal Facebook page. The director was understandably caught off guard and of course did not "friend" the client. But the director later realized that the use of Facebook might be an untapped resource, so the agency established a page. With regard to your use of your personal Facebook page and using social networking as a way of making your "friends" aware of social issues, Facebook can be an important macro-level practice tool. This was seen in the significant role Facebook and twitter played in organizing protesters during the Arab Spring which began in 2010. However, it is very important to discuss with your field instructor your interest in using Facebook to increase awareness of issues and specifically how to maintain confidentiality with regard to your agency and the clients you serve when doing so. For instance, it is not appropriate to post specific client-based situations as your status. Second, if you want to increase your Facebook "friends" awareness of an issue or a need, do so very generally and always make sure it is okay with your agency. For instance, if your agency is having a fund-raising event that is open to the community, ask your field instructor if you can post the event on your Facebook page. With your field instructor's approval, it is okay. If you want to comment on something that is happening in the news and is impacting your agency, make sure you do not officially identify yourself as a representative of the agency. This is because many agencies have individuals who are approved for media contact, and although Facebook is not the media, you have no idea who is "friends" with whom and the impact your passionate post could have on your agency.

If a client sends you a "friend" request (yes, this can happen), make sure you ignore the request and discuss with the client why you can't be friends on Facebook. Also, reset your privacy settings to ensure that clients cannot inadvertently access your personal information. When posting photos that could link you to your agency, discuss this with your field instructor to determine if it is appropriate. I generally recommend that there are no circumstances where that would be appropriate, but there could be some gray areas, such as a community-based rally or walk that you participated in. Nonetheless, always discuss this with your field instructor ahead of time. Last, if and when you have a bad day, you think your field agency is crazy, your agency just lost all its funding, or your director suddenly quit, pause before you Tweet or post a status that could inadvertently breach confidentiality or show a lack of professionalism on your part.

Computer Systems

Another possible use of technology in your field agency could be the use of computer-based client records and documentation. Using the computer to maintain client records and document client contacts could be in addition to paper-based files or the sole format. Whatever the case, it is important for you to discuss how this is done and develop a plan to be trained on the computer system and required databases. Most important, the type of access you will have to the computer system needs to be addressed. This is extremely important given that a students' learning may be compromised by failing to address this issue early on in the placement. If you are not trained or do not have access to your client records, this will hamper the learning process.

REFLECTION QUESTION 6.3

Now that you have had a chance to consider the use of technology in field, what are your thoughts about the appropriate use of technology in social work practice such as e-mail, cell phones, social networking, and computerized records? What is your current level of competence in the use of technology, and what are any specific needs in this area?

COMMUNICATION CHALLENGES IN FIELD

From time to time, challenging situations will come up when communicating with clients that will require a more thoughtful response. For instance, you may experience a client who becomes verbally aggressive and angry and expresses intense emotions. These situations have happened to students I have worked with and require skill to manage. For instance, a student who was working at a child welfare agency was supervising a visit between a mother and her children when the mother became very angry and starting yelling at the student. The situation escalated to the point that the client began shouting, cussed at the student, and called her a derogatory name. The student was able to remain calm and use the verbal deescalation skills she had learned during her training. She reflected back to the client that she could hear she was very upset and felt it would be a good idea for the client to speak to her supervisor, who would be better able to address her concerns. She asked the client to wait in the room, took the children with her, and got her supervisor. The student reported later that she was caught off guard and was scared, but she also knew that if she acknowledged the client's anger using her active listening skills and got assistance from her supervisor, she would be able to manage the situation. In another similar situation, a student reported that her client became extremely angry during an interview, and again the student used her active listening skills, acknowledged the client's anger, and sought assistance of her supervisor. Both of these situations demonstrate that even in a situation where you may be caught off guard, it is always useful to go back to the basics and use active listening and reflecting back.

Another situation that can be challenging, particularly the first time a student experiences it, is when a client displays intense emotion such as crying uncontrollably during an interview or in group session. Although displaying intense emotion such as crying is normal and expected, many students report that when faced with this situation they do not know how to respond. The best plan of action is again to go back to the basics, acknowledge your client's feelings, allow the client time to experience the feelings by using silence, and reflect the feelings back to the client by saying something as simple as, "I can see how upsetting this is for you." All of these techniques can be very helpful to a client and let him or her know that you understand and require the ability of the social work student to be comfortable with experiencing intense emotions. Once a client's feelings are acknowledged and understanding is established, it is more likely that you will be able to redirect the client to the task and continue your work.

The last challenge that students can face when communicating with clients relates to the students' desire to assist their client. This can take the form of jumping to problem solving by giving advice or monopolizing the interview by only asking questions or talking too much. Both actions can result in the student missing opportunities for reflecting feelings or content back to a client, which is an important part of interviewing. Reflecting back what you are hearing gives the client important information and an opportunity to process their situation. It is very important to relax and allow the client to tell his or her story, to seek out opportunities for the client to engage in problem solving by reflecting back what you are hearing, and last, to allow for silence. Allowing for silence, particularly after you have reflected something back to a client, gives the client time to think and process the conversation, which often will result in the client having a realization or developing a plan. By rushing to problem-solving or information giving you may inadvertently prolong the process and, worse, miss the opportunity to engage the client fully. For the social work student this can be challenging because in all likelihood he or she has a genuine desire to assist the client and perhaps even excellent ideas and resources; however, if he or she has not engaged the client, the client may not be able to benefit from what the student and agency has to offer. Lastly, the opposite can hold true as well, where the social work student can allow the client to prolong the process and inadvertently delay the helping process. In this case, the student must develop the skill at using positive confrontation to redirect focus back to the task at hand.

The challenges discussed above become excellent sources for a process recording and analysis in supervision. So do not be afraid to bring these challenges to the attention of your field instructor, faculty field liaison, and peers if you are taking an integrative seminar course.

REFLECTION QUESTION 6.4

As you reflect on the challenges that can present themselves related to multilevel communication in field, what, if any, challenges do you face? What is your level of competence with regard to oral and written communication? What are your communication strengths and weaknesses, and what do you need to develop your competence?

Suggested Field Tasks

- Communicate with clients and at the organizational level using verbal, nonverbal, and written skills
- Evaluate professional communication skills
- Complete documentation, professional writing
- Intake and engage individuals, families, groups—task and treatment, organizations, and communities via phone and in person
- Use empathy and effective interpersonal skills
- Practice a wide variety of communication skills with clients

Competency Notes

The following identifies where the CSWE *EPAS* (2008) Educational Policy (EP) and practice behaviors are discussed in the chapter.

EP 2.1.3c Demonstrate effective oral and written communication in working with individuals, families, groups, organizations, communities, and colleagues (p. 84): Social workers must engage in multilevel communication both orally and in writing and assess their communication skills in order to develop competence.

EP 2.1.10b Use empathy and other interpersonal skills (p. 85): Social workers must develop competence in interviewing and interpersonal skills to be able to demonstrate competence.

References

Beall, A. E. (2004). Body language speaks. *Communication World*, *21*(2), 18–20.

Chang, V., Scott, S., & Decker, C. (2009). *Developing helping skills: A step-by-step approach.* Belmont, CA: Brooks/Cole.

Finn, J., & Krysik, J. (2007). Agency-based social worker's attitudes and behaviors regarding service-related unsolicited e-mail. *Journal of Technology in Human Services, 25*(3), 21–38.

Graybeal, C. T. (1995). Process recording: It's more than you think. *Journal of Social Work Education, 31*(2), 169–181.

Ishizuki, T., & Cotter, J. (2008). Social worker's use of the Internet and e-mail to help clients in Virginia. *Journal of Technology in Human Services, 27*, 127–140.

Kagel, J., & Kopels, S. (2008). *Social work records* (3rd ed.) Long Grove, IL: Waveland Press, Inc.

Mullin, W. J., & Canning, J. J. (2007). Process recording in supervision of students learning to practice with children. *Journal of Teaching in Social Work, 27*(3/4), 167–183.

Murphy, B., & Dillon, C. (2008). *Interviewing in action in a multicultural world.* Belmont, CA: Brooks/Cole.

Nartz, M., & Schoech, D. (2000). *Use of the Internet for community practice: A Delphi study. Journal of Community Practice, 8*(1), 37–59.

Neuman, K. M., & Friedman, B. D. (1997). Process recordings: Fine-tuning an old instrument. *Journal of Social Work Education, 33*(2), 237–243.

Sheafor, B., & Horejsi, C. (2008). *Techniques and guidelines for social work practice.* Boston: Pearson Education, Inc.

Sidell, N., & Smiley, D. (2008). *Professional communication skills in social work.* Boston: Pearson Education, Inc.

Schubert, M. (1996). *Interviewing in social work practice: An introduction* (rev. ed.). VA: Council on Social Work Education, Inc.

CHAPTER 7

Ethical Practice in Field

S ocial work practice is grounded in the values of the profession. The ethical practice demonstrated by a social worker reflects those values and is integral to competent practice. As a student in field, you will become immersed in these values and will have opportunities to demonstrate ethical decision making, particularly in the area of resolving ethical dilemmas. This chapter will explore several important content areas such as values and ethics in field, the ethics audit, ethical decision making, resolving ethical dilemmas, and last, the role of the law in ethical decision making.

VALUES AND ETHICS IN SOCIAL WORK

The National Association of Social Worker (NASW) delegate assembly initially approved the current Code of Ethics in 1996 and revised it in 1999. Reamer (1998) describes the code as "the most ambitious set of ethical guidelines in social work's history" (p. 488). Congress (2002) states that, "The NASW Code of Ethics with 155 ethical standards is the most comprehensive ethical code for social workers and represents a dramatic change from previous codes" (p. 162).

EP 2.1.2a

 The NASW Code of Ethics outlines several overarching ethical principles, which are grounded in the profession's core values of

- service,
- social justice,
- dignity and worth of the person,
- importance of human relationships,
- integrity, and
- competence (p. 1).

The ethical principles are as follows,

- Social workers' primary goal is to help people in need and address social problems.
- Social workers challenge social injustice.

- Social workers respect the inherent dignity and worth of the person.
- Social workers behave in a trustworthy manner.
- Social workers practice within their areas of competence and develop and enhance their professional expertise . . . (NASW Code of Ethics, p. 5–6).

In addition to the preceding ethical principles, the code identifies multiple ethical standards that relate to social workers' activities. The standards fall within six broad categories and reflect a social worker's responsibilities to clients, colleagues, practice settings, themselves as professionals, the profession, and the broader society. The code also identifies six purposes, which are to,

- name the core values on which the profession's mission is based,
- summarize the board ethical principles that reflect the core values and establish a set of ethical standards that guide social work practice,
- help social workers identify relevant considerations when their professional obligations conflict or ethical uncertainties arise,
- provide ethical standards the general public can hold the profession accountable to,
- socialize practitioners new to the field to the mission, values, ethical principles, and ethical standards, and
- articulate standards that the social work profession itself can use to assess whether social workers have engaged in unethical conduct (NASW Code of Ethics, p. 2).

EP 2.1.2c

One of the most important purposes of the NASW Code of Ethics is to offer "a set of values, principles, and standards to guide decision making and conduct when ethical issues arise" (NASW Code of Ethics, p. 2). However, the code is not prescriptive in nature. This means that the code is not going to tell a social worker what should be done in any given situation; instead, it provides direction for thinking about the context of any given practice situation and the likely conflicts that will arise even within the standards themselves. Furthermore, the code does not identify which standard is more important or which standard should outweigh another. It is critically important that social workers be competent in their ethical decision-making process, as well as, how to resolve the ethical dilemmas that present themselves when practicing.

REFLECTION QUESTION 7.1

As you enter field and consider your values and the values of the profession, what stands out to you? Where do you see congruence, and where is there possible dissonance between your values and those of the profession?

THE ETHICS AUDIT

EP 2.1.2b

A useful activity for you to engage in to develop your understanding of ethics in field and assist you in the development of your competence as an ethical practitioner is to conduct an "ethics audit" (Reamer, 2000) of your agency. Reamer (2000) states that an ethics audit should focus on two main areas,

1. knowledge of social work ethics and how they relate to the practice setting, and
2. assessment of risk level and engagement in ethical decision making.

Although Reamer's (2000) ethics audit primarily targets risk management, this task is extremely beneficial to you in field in that the two main areas of the audit, knowledge of ethics related to your agency and consideration of risk level and ethical decision making are extremely important areas to consider as you develop and demonstrate competence in the area of ethical practice.

The first task of the audit is to review and develop your knowledge related to ethics and particularly ethical practice in your agency. To accomplish this goal, review the NASW Code of Ethics, which can be found at www.socialworkers.org, and any other pertinent codes of ethics specific to your agency. In the NASW Code of Ethics, several standards in the area of social worker's responsibility to clients are important to focus on:

- competence,
- cultural competence,
- conflicts of interest, particularly in the area of dual or multiple relationships, and
- confidentiality.

In your supervision session, discuss these ethical standards in the context of your practice setting. This can be done by asking your field instructor to share some of the common ethical issues that may be inherent to the agency and that relate to each of the areas identified above.

I had a student who conducted a weekly review of the NASW Code of Ethics in her supervision session. This consisted of reviewing one of the standards each week and discussing how this standard was met in the agency, any ethical issues that might have arisen related to the standard, and how that was handled. Both the student and field instructor reported that this was an extremely beneficial task for field supervision.

Next, review the agency's policies and practices to determine the level of risk those practices present to clients, the workers and students, and the agency. Reamer (2000) identifies four risk levels that can be applied to the areas audited: (1) no risk, (2) minimal risk, (3) moderate risk, and (4) high risk. The purpose of assigning a risk level is to identify those procedures or practices within the agency that are strong and thus represent no risk and those that may increase risk to the clients and agency and thus represent a high risk. Reamer (2000) identified several areas that you can explore as you conduct this part of the audit: "clients rights, confidentiality and privacy, informed consent, service delivery, boundary issues, conflicts of interest, documentation, defamation of character, supervision, training, consultation, referral, fraud, termination of services, and practitioner impairment" (p. 357). By exploring the practices and procedures that your agency employs in any of the preceding areas and assigning a risk level, you develop your understanding of the agency's overall ethical practice. It is important to note that not all of the preceding areas will be relevant given your agency and practices. You may want to discuss with your field instructor the areas that you will be auditing.

The last area that Reamer (2000) identified in the ethics audit is ethical decision making. This is a critically important competence and an important part in resolving ethical dilemmas, so this will be explored separately.

Integrative Activity 7.1: The Agency Ethics Audit is an opportunity to apply all of the preceding information to your agency. This activity asks you to consider specific areas related to ethical practice, assess the current level of risk or successful practices of the agency in a particular area, and address any needed action within the agency to reduce risk.

INTEGRATIVE ACTIVITY 7.1

The Agency Ethics Audit

Purpose: The purpose of this activity is to audit key ethical practices and procedures of your agency.

Directions: For each of the following key ethical areas, gather information through interview or observation of the practices and procedures of your agency related specifically to that area and ask yourself the identified questions. Then give each area a rating of **1 = no risk, 2 = minimal risk, 3 = moderate risk, or 4 = high risk** related to your assessment of the risk this area presents to clients and employees of the agency. *Risk* refers to practices or procedures that could directly or indirectly harm clients or create the potential that the ethical values and standards set forth in the NASW Code of Ethics may not be met by the agency. For each area, provide any comments that you would like to discuss in supervision based on the audit. Once you have looked at all relevant areas, provide an overall assessment of the ethical practice and procedures of your agency and potential for risk.

Source: From "The Social Work Ethics Audit: A Risk-Management Strategy," by F. Reamer, 2000, *Social Work, 45*(4), pp. 355–366.

Key Ethical Areas of Potential Risk	1	2	3	4	Comments
Client's Rights: Does the agency have a client's rights statement? A client's rights statement typically addresses confidentiality, release of information, informed consent; access to services, access to records, service plans, service provision; and options for alternative services and referrals, the right to refuse services, potential for harm by receiving services, termination of services, and grievance procedures. Also, assess how frequently and competently the agency informs clients of their rights.					
Confidentiality and Privacy: Does the agency have practices and procedures for releasing and obtaining information about the client, and outline the limits of confidentiality, meaning identifying when confidentiality must be breached? Also, assess the practice and procedures for protecting written (secure client files) and electronic information as well as use of electronic devices such as faxes, e-mail, and texting. Consider the privacy practices that prevent sharing of confidential information in public (corresponding with clients and staff maintaining confidentiality), and the practices of informing clients of the confidentiality policies.	1	2	3	4	

(Continued)

Informed Consent: Does the agency have informed consent documents and procedures? Also, are clients informed of the right and procedure for withdrawing consent to receive services? Do the policies and practices of the agency ensure that clients are mentally capable of providing consent?	1	2	3	4	
Service Delivery: How are services provided? Do social workers present as competent and practice only within their education, training, and license? Is the agency delivering the services that they say they are?	1	2	3	4	
Boundary Issues and Conflicts of Interest? Do the social workers establish and maintain proper boundaries with respect to multiple or dual relationships, such as encounters in public, physical contact, receiving gifts, delivery to two or more clients who have a relationship (couple or family), attending social community events, and self-disclosure?	1	2	3	4	
Documentation: Does the agency have established practices and procedures for documentation? Is the documentation produced by the social workers timely, accurate, and client driven? Are the social workers following the procedures for documentation? Is the documentation such that should a worker become ill or unavailable, client services would continue? Are records routinely reviewed to ensure compliance with documentation policies and procedures?	1	2	3	4	
Supervision: Does the agency have policies and procedures for supervision? Do the social workers regularly attend and use supervision? Do the supervisors provide needed information to the social workers to serve their clients? Is there a plan for supervision in the absence of the supervisee? Does the supervisor routinely review the work of the social worker, such as documentation, assessments, service plan, and treatment summaries, to name a few?	1	2	3	4	

(Continued)

	1	2	3	4	
Training: Does the agency provide training directly or indirectly for the social workers?	1	2	3	4	
Referral: Does the agency have practices and procedures that address client referral when the social worker or agency cannot service the client?	1	2	3	4	
Termination of Services: Does the agency have practices and procedures for when and how client services are terminated? Does the agency have practice and procedures for how clients can obtain services in the event of an emergency or if they cannot contact their social worker?	1	2	3	4	

Overall Assessment of Agency's Ethical Practices and Procedures and Level of Risk

In the space, provide your thoughts about the agency's ethical practices and procedures, include your assessment of their overall risk and any specific areas that you feel need to be addressed, and identify your plan, if any, for how to address the areas of risk.

REFLECTION QUESTION 7.2

Now that you have conducted your agency ethics audit, what did you learn about the ethical practices of your agency? What were the areas of significant risk and of no risk? What would you recommend that the agency do to address the areas you identified as being at high risk?

ETHICAL DECISION MAKING

EP 2.1.2b

Ethical decision making is a process that involves several important considerations. Rothman (2005) identifies several components of ethical decision making: defining the ethical problem, gathering information relevant to the problem, determining a theoretical base, exploring professional values, understanding client values, and finally, considering the impact of the personal values that are identified. Congress (1996) developed the ETHICS model: (1) examine your values, (2) think about the ethical standards, (3) hypothesize different courses of action, (4) identify who may be harmed and who may be helped, and (5) consult with your supervisor or colleagues. Mattison (2000) states that "ethical decisions made by social workers are shaped by the decision maker and the process used to resolve ethical dilemmas" (p. 201), thus emphasizing the person in the process of ethical decision making. This emphasis considers both the impact of the practice setting and who the decision maker is as well as how that person makes decisions. It is important for you, through reflection and supervision, to increase your understanding of how you resolve dilemmas and how those decisions are unique to your practice setting and who you are becoming as a social worker.

As a student in field, you may experience a wide variety of ethical dilemmas that will require critical thinking, effective use of supervision, and competence in ethical decision making such that you can successfully resolve the dilemma. As a field director, every year I work with students who experience multiple ethical dilemmas that reflect the competing obligations that social workers have to their clients, colleagues, practice setting, themselves as professionals, the profession, and society. A dilemma can be straightforward or extremely complex and multifaceted. The following situations have come up over the years and will give you an idea of what you might encounter. As you read the various scenarios, notice what stands out to you as you think about the situation, as well as what you might do if you found yourself in a similar situation.

EP 2.1.1f, 2.1.3a

The first situation involved a student who was working with older adults in an apartment complex that offered social work services. One day the student arrived to work and it happened to be his birthday. This news spread throughout the center, and he was greeted with many birthday wishes. During one of these birthday wishes, one of residents gave him a five-dollar bill, and said, "Happy birthday! Buy yourself something nice." The student replied that the gift wasn't necessary and attempted to return the five-dollar bill. To this, the resident insisted and again placed the money in the student's hand. The student walked away knowing that he should not accept the money but also not knowing exactly how to handle the situation. The student discussed the situation with his field instructor, who recommended that he go back to the client and explain how much he appreciated the gesture, but the agency's policy is that staff cannot accept gifts from clients. The student felt very comfortable with the plan and expected it to go smoothly. However, when the student explained the policy and attempted to return the money, the client became upset, expressed feeling offended, stated that the whole situation was ridiculous, and refused to take the money. At this point, the student, too, was frustrated and went back to his supervisor. The field instructor then spoke to the client and suggested that the money be used to purchase cookies for everyone, to which the client stated that he didn't really care what they did.

EP 2.1.2c

As a result of the student and field instructor processing this ethical dilemma, it was determined that the agency would institute a birthday celebration to formalize the acknowledgment of the birthdays of both staff and residents as a way to allow celebrations to occur. This institutional change was the result of both the student and field instructor realizing that at the heart of this dilemma was the social need to acknowledge and recognize something as simple as a birthday. However, this normal social exchange was happening within a professional context that involved professional relationships and boundaries as well as a clear agency policy, hence the dilemma. In a follow-up, the student reported that the birthday celebrations were going well and if a client wanted to acknowledge someone's birthday, he or she could contribute to the birthday fund from which cookies were purchased and offered to all the residents and staff.

When the student processed the situation and dilemma, he could clearly see the competing values and ethical obligations, that is, the value of human relationships and the standard of commitment to clients versus the value of competence and the standard of the commitment to employers. It was clear to the student that he needed to adhere to the policy of the agency, which stated that staff could not accept gifts from the residents.

But at the same time, he saw the need for acknowledging the importance of the value of human relationships. The agency instituted the birthday program as a way to strike a balance between the needs of the residents and staff to share in normal human experiences while also maintaining an agency policy that they felt was equally important to preserve the integrity of the agency and the professional conduct of the staff.

In addition to the preceding scenario, I have had students experience extremely challenging situations that have required consultation from multiple sources. For instance, students have had dilemmas arise with regard to their responsibility as mandated reporters of suspected abuse or neglect on the one hand and their commitment to their client and the standard of maintaining confidentiality on the other. In these situations, although the students involved could clearly point to their legal responsibility as a mandated reporter, the experience was nonetheless challenging for them, particularly when placed in the context of their relationship with their client and the need to breach confidentiality. Again, this dilemma generated extremely helpful discussion in class for the student involved as well as the class as a whole. For even when we, as professionals, know we are acting appropriately, it can still be challenging and require support. That is why supervision, consultation, and support are so important when dealing with ethical dilemmas.

Last, it is not uncommon for a student to observe or be exposed to the questionable conduct of a coworker or question the practices of the agency. The dilemmas that result from these kinds of situations are extremely challenging. For instance, I had a student who was exposed to illegal behavior on the part of a coworker. Again, although the student knew that she had to tell his field instructor what had happened, it was still stressful as she worried about what would happen to the coworker and even questioned if she would be able to continue at the agency. With a great deal of support and consultation, the student informed her field instructor, the situation was handled well by the agency, and the student did not feel the need to leave the agency.

These are only a few of the many dilemmas that my students over the years have experienced. Before moving on to developing your competence in resolving the ethical dilemmas you will experience, consider the following reflection question.

REFLECTION QUESTION 7.3

As you reflect on the presented scenarios, how would you have handled the situations? What ethical dilemmas could you see happening in your agency?

Resolving Ethical Dilemmas

Now that you have had a chance to think about the types of dilemmas you might face as a student, the next step is to develop your competence in resolving ethical dilemmas. The first step in developing your ability to resolve an ethical dilemma is to be able to recognize the dilemma. An ethical dilemma is defined as a practice situation in which you have to choose between two arguably correct yet competing courses of action (Royse, Dhooper, & Rompf, 2007). Ethical dilemmas are often those practice situations that stick with you or gnaw at you. A dilemma can be between you and your client or involve policies and procedures of your agency that impact your clients or involve your obligation to uphold laws even if that potentially harms your client.

For instance, I had a student whose client violated the safety policy of the shelter and the violation resulted in the client being removed from the shelter. The student knew that this could potentially put the client at risk, particularly if the client returned to her abuser. But the student also knew that the client, who had been informed of the policy and the consequences of violating the policy, put the other clients at risk and therefore had to be removed. This dilemma was difficult for the student, yet fairly straightforward given the fact that the policies of the shelter and the need for client to uphold them trumped the individual needs of the client.

The ethical dilemmas that students experience are often not as dramatic and clear as the preceding one and thus require more attention. For instance, some of my students were asked by their clients to do something that may not have been within their role, such as attending a social event. The tendency of the student is to be torn between accepting the invitation to express caring and not accepting to maintain clear boundaries. One student was working with a family, providing in-home parent education services, and the client invited her to her daughter's birthday party. At first, the student wanted to say yes, because she knew that the client saw her as a support in her life. But she also wondered if it would be appropriate to do so. Thus the student considered the situation carefully using the steps of an ethical decision-making process to guide her examination. She determined that the request did not fall within her role and was purely social. So she declined the invitation. She felt that had the social event been linked to the work she was doing with the client, it may have been appropriate. But given the fact that attending her client's daughter's birthday party had no relation to the work she was doing, she informed the client that she could not attend the party. In discussing the situation with her field instructor, the field instructor shared that she had once been invited by a client to attend the client's GED graduation. Given the fact that achieving a GED was one of the goals they were working on, the field instructor felt it would be appropriate to attend the graduation but not go to the reception. Thus similar situations had very different outcomes, both of which were appropriate given the specifics of the situation and the case.

The next step is to engage in an ethical decision-making process to resolve the dilemma. The steps are as follows:

EP 2.1.2d

1. *Recognize* that you are experiencing an ethical dilemma.
2. *Identify* the two competing but arguably correct courses of action.
3. *Gather* all relevant information regarding the situation. This could include agency-based policies and procedures and information specific to the case that might inform the situation.
4. *Consult* the code of ethics to determine the standards that support each course of action and your field instructor for information you may not have considered.
5. *Reflect* on your own values and consider where you are coming from as you think about the situation.
6. *Consider* the potential outcome of each course of action in terms of the impact on the client, on you the student and your field instructor, the agency, and society.
7. *Decide* the course of action you want to take based on all of the preceding.
8. *Analyze* the decision you made, its outcome, and whether or not you would do anything differently.

Figure 7.1 illustrates the critical steps of resolving an ethical dilemma using the previous case example.

Now that you have had a chance to review ethical decision making and considered a step-by-step process in resolving ethical dilemmas, it is important in the development of your competence in resolving ethical dilemmas to engage in the process of resolving

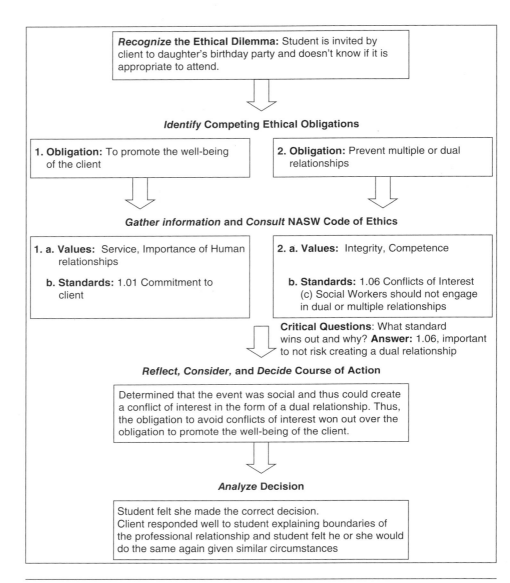

Figure 7.1 Resolving an Ethical Dilemma

a dilemma you have directly experienced in field. Integrative Activity 7.2: Resolving Ethical Dilemmas will provide you the necessary framework to engage in this process and thus demonstrate your competence.

INTEGRATIVE ACTIVITY 7.2

Resolving Ethical Dilemmas

Purpose: The purpose of this activity is to develop your ethical decision-making skills and demonstrate competence in your ability to resolve an ethical dilemma.

Directions: Using the following ethical decision-making process and flow chart to guide your thinking, resolve an ethical dilemma you have experienced or are experiencing in field.

Ethical Decision-Making Steps to Resolve and Ethical Dilemma

1. **Recognize** that you are experiencing an ethical dilemma, and describe the dilemma.
2. **Identify** the two competing but arguably correct courses of action.
3. **Gather** all relevant information regarding the situation, this could include agency-based policies and procedures and information specific to the case that might inform the situation.
4. **Consult** the code of ethics to determine the standards that support each course of action and your field instructor for information you may not have considered.
5. **Reflect** on your own values and consider where you are coming from as you think about the situation.
6. **Consider** the potential outcome of each course of action in terms of the impact on the client, you the student and your field instructor, the agency, and society.
7. **Decide** the course of action you want to take based on all of the preceding.
8. **Analyze** the decision you made, its outcome, and whether or not you would do anything differently.

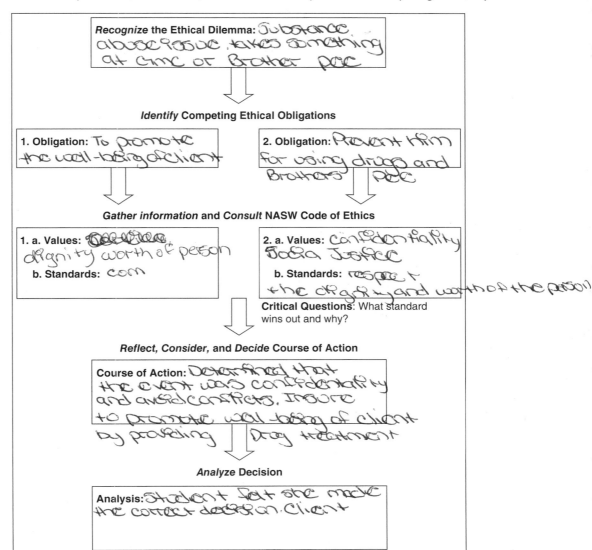

Recognize the Ethical Dilemma: Substance abuse issue takes something at clinic or Brother poc

Identify Competing Ethical Obligations

1. Obligation: To promote the well-being of client

2. Obligation: Prevent him for using drugs and Brothers poc

Gather information and Consult NASW Code of Ethics

1. a. Values: dignity worth of person
   b. Standards: com

2. a. Values: Confidentiality Social Justice
   b. Standards: respect the dignity and worth of the person

Critical Questions: What standard wins out and why?

Reflect, Consider, and Decide Course of Action

Course of Action: Determined that the event was confidentiality and avoid conflicts. Insure to promote well-being of client by providing Drug treatment

Analyze Decision

Analysis: Student felt she made the correct decision. Client

REFLECTION QUESTION 7.4

Now that you have had a chance to resolve an ethical dilemma, as you will recall Mattison (2000) states that the person (you) is an important factor in the ethical decision-making process, thus, what have you learned about yourself as a ethical decision maker and how did that translate into how you resolved your dilemma?

The Role of the Law in Resolving Ethical Dilemmas

Many times during the process of resolving an ethical dilemma, you will identify a legal obligation that will trump all other ethical obligations. For instance, your legal obligation to report suspected abuse or neglect, prevent harm or warn, and last, report a felony will override other ethical obligations. In a situation in which one of these legal obligations exists, it is necessary to follow the law. It is critically important to be aware of any laws that pertain to your agency and role, and always consult your field instructor should a legal obligation present itself.

Suggested Field Tasks

- Review related course work.
- In supervision, identify and discuss personal values and distinguish personal and professional values.
- Read and review the NASW Code of Ethics and any agency-based code of ethics.
- Discuss ethical principles and standards and any agency-based ethical standards.
- Discuss state and local laws that may govern practice at your agency.
- Identify and discuss common ethical dilemmas in practice setting.
- Conduct an agency audit regarding ethical practices.
- Identify, analyze, and resolve ethical dilemmas using the NASW Code of Ethics standards as a guide.

Competency Notes

The following identifies where the CSWE *EPAS* (2008) Educational Policy (EP) and practice behaviors are discussed in the chapter.

EP 2.1.1f Use supervision and consultation (p. 107): Social workers must develop competence in using supervision and consultation as a part of resolving an ethical dilemma.

EP 2.1.2a Recognize and manage personal values in a way that allows professional values to guide practice (p. 101): Social workers must develop competence in identifying their own values and developing the skills necessary to identify value conflicts that come up in practice, thus developing competence in differentiating personal and professional values and allowing professional values to direct practice decisions.

EP 2.1.2b Make ethical decisions by applying standards of the National Association of Social Workers Code of Ethics and, as applicable, of the International Federation of Social Workers/International Association of Schools of Social Work Ethics in Social Work, Statement of Principles (pp. 102, 106): Social workers must develop an understanding of the common ethical issues and dilemmas that impact practice in their setting, and review and discuss the NASW Code of Ethics and be able to apply the Code of Ethics and specific ethical standards to ethical dilemmas, thus demonstrating competence in applying the Code of Ethics to practice situations.

EP 2.1.2c Tolerate ambiguity in resolving ethical conflicts (pp. 102, 107): Social workers need to be able to manage their personal and professional obligations to their clients and agency and thus competently tolerate the ambiguity that is often inherent in professional practice.

EP 2.1.2d Apply strategies of ethical reasoning to arrive at principled decisions (p. 109): Social workers must develop the skills necessary to competently engage in an ethical decision-making process in order to resolve ethical dilemmas.

EP 2.1.3a Distinguish, appraise, and integrate multiple sources of knowledge, including research-based knowledge, and practice wisdom (p. 107): Social workers must develop competence in the ability to engage in a step-by-step process to resolve an ethical dilemma that integrates multiple sources of information with practice experiences.

References

Congress, E. (1996). *Social work values and ethics*. Chicago: Nelson-Hall.

Congress, E. (2002). Social work ethics for educators: Navigating ethical change in the classroom and in the field. *Journal of Teaching in Social Work*, *22*(1/2), 151–166.

Mattison, M. (2000). Ethical decision making: The person in the process. *Social Work*, *45*(3), 201–212.

National Association of Social Workers. (1999). *Code of ethics*. Washington, DC: NASW.

Reamer, F. (1998). The evolution of social work ethics. *Social Work*, *43*(6), 488–500.

Reamer, F. (2000). The social work ethics audit: A risk-management strategy. *Social Work*, *45*(4), 355–366.

Rothman, J. (2005). *From the front lines: Student cases in social work ethics*. Boston: Pearson Education, Inc.

Royse, D., Dhooper, S., & Rompf, E. (2007). *Field instruction: A guide for social work students*. Boston: Pearson Education, Inc.

Strom-Gottfried, K. (2007). *Straight talk about professional ethics*. Chicago: Lyceum.

CHAPTER 8

Diversity and Social and Economic Justice in Field

EP 2.1.1e

Developing your understanding of and competence in engaging diversity and advancing social and economic justice in field is critical to effective practice. In fact, diversity and social and economic justice permeate all aspects of field. For instance, you cannot sufficiently know your agency and the services you will be trained to provide and deliver competently without considering them within the context of diversity and social and economic justice.

With regard to diversity and particularly cultural competence, many years ago I and several other social workers had the opportunity to have an informal discussion with one of the members of the National Association of Social Workers (NASW) committee that was developing the cultural competence standards. I remember a few social work practitioners expressing concern with regard to the move from cultural sensitivity to competence. Even though this discussion was more than a decade ago, it remains relevant today. A few social workers were concerned about including cultural competence in the code of ethics and questioned their ability to be truly culturally competent. This is an understandable anxiety for all social workers and reflects the awesome responsibility inherent in the work we do as social workers, particularly in our increasingly diverse world. On the other hand, the same social work practitioners applauded the efforts of the committee and the NASW to advance the expectations for professional social workers to be culturally competent. In my opinion, the expectation of cultural competence is grounded in the professional expectation that social workers be lifelong learners because our development as culturally competent social workers is a career-long endeavor, and in all likelihood, we are never done.

Given this daunting expectation, you are most likely asking yourself, OK, so where do I begin? This chapter will provide an overview of diversity with specific emphasis on cultural competence as well as social and economic justice. The purpose of this overview is to ground your thinking and prepare you to apply the knowledge, values, and skills in your practice in field. This will be accomplished through your use of the chapter's integrative activities and your consideration of the reflection questions. It may be helpful to note that diversity and social and economic justice have intentionally been grouped together, because in my opinion they are intricately linked. The rationale behind this will become evident later in the chapter.

Rothman (2008) conceptualizes cultural competence as being made up of two different things, a process that can be learned through the acquisition of knowledge and skills as well as content that is specific to a specific population. This useful conceptualization will ground you as you develop your competence in this important area in field.

UNDERSTANDING DIVERSITY, CULTURE, AND CULTURAL COMPETENCE

Human diversity is vast, and the client systems you will interact with in field will reflect this vastness. That is, in field you will encounter clients who represent all ages, economic backgrounds, races, ethnic groups, religions, mental and physical abilities, gender, and sexual orientation. It is critical that you develop your understanding of diversity, culture, and cultural competence. As Sheafor and Horejsi (2012) state, ". . . diversity brings richness to the quality of life, and failure to accept and appreciate difference creates barriers to helping" (p. 49). Kirst-Ashman and Hull (2012) provide a comprehensive list of dimensions of diversity, which include age, class, race, ethnicity, (people) of color, culture, disability, gender, gender identity, gender expression, sex, sexual orientation, immigration status, political ideology, and religion (p. 26). Given that culturally competent practice is grounded in an understanding and appreciation of diversity and is an expected outcome of both social work education and field, it is also helpful to define culture and cultural competence.

There are many definitions of culture. However, the one that provides the best context for the social work student in field says that culture is a,

> … set of interrelated behaviors, beliefs, values, patterns of behavior, and practices that strongly influence how a group of people meet their basic needs, cope with the ordinary problems of life, make sense out of their experiences, and negotiate power relationships both within and outside their own group. (Sheafor & Horejsi, 2003, p. 173)

This definition is helpful in that it places a person's behaviors, beliefs, and values at the center of his or her ability to meet needs or respond to life's challenges which is often the point at which a social worker interacts with a client. Thus, this definition encourages the social work student to view the client's culture as being in a dynamic relationship with his or her experiences and, therefore, must be considered as the social work student attempts to understand the client's needs and assist them in meeting their needs.

Sheafor and Horejsi (2008) conceptualize culture as a lens. They state that,

> A culture is like a lens or screen through which people view life. That lens typically becomes so internalized and such a part of his or her way of interpreting experiences that he or she may not even recognize its existence and its power in shaping his or her thoughts, behaviors, and judgment about self and others. (p. 174)

It is incredibly important that you realize that all people have a cultural lens and that your exploration of culture and development of culturally competent practice skills begins with considering your own. Self-reflection has been recognized as an important part of developing cultural competence (*NASW Standards for Cultural Competence in Social Work Practice*, 2001; Sheafor & Horejsi, 2008).

Cultural competence can be defined as,

> the process by which individuals and systems respond respectfully and effectively to people of all cultures, languages, classes, races, ethnic backgrounds, religions, and other diversity factors in a manner that recognizes, affirms, and values the worth of the individual, families, and communities and protects and preserves the dignity of each. (*NASW Standards for Cultural Competence in Social Work Practice*, 2001, p. 11)

In fact, the NASW Code of Ethics includes "cultural competence and social diversity" (p. 9) as one of the ethical standards. The standard reads as follows:

1.05 Cultural Competence and Social Diversity

> (a) Social workers should understand culture and its function in human behavior and society, recognizing the strengths that exist in all cultures.
> (b) Social workers should have a knowledge base of their clients' cultures and be able to demonstrate competence in the provision of services that are sensitive to clients' cultures and to differences among people and cultural groups.
> (c) Social workers should obtain education about and seek to understand the nature of social diversity and oppression with respect to race, ethnicity, national origin, color, sex, sexual orientation, age, marital status, political belief, religion, and mental or physical disability. (NASW Code of Ethics, 1999, p. 9)

EP 2.1.4b

Developing your understanding of the role culture plays in field will increase your ability to practice in a culturally competent manner and is a complex, multifaceted endeavor. The *NASW Standards for Cultural Competence in Social Work Practice* (2001) identify five elements that must be present for a system to be culturally competent (p. 12). These five elements have been adapted to individual practice in field. They are as follows

1. the need to value diversity,
2. the need to increase one's awareness of his or her own cultural identity and worldview,
3. the need to develop an understanding of what can happen when cultures interact,
4. the need to internalize knowledge of various cultures, and
5. the need to develop and implement services that reflect an understanding of diversity between and within cultures.

Integrative Activity 8.1: Developing an Understanding of Diversity, Culture, and Cultural Competence in Field: A Multilevel Approach will assist in the process of developing a better understanding of yourself and your clients and thus begin your process of understanding cultural competence. "Effective cross-cultural social work practice depends upon the worker's ability to accept and respect human differences as well as accept and respect human similarities" (Harper and Lantz, 1996, p. 3). Harper and Lantz (1996) go on to say that "A social worker who is competent in cross-cultural practice moves beyond assessing cultural differences and develops awareness of processes people use in meeting needs and solving problems" (p. 4).

INTEGRATIVE ACTIVITY 8.1

Developing an Understanding of Diversity, Culture, and Culture Competence in Field: A Multilevel Approach

Purpose: The purpose of this activity is for you to develop your understanding of culture in field using a multilevel approach that involves both reflection and building experience.

Directions: For each area, explore the prompt statement and answer any questions; then discuss in supervision with your field instructor. Last, engage in any identified experiential activities.

Individual and Family Level

1. Identify and reflect on the cultural/ethnic/special population group(s) you belong to taking into account your family of origin. In what ways is your cultural identity similar to and different from your family of origin and others who represent similar categories as you?

2. How would you describe your comfort level and personal experience with diversity? That is, consider the amount of experience you have had with diverse population groups and your comfort level when interacting with diverse population groups.

3. Identify your knowledge base and opportunities for exposure to diverse populations. Develop a plan for increasing your knowledge base and exposure (i.e., reading research, attending cultural activities, interviewing individuals who represent diverse population groups).

Agency Level

1. Identify the cultural/ethnic/special population groups served by your agency.

2. Explore the agency's policies, procedures, and practices from the standpoint of cultural competence. Consider the physical environment of the agency, diversity of staff, mission, policies and procedures, access to services, assessment tools used by the agency, models and theories used, and availability of resources/referrals to address the needs of clients.

Community/Societal Level

1. Identify issues, strengths, and struggles at the community level that may or may not be impacting the diverse clients with whom you work.

2. Identify issues at the societal level, including social problems, policies, politics, and trends that may or may not be impacting the diverse clients with whom you work.

REFLECTION QUESTION 8.1

As you think about the previous definition of culture and the metaphor of culture as a lens through which an individual views the world, what is your cultural lens? How do you see the world? What has impacted your view? How do you see the problems your client systems are experiencing? How do you view helping and the helping process?

DEVELOPING CULTURALLY COMPETENT PRACTICE SKILLS

Now that you have had a chance to consider the elements that are important to developing your understanding of cultural competence, the next step is to put that understanding into practice in field and develop and demonstrate culturally competent practice skills. Rothman (2008) states that the commitment to cultural competence is a challenge for each worker in that it is a "commitment to personal awareness, to personal growth, to understanding, and to unlearning (as possible) any biases, stereotypes, or prejudices that may interfere with the worker's ability to assist the client toward culturally appropriate personal goals" (p. 15). A concept that is useful in the process of translating your understanding of diversity and cultural competence into culturally competent practice is to first conceptualize the worldview of your client system.

EP 2.1.4c

According to Coggins and Hatchett (2002), worldview refers to a variety of concepts that shape how people perceive their relationship to the natural environment, objects, institutions, and people. They go on to say that this worldview impacts people's beliefs, behavior, and expectations. The ability to gain an understanding of a client's worldview is critically important and grounded in many of the competencies necessary for effective practice. Examples include the ability to effectively communicate verbally and nonverbally with a client, use culturally competent assessment tools that consider the types of questions needed to elicit an understanding of the client's culture, and last, the ability to use intervention strategies that are culturally competent and sanctioned as such by the client.

Many models have been developed to assist the social worker in developing cultural competence skills; one such model is the Reciprocal Exploration Model (Coggins & Hatchett, 2002). Coggins and Hatchett (2002) describe the model as, "an approach to information gathering that has been adapted from a long established style of gaining cultural knowledge among and between different Native American groups" (p. 136). The model is grounded in the idea that it is important to engage in a process of understanding cultural differences, a tradition for thousands of years among Native Americans, where the sharing of information focuses on what is common among the participants as well as different. The conversation or exploration is grounded in "genuine interest and a nonjudgmental attitude on the part of participants in the discussion" (Coggins & Hatchett, p. 136). In the context of the social worker–client relationship, through the process of sharing information about the situation at hand, the social worker and client "build a more solid understanding of the cultural values, beliefs, and problem-solving practices of each other's cultures" (p. 136). It is important to note that for the reciprocal model to work, the worker must be clear on his or her own culturally based beliefs, practices, and expectations for behavior. The idea of this model builds nicely on the development of your understanding of cultural competence, which was the result of Integrative Activity 8.1.

EP 2.1.4d

Another tool that you can use to develop your cultural competence in field is Devore and Schlesinger's (1999) ethnic-sensitive generalist practice model, which identifies seven layers of understanding determined to support ethnic-sensitive practice. The seven layers are,

1. social work values
2. a basic knowledge of human behavior
3. knowledge of and skill in using social welfare policies and agency policy that determines what services can be offered

EP 2.1.4a

4. self-awareness, including awareness of one's own ethnicity and an understanding of how it may influence professional practice

5. the impact of the ethnic reality upon the daily life of clients

6. an understanding that the route taken to the social worker has considerable impact on the manner in which social services will be perceived and delivered

7. adaptation and modification of skills techniques in response to the ethnic-reality (p. 93).

This perspective is particularly useful in field because it provides a comprehensive and integrated approach to assist you in developing your cultural competence and is grounded in generalist practice. Each layer emphasizes a core aspect of generalist social work practice such as the values and roles of the profession, understanding of human behavior, and knowledge of social welfare policies and services with specific emphasis on the agency and the need to ". . . become aware of the ways in which the organization may constrain as well as facilitate effective practice" (Devore & Schlesinger, 1999, p. 99). In addition, the perspective places emphasis on self-awareness of the worker's own ethnicity and how that might impact practice. But, the two layers from Devore and Schlesinger's (1999) ethnic-sensitive generalist practice model that are particularly important to consider as you work toward being culturally competent in field are the impact of the ethnic reality of the client and the route the client has taken to become a client. According to Devore & Schlesinger (1999), one's ethnic reality results in identifiable behaviors and dispositions that are the result of "(1) a group's cultural values as embodied in its history, rituals, and religion; (2) a group's migration experience or other processes through which the encounter with mainstream culture took place; and (3) the way a group organizes its family system" (p. 55). A client's ethnic reality will impact many facets of his or her life, which may be related to the problem(s) the client is seeking assistance for, such as parenting, homelessness, and addiction. Similarly, it is important to consider how the client became a client and reflect on the fact that clients come to the attention of agency services and social workers in many ways along a continuum of voluntary to mandated, and regardless of the route, it is important for the social worker to elicit the client's understanding of the problem.

EP 2.1.3b

The last layer offered by Devore & Schlesinger (1999) is to adapt and modify what you do to assist your client. They state, ". . . intervention must be reviewed, reconsidered, adapted, and modified in relation to the ethnic reality" (p. 169). When you are working with a client system, gaining a sense of the client's ethnic reality will be critical to understanding the problem and how to adapt the interventions that are offered by your agency. Chapter 10 will discuss how to integrate cultural competence into the planned change process.

But first it is important to gain experience in gathering and reflecting on the preceding information from the point of view of a client. To do this, see Integrative Activity 8.2: Developing Culturally Competent Practice Skills in Field. Gather information on a client, and reflect on that information particularly in the context of developing your understanding of the client's worldview and ethnic reality. Last, reflect on how the client became a client and the impact the agency's policies, particularly with regard to the possible services available to the client, may have on what you can do for your client.

INTEGRATIVE ACTIVITY   8.2

Developing Culturally Competent Practice Skills in Field

Purpose: The purpose of this activity is to develop culturally competent practice skills, through a process of gathering information on a client and reflecting on that information in the context of the services you hope to provide.

Directions: Select a client with whom you can gather the following information, and reflect on the information gathered. Following your reflection, consider and discuss with your field instructor the impact this information may have on the services you hope to offer.

Note: This worksheet is grounded in Devore and Schlesinger's (1999) ethnic-sensitive generalist practice perspective.

1. Describe the client in terms of his or her diversity (see Kirst-Ashman and Hull's list from earlier). Consider how the client would describe him- or herself in terms of diversity. Is this description similar or different from yours?

2. Describe the client's worldview. How does the client see the world, and specifically how does the client see his or her problem and the helping process?

3. Describe the client's "ethnic reality," that is, the impact his or her diversity is having on the client's situation and worldview:

4. Explain how the client became a client and what, if any, role his or her diversity has played in the client becoming a client:

5. Identify any issues related to agency policies and service constraints that need to be considered as you reflect on what you feel the client needs. State how you might go about addressing those needs.

UNDERSTANDING SOCIAL AND ECONOMIC JUSTICE IN FIELD

EP 2.1.4a

The concepts of social diversity and the impact of oppression identified in standard 1.05 (c) of the NASW Code of Ethics link diversity to social and economic injustice. This is best understood in the context of the negative effects that people can experience in society solely based on their membership in a group determined by the majority to be the "other." Membership as the "other" is often determined by categories of gender, race, ethnicity, creed, age, sexual orientation, socioeconomic status, and ability, to name a few. People who represent certain groups within the categories listed above often experience societal *-isms* such as racism, elitism, classism, sexism, heterosexism, ageism, and ableism as a result of their particular categorization. According to Dubois and Miley (2008):

> Societal isms are the prejudicial attitudes directed against groups that society identifies as "lesser"—less capable, less productive, and less normal. The isms provide rationalization for stratified social structures that provide fewer prospects—fewer opportunities, fewer possibilities, and fewer resources— for those with lower status. Stratified structural arrangements perpetuate exploitation and dominance of some segments of society by others. Some groups of people have access to power, prestige, and resources, and others do not. (p. 139)

EP 2.1.5a

In field you want to become aware first of the diversity of your clients and second of the *-isms* that your clients may be experiencing. By doing so, you are developing your understanding of the social injustices that may be directly or indirectly impacting your clients. Last, you will want to develop ways to challenge social and economic injustice in your practice in field. As Cordero and Rodriguez (2009) state:

> In short, the development of cultural competency is a journey of cross-cultural learning through the development of critical self-consciousness, an appreciation and respect for difference, understanding the sociopolitical context in which cross-cultural interactions takes place and a commitment to advocacy for social justice. (p. 137)

Social Justice is one of the core values of the profession of social work and the NASW Code of Ethics (1996) defines the broad ethical principle based on this value as

> *Social workers challenge social injustice.*
> Social workers pursue social change, particularly with and on behalf of vulnerable and oppressed individuals and groups of people. Social workers' social change efforts are focused primarily on issues of poverty, unemployment, and other forms of social injustice. These activities seek to promote sensitivity to and knowledge about oppression and cultural and ethnic diversity. Social workers strive to ensure access to needed information, services and resources; equality of opportunity; and meaningful participation in decision making for all people. (p. 5)

The NASW Code of Ethics (1996) goes on further to identify "social workers' ethical responsibilities to the broader society," in the following standard:

6.01 Social Welfare

Social workers should promote the general welfare of society, from local to global levels, and the development of people, their communities, and their environments. Social workers should advocate for living conditions conducive to the fulfillment of basic human needs and should promote social, economic, political, and cultural values and institutions that are compatible with the realization of social justice. (pp. 26–27)

and,

6.04 Social and Political Action

(a) Social workers should engage in social and political action that seeks to ensure that all people have equal access to the resources, employment, services, and opportunities they require to meet their basic human needs and to develop fully. Social workers should be aware of the impact of the political arena on practice and should advocate for changes in policy and legislation to improve social conditions in order to meet basic human needs and promote social justice.

(b) Social workers should act to expand choice and opportunity for all people, with special regard for vulnerable, disadvantaged, oppressed, and exploited people and groups (p. 27).

Barker (2003) defines social justice as "an ideal condition in which all members of a society have the same basic rights, protection, opportunities, obligations, and social benefits" (pp. 404–405). As a student in field, it is very likely that you will witness instances of social injustice, which are

> evident when a society denies certain population groups civil rights by excluding them from full participation in decision making, when it distributes institutional resources in deference to privilege and power, or when its members show prejudicial attitudes and discriminatory actions toward each other. (Miley, O'Melia, & Dubois, 2011, p.7)

Advancing social and economic justice can be challenging for a variety of reasons. First, in the current societal and political environment, the views of the role of government and social welfare programs are polarized around those arguing for smaller government and less social welfare programs and those arguing for what they see as government's necessary role in promoting the social well-being of its members. Second, society is unable to effectively eradicate social systems and structures that directly discriminate and oppress various groups, as seen in the fact that women continue to be paid less than men for the same job. Third, there is a lack of focus on social action and advocacy taken by many agencies in their service delivery. Yet Blundo (2010) advocates that students "learn to understand the complexity and unique ways social justice is a part of their practice and the lives of their clients" (p. 99). When you are working with your clients in field, you want to first identify instances of social and economic injustice and second reflect on the ways in which you can intervene and advocate for social and economic justice.

This is accomplished by engaging in Integrative Activity: 8.3 Identifying Social and Economic Injustice in Field, considering the questions posed, and discussing your reflection in supervision with your field instructor.

INTEGRATIVE ACTIVITY   8.3

Identifying Social and Economic Injustice in Field

Purpose: The purpose of this activity is to help you identify specific instances of social and economic injustice impacting the clients with whom you work and consider strategies for practices that advance social and economic justice.

Directions: Consider the following areas, and discuss in supervision with your field instructor.

1. Referring back to Integrative Activities 8.1 and 8.2, and the diverse clients with whom you work, what, if any, issues of social or economic injustice are your clients experiencing?

2. How are the instances of social and economic injustice experienced by your clients impacting the problems they are having as well as the options for addressing those problems?

3. If your agency provides specific services that directly target issues of social and economic justice, what specific strategies might you engage in to address the instances of social and economic injustice experienced by your clients?

4. If your agency does not provide specific services that target social and economic injustice, what specific strategies might you engage in to assist your clients?

REFLECTION QUESTION 8.2

As you think about the clients you work with, what -*isms* do you think they experience and how do these -*isms* impact the problems they are experiencing and their ability to address these problems? What specific issues of social injustice are impacting your clients? How might you begin to address these issues?

ADVANCING SOCIAL AND ECONOMIC JUSTICE IN FIELD

Although identifying instances of social and economic injustice is an important first step in developing your understanding of the role that social and economic justice will play in your practice, it is equally important to intervene to advance social and economic justice. Interventions that target social and economic injustice or advance social and economic justice can happen at the individual, family, group, organization, community, professional, and societal levels. In fact, it is important to identify all the ways in which you can address the issues of social and economic injustice that may be impacting your client's ability to meet their goals and needs and to realize that interventions that target social and economic injustice occur at all levels of practice not only at the macro or larger system level. The reason this is important is because only viewing interventions that address social and economic injustice at the macro level perpetuates what Melia, O'Melia, and Dubois (2011) identify as the division of the social work profession into two mutually exclusive practice areas, one focusing on individual or micro practice, and the other on larger system or macro practice. It is critically important to develop the skills necessary to identify the social and economic justice issues that may be impacting clients and to target interventions at all levels of service.

EP 2.1.5c

Advocacy and Policy Practice

Two practice interventions that cut across all system levels and are effective when advancing issues of social justice are *advocacy* and *policy practice*. The foundational role of advocacy was discussed in Chapter 3, and you were encouraged to identify (1) how your agency uses the role of advocacy, and (2) identify opportunities for you to engage in advocacy with client systems. You want to consider how to use advocacy when addressing issues of social and economic injustice. Sheafor and Horejsi (2012) identify two activities a social worker might engage in as they use the role of advocacy; they are client or case advocacy, and class advocacy.

EP 2.1.5b

Client or case advocacy is used to ensure that the client is receiving the service they are entitled to. An example of this might be the student who accompanies a client to the Social Security Administration to assist the client in the application process for Social Security disability benefits. Class advocacy is when a social worker is serving a group of clients or a segment of the population with the goal of removing obstacles or barriers to receiving rights or services. These efforts might take the form of building a coalition of concerned citizens or organizations to effect change at the societal level. For instance, a student might become a member of a coalition of organizations that advocate for the development of affordable housing units within a neighborhood that is experiencing gentrification. Class advocacy can also involve the next intervention, which is policy practice.

Policy practice can be extremely effective in addressing issues of social and economic injustice. Figueira-McDonough (1993) states that "Progress toward social justice requires direct involvement in the formation and modification of social policy" (p. 180). Yet the ability of social workers to directly intervene in matters of policy development can be challenging, and in fact, policy decisions that are impacting individuals are often made by those who lack a full understanding of those impacted and their unique circumstances.

EP 2.1.8a

The first step in developing your skills for policy practice in field is to conduct a policy analysis. Policy can be thought of in two ways: agency-based policies and social policies. During your orientation, you were asked to become proficient with regard to your agency's policies. Now you will want to consider how those policies serve the clients of your agency and reflect local, state or federal policies directly or indirectly.

EP 2.1.8b

EP 2.1.3a

The next step is to identify opportunities for policy practice to address issues of social injustice or to advance social justice that may be available to you in your field agency. Students can engage in a variety of tasks that target policy development, such as supporting new legislation or working to ensure the continuation of current legislation.

As you consider your efforts to address issues of social and economic injustice in field, it is critical that you develop the ability to (1) identify the issues of social and economic injustice that are impacting your client system, and (2) consider all possible interventions that target individuals, families, groups, organization, communities, and society through the use of advocacy and policy-based practice. This can be accomplished by engaging in Integrative Activity 8.4: Policy Analysis and Practice. This integrative activity will enable you to increase your understanding of how the policies of your agency impact your clients, as well as the impact of local, state, and federal policies on the policies and services offered clients to address their problems. In addition, this activity will assist you in identifying ways to engage policy practice at your field site and thus demonstrate competence in this important area of social work practice.

INTEGRATIVE ACTIVITY 8.4

Policy Analysis and Practice

Purpose: The purpose of this activity is to guide you in (1) conducting an analysis of an agency policy within the context of state or federal policy in order to better understand the link between policy and practice, and (2) identify opportunities for policy practice in your field agency. Both of these will contribute to the development of competence in policy analysis and practice.

Directions: Address each of the following areas by providing a brief description of the requested information, and discuss in supervision with your field instructor.

1. Identify and explain an agency policy that directly impacts your clients and is grounded in or reflects a state or federal policy (attach a copy of the policy if possible):

2. Identify the state and or federal policy that relates to the agency policy identified in question 1 (include the name and number of the policy):

3. Explain the history and basic tenets of the state or federal policy:

4. Explain how the state or federal policy led to the agency policy or how the agency policy reflects the state or federal policy:

5. Explain how the policy impacts your clients and your agency (be specific and use examples):

6. Identify your analysis of the agency policy in general and whether or not it serves your clients and supports your work:

7. Identify any changes you would recommend to the policy:

8. If any, specifically identify a plan of action to engage in policy practice:

9. Identify an opportunity for policy practice at your agency (this could involve the development of new policy or efforts to maintain current policy both at the agency level and state or federal level):

10. Identify any policy needs you see of your agency or clients and how you would address that need through policy practice:

REFLECTION QUESTION 8.3

Now that you have had an opportunity to analyze a policy and consider both advocacy and policy practice to address social and economic injustice, what do you see as the role of social justice in your practice in field and the lives of the clients you work with? Last, what specifically can you do in your agency to address issues of social and economic injustice and advance social and economic justice?

Suggested Field Tasks

- Attend agency-based, community, or campus trainings and events.
- Present and analyze client system information through the lens of diversity and social and economic justice.
- Review related course work on diversity and social and economic justice.
- Identify diversity at the agency and client system levels.
- Increase knowledge of special population(s) served by agency.
- Identify value-based issues related to diversity.
- Review standards of cultural competence as set forth by NASW.
- Develop cultural competence skills in practice.
- Design and implement cultural competence practice interventions.
- Identify and discuss issues of oppression and discrimination that directly impact clients in the agency at all levels.
- Identify how the role of advocacy is used at the placement site to advance social and economic justice.
- Design and implement interventions that target advocacy to address oppression and discrimination and issues of human rights and social and economic justice.

Competency Notes

The following identifies where the CSWE *EPAS* (2008) Educational Policy (EP) and practice behaviors are discussed in the chapter.

EP 2.1.1e Engage in career-long learning (p. 114): Social workers must identify and engage in learning activities that develop their understanding of diverse clients, and thus develop competence as career-long learners seeing the link between career-long learning and culturally competent practice.

EP 2.1.3a Distinguish, appraise, and integrate multiple sources of knowledge, including research-based knowledge, and practice wisdom (p. 126): Social workers must develop the skills necessary to integrate information from a variety of sources, personal, professional, and experiential, to develop and demonstrate culturally competent practice and to advance issues of social and economic injustice.

EP 2.1.3b Analyze models of assessment, prevention, intervention, and evaluation (p. 120): Social workers must understand the diverse client populations with whom they work and specifically the client's worldview, which is necessary to develop culturally competent interventions.

EP 2.1.4a Recognize the extent to which a culture's structures and values may oppress, marginalize, alienate, or create or enhance privilege and power (pp. 119, 122): Social workers must competently identify the social and economic justice issues impacting the diverse clients with whom they work in order to see the link between diversity and social and economic injustice.

EP 2.1.4b Gain sufficient self-awareness to eliminate the influence of personal biases and values in working with diverse groups (p. 116): Social workers must understand their own diversity and cultural background in order to develop the practice skills necessary to address potential personal bias when working with clients.

EP 2.1.4c Recognize and communicate their understanding of the importance of difference in shaping life experiences (p. 119): Social workers must competently identify and articulate how diversity impacts and shapes a client's worldview and experience of an issue(s) he or she is facing, thus demonstrating an understanding of how difference shapes a client's life.

EP 2.1.4d View themselves as learners and engage those with whom they work as informants (p. 119): Social workers must develop the skills necessary to seek out and develop an understanding of a client by engaging that client, thus demonstrating competence in seeing him- or herself as a learner and the client as an important source of learning.

EP 2.1.5a Understand the forms and mechanisms of oppression and discrimination (p. 122): Social workers must develop and demonstrate an understanding of oppression and discrimination as it impacts the clients with whom they work.

EP 2.1.5b. Advocate for human rights and social and economic justice (p. 125): Social workers must identify and engage in advocacy with and on behalf of clients.

EP 2.1.5c. Engage in practices that advance social and economic justice (p. 125): Social workers must develop interventions that advance social and economic justice with the clients with whom they serve.

EP 2.1.8a. Analyze, formulate, and advocate for policies that advance social well-being (p. 125): Social workers must develop the skills necessary to analyze a policy at the agency or larger system level in order to understand how policy impacts client systems.

EP 2.1.8b. Collaborate with colleagues and clients for effective policy action (p. 126): Social workers must develop the skills necessary in order to engage in practice that targets policy.

References

Barker, R. L. (2003). *The social work dictionary*. Washington, DC: NASW Press.

Blundo, R. R. (2010). Social justice becomes a living experience for students, faculty, and community. *Journal of Teaching in Social Work, 30*(1), 90–100.

Coggins, K., & Hatchett, B. (2002). *Field practicum: Skill building from a multicultural perspective*. Peosta, IA: Eddie Bowers Publishing Co., Inc.

Cordero, A. A., & Rodriguez, L. N. (2009). Fostering cross-cultural learning and advocacy for social justice through an immersion experience in Puerto Rico. *Journal of Teaching in Social Work, 29*(2), 134–152.

Council on Social Work Education. (2008). *Educational policy and accreditation standards*. Alexandria, VA: Council on Social Work Education.

Devore, W., & Schlesinger, E. (1999). *Ethnic-sensitive social work practice,* (5th ed.). Boston: Allyn and Bacon.

Figueira-McDonough, J. (1993). Policy practice: The neglected side of social work intervention. *Social Work, 38*(2), 179–188.

Harper, K., and Lantz, J. (1996). *Cross-cultural practice: Social work with diverse populations.*
Chicago, IL: Lyceum Books, Inc.

Kirst-Ashman, K. K. & Hull, G. H. (2012). *Understanding generalist practice,* (6th ed.). Belmont: Brooks/Cole.

Lum, D. (2003). *Culturally competent practice: A framework for understanding diverse groups and justice issues.* Pacific Grove, CA: Brooks/Cole.

Miley, K., O'Melia, M., & DuBois, B. (2007). *Generalist social work practice: An empowering approach.* Boston: Allyn and Bacon.

National Association of Social Workers. (1999). *Code of ethics.* Washington, DC: NASW.

National Association of Social Workers. (2001). *National standards for cultural competence in social work practice.* Washington, DC: NASW Press.

Parker, L. L. (2003). A social justice model for clinical social work practice. *AFFILIA: Journal of Women and Social Work, 18*(3), 272–288.

Petrovich, A., & Lowe, M. (2005). Developing cultural competence: Student and alumni perspectives. *Journal of Teaching in Social Work, 25*(3/4), 157–176.

Rothman, J. (2008). *Cultural competence in process and practice building bridges.* Boston: Allyn and Bacon.

Sheafor, B., & Horejsi, C. (2003). *Techniques and guidelines for social work practice,* (6th ed.). Boston: Pearson Education, Inc.

Sheafor, B., & Horejsi, C. (2008). *Techniques and guidelines for social work practice,* (8th ed.). Boston: Pearson Education, Inc.

Sheafor, B., & Horejsi, C. (2012). *Techniques and guidelines for social work practice,* (9th ed.). Boston: Pearson Education, Inc.

CHAPTER 9

Critical Thinking in Field

C ritical thinking is at the heart of liberal arts education and is the foundation of social work education and social work practice. According to Gambrill (2006) critical thinking . . .

> . . . encourages us to reflect on how we think and why we hold certain beliefs. It requires an acceptance of well-reasoned conclusions even when they are not our preferred ones. Critical thinkers question what others take for granted. They challenge accepted beliefs and ways of acting. (p. 121)

Critical thinking is the ability to analyze information, make a determination about a situation, and engage in problem solving. Critical thinking is an important skill for being able to practice effectively in field and learn from your practice experiences. Several activities will develop your critical-thinking skills,

1. developing knowledge, values, and skill through coursework,
2. observing practice tasks in field,
3. writing reflection journals,
4. discussing practice tasks in supervision,
5. linking course work and academic assignments with practice experiences of field,
6. consulting with peers in field and in the classroom, and
7. engaging in focused task analysis.

Many of the preceding activities have already been discussed in previous chapters. This chapter will focus specifically on task analysis and linking course work with the practice tasks of field as well as provide an overview of evidenced-based practice.

TASK ANALYSIS

Critical thinking is linked with experiential learning (Gibbons & Gray, 2004), provides the foundation for your learning in field, and is distinct from training. Chapter 2 discussed your training and identified it as an important part of orientation. However, being trained to complete a task is only one part of learning in field. In fact, Rogers (1995) advocates for a paradigm shift in field from training to learning, and states,

> Requiring students to simply engage in the experience of the practicum is not enough for quality learning to be realized. To transform *doing*, that is, the acts or skills of practice, into learning, that is, the understanding and critique of the accumulated experiences, requires a process of dialogue and reflection. This is the paradigm that quality field education encompasses. (pp. 529–530)

This is best exemplified by an experience a student shared in a seminar class. This particular student was working at a neighborhood-based social service agency that provided a variety of services. The primary work the student was engaged in was running the youth program. One day the student arrived to field and learned that the agency was to be audited the next day and the computers were down. Everyone in the agency was hand-counting intake information to include in the report. The student was asked to assist and was trained on how to count the data and tally the results on the data sheets. At first, the student reported being irritated by having to conduct such a mundane task and being pulled away from her normal tasks. But then the student reported that as she was counting each client served and placing hash marks in the various demographic area boxes, she began to realize that each hash mark represented a person who had sought out services of the agency.

She then began to focus on who these hash marks represented and noticed that the majority were African-American males between the ages of 18 and 24. She reflected on this data and developed several questions. Why were there so many clients in this demographic group? What were the particular needs of this demographic group? Was the agency adequately serving this group? And last, was there anything the agency could do to reduce the needs of this demographic group? The student took her observation and questions to her next supervision session and engaged in a focused discussion, targeting this demographic group. As a result, the agency began to focus on this demographic group and provide services that targeted their specific needs. The student reported that what started as a mundane and bothersome task became an excellent learning experience and one that was grounded in critical thinking. This experience exemplifies the need for students to differentiate between learning and simply performing a task. This is not to say that every task or experience you engage in while in field will result in significant learning, but it is important to lay the foundation such that you will be able to discern the tasks that can provide excellent learning and engage in a process that will increase your ability to elicit learning from a task.

To do this, see Integrative Activity 9.1: Task Analysis. Engaging in this activity while in field will provide you with an opportunity to develop, demonstrate, and use your critical-thinking skills such that you can learn from your practice experiences. The

EP 2.1.3a

INTEGRATIVE ACTIVITY **9.1**

Task Analysis

Purpose: The purpose of this activity is to guide you in the process of analyzing a field task you are engaging in, to both develop and demonstrate your critical-thinking skills and increase your overall learning.

Directions: Identify a task of field that you would like to analyze on your own or in supervision, and address each distinct area, 1–6. Each area has specific suggestions or questions for you to consider, as well as an identified goal. The worksheet is grounded in Bogo and Vayda's (1998) Integrative Processing Loop and Kiser's (2008) Integrated Processing Model. You may find that you want to analyze several tasks throughout your field experience. If this is the case, make copies or use a separate sheet of paper on which you can take notes.

	Notes:
1. Task a. Select a task to analyze. b. Set the stage. c. Based on your observations, share any and all information that will be helpful in the discussion. Goal: Increase your observation skills.	Notes:

2. Reflection
a. Share your reaction to the task, and answer the following questions:
  1. How did it go?
  2. What went well?
  3. What was difficult or uncomfortable?
  4. What specifically did the client do?
  5. What did you do?
  6. What assumptions did you make about the situation, the client, and anyone involved in the experience, including yourself?
 	
Goal: Increase your awareness of what is going on for you in relation to the task.
	Notes:

3. Linking Curriculum to Task a. What knowledge, values, and skills did you draw on when engaging in the task? b. Were there any gaps in your knowledge, values, and skills as you attempted to complete this task? c. What do you currently know about this task or experience? d. What knowledge, values, and skills do you need to acquire for the next time you complete this task? Goal: Increase ability to integrate curriculum with task and identify gaps.	Notes:
4. Review and Process Learning Tools a. Look over any and all learning tools such as case notes, interview checklist, process recording, assessment tools— ecomap, genogram, social history, interventions that were used when conducting the tasks. Goal: Develop ability to use learning tools effectively.	Notes:
5. Verbalize Learning a. What, if anything, stood out to you while you were engaged in the task? b. What specifically did you do? c. What is one specific thing you learned? d. What was your primary role in the task? e. How did you execute that role? f. What, if any, personal reactions did you have while you were engaged in the tasks? g. As you look back on the task, what if anything would you do differently? Goal: Develop ability to verbalize learning.	Notes:

6. Next Steps/ Plan
a. Identify a specific plan targeting
  1. the client system,
  2. the task, and
  3. the role the task is playing in your overall learning by asking yourself, what needs to happen next.
b. What do you need to know to execute your plan?
 	
Goal: Develop ability to develop a plan specific to the analysis of the task.
	Notes:

activity identifies several steps to follow to analyze a task. Each step offers suggested activities or questions to consider, as well as an identified goal.

EP 2.1.3c

As you can see, the first step is to identify a task to analyze. This involves three activities: first, select a task; then set the stage, that is, provide the necessary background; and finally, based on your observations, share any and all information that will be helpful in the analysis. When conducting the task analysis in supervision, these three activities are particularly important for two reasons. First of all, it is helpful for your field instructor to gain a sense of the task from your perspective. Second, once you are practicing independently, or if you are in a setting where you don't work closely with your field instructor, providing the overview will give your field instructor the necessary background information to assist you in your analysis. The goal of this step is to increase your observation and task presentation skills.

When considering a task to analyze, it is important to realize that a task can also be an experience, that is, something significant that happened in field that requires analysis. Furthermore, not all the tasks and experiences you have in field will require the use of your critical-thinking skills or garner significant learning, but without developing a structure and format for processing the tasks of field, you may miss important learning opportunities. Last, it is often the unexpected tasks, as in the previous example, that garner the most significant learning.

EP 2.1.1b

The second step is reflection and sharing of your reaction to the task. In your reflection consider several questions, such as how the task went, what went well, what was difficult or uncomfortable, what the client did or did not do, what you did or did not do, and last, any assumptions you made about the situation, the client, and anyone involved in the task, including yourself. The goal of this step is to increase your awareness of what is going on for you in relation to the task and your reactions.

The third step is to link the task to your curriculum. This step is at the heart of both field education and generalist practice in two ways. First, the purpose of field is the integration of the knowledge, values, and skills acquired in the classroom with the practice tasks experienced in field. Second, generalist practice is ground in the knowledge, values, and skills acquired in the classroom. This step is accomplished by referring to the Integrative Activity 2.3: Curriculum Review and identifying the knowledge, values, and skills, from your curriculum that you drew on when engaging in the task. It is equally important to identify whether there were any gaps in your knowledge, values, and skills as you attempted to complete this task. The last activity is to identify what knowledge, values, and skills you will apply or need to acquire to take the next step in the task or complete this task in the future. The goal of this step is to increase your ability to integrate your curriculum with the tasks of field and identify gaps. A useful question to ask is, What do I currently know about this task or experience? For instance if you are cofacilitating a group, identify your current knowledge base about running groups. By doing so, you are applying critical-thinking skills to task analysis. We will say more about knowledge and focus specifically on evidence-based practice later in the chapter.

The fourth step is to review and process any learning tools used when completing the task. This can be accomplished by reviewing your case notes; an interview checklist or process recording; any assessment tools, such as an ecomap, genogram, or social history completed during the task; and an intervention you used, such as an anger management activity. The goal of this step is to develop your ability to use learning tools to enhance your analysis as well as see how the various learning tools relate to the tasks of field.

The fifth step is to identify your learning from the analysis of the task. This may be done while thinking, in writing, or verbally. As Kiser (2008) states,

> Using words to explain and describe what you have learned pushes you to conceptualize your learning . . . . You then have a greater command over this learning as a more tangible, concrete, and lasting "possession" that you can retrieve and use as needed. (p. 79)

To articulate your learning in supervision or other settings such as the classroom, ask and answer the following questions. What, if anything, stood out to you while you were engaged in the task? What specifically did you do? What was one specific thing you learned as a result of conducting this task? What was your primary role in the task? How did you execute that role? What, if any, personal reactions did you have while you were engaged in the task? And as you look back on the task, what, if anything, would you do differently? The goal of this step is to develop your ability to verbalize and explain your learning. This skill will become extremely important in your professional development and a tool as you prepare for your professional or academic life after field.

The last step in the task analysis process is to identify a specific plan for what to do next. The plan you develop should be grounded in the outcome of the first five steps, and take into consideration three specific entities,

1. the client system,
2. the task, and
3. the role the task is playing in your overall learning.

In terms of the plan for the client system, this will vary depending on the client system. For instance, if the client system is the members of the social-skills-building group you are cofacilitating, you will want to consider the plan for those group members. If your client system is an individual, you can determine what you need to do next on behalf of that person. Last, if your client system is the agency and specifically the client satisfaction survey you conducted, you will want to determine the next step in how to address the agency's needs. Thus the plan will vary depending on the client.

Next, focus on the task itself and consider what your plan is for the task, that is, what you need to do next in relation to the task. Using the example of the group, the plan would be to develop the next group session, taking into consideration the members of the group and your knowledge, values, and skills related to cofacilitation of a group. You may determine, as a result of exploring the earlier steps in the process, that you need to develop your skill in managing the group's session time and keeping the participants on task. So you decide to develop a timeline to follow as well as identify specific things you can say to group members who go off task, to redirect the group back to the task at hand.

Last, consider the role the task is playing in your overall learning. This is important in that it can assist in the process of refining your activities while in field. You may determine that you have maximized your learning with regard to a particular task and plan to not engage in that task anymore to allow you to engage in other tasks. Or conversely, you may determine that you have much to learn and thus will continue to focus your attention and time on this particular task. Considering the role the task plays in your learning provides that necessary pause you may need particularly in a hectic agency or one that offers many exciting learning opportunities. Last, the task or experience you identified may have been a onetime task or experience, and therefore, there is no specific next step in relation to the task. The plan for this task is to articulate the learning and identify the role the task played in your overall learning; once that is completed, your focus on that task is done.

The goal of this final step is to develop and demonstrate your ability to develop plans related to the tasks you are engaging in while in field.

EVIDENCE-BASED PRACTICE IN FIELD

Critical thinking is grounded in knowledge, as Gibbons and Gray (2004) state, ". . . knowledge is a social construction; where the limits of knowledge are recognized; and where knowledge is seen as ever changing, even shifting and unstable" (p. 19). They go on to state that students, "are 'constructing' their own knowledge by testing ideas and approaches based on their prior knowledge and experience, sharing these with one another, applying them to a new situation, and integrating the new knowledge gained with preexisting intellectual constructors" (p. 27). Hutchison (2011) identifies four things that social workers need to know to practice effectively: "knowledge about the case, knowledge about the self, values and ethics, and scientific knowledge" (p. 23). We have touched on the first three, so let's bring our attention to scientific knowledge. Hutchison states that scientific knowledge comes from scientific inquiry, which she defines as, "a set of logical, systematic, documented methods for answering questions about the world" (p. 26). Two important types of scientific knowledge undergird your practice in field; they are *theory* and *empirical research*. A theory is a, "logically interrelated set of concepts and propositions, organized into a deductive system, which explains relationships among aspects of the world" (Hutchison, 2011, p. 26). Although the idea of applying a theory to your practice in field can seem overwhelming, in all likelihood, you have already done so but may not have identified it as such.

EP 2.1.3b

For instance, you may have immediately thought that you needed to prioritize the issues and needs of your client who is in crisis and help the client draw on his or her resources, thus using a tenet of the Crisis Intervention Model. Or you may notice that you have developed your own thoughts as to why your client is experiencing his or her difficulties and what you think your client should or should not do, thus developing your own theory about the case. However, it is important to take the happenstance and make it systematic. This can be accomplished through a critical-thinking process directed at reflection and analysis that will enable you to systematically apply what you know and seek out the information that is necessary to practice effectively in field.

Empirical research is often associated with science and is widely held as the most rigorous and systematic way of understanding something. There are two predominant types of empirical research. First, quantitative research, which emphasizes quantifiable measures of a concept, systematically collects data, focuses on identified variables, and uses statistics to draw conclusions. Qualitative research is more experiential and flexible, and attempts to gather the participant's understanding or experience of something through interviewing or observation as opposed to responding to the researchers predetermined criteria (Hutchison, 2011). Both of these types of research will become important and useful to you in your practice in field and reflect what is meant by evidence-based practice.

EP 2.1.6a

Evidence-based practice can be defined as practice that is grounded in the "strongest documented information to guide . . . practice-related judgments and decisions" (Sheafor & Horejsi, 2008, p. 119). Evidence-based practice states that social workers will use the most effective interventions and discontinue use of interventions that don't work. Furthermore, evidence-based practice reflects the value of competence and the ethical practice of using knowledge that is empirically based as identified in the NASW Code of Ethics. Rubin and Parrish (2007) define evidence-based practice as,

a process in which practitioners attempt to maximize the likelihood that their clients will receive the most effective interventions possible by engaging in the following five steps:

1. Formulating an answerable question regarding practice needs
2. Tracking down the best evidence available to answer that question

3. Critically appraising the scientific validity and usefulness of the evidence
4. Integrating the appraisal with one's clinical expertise and client values and circumstances and then applying it to practice decisions
5. Evaluating outcome (with the use of single-case designs if feasible). (p. 407)

It is also important to note that evidence-based practice, like all sound practice interventions, must be, "adapted to the client's unique or particular circumstances" (Thomlison & Corcoran, 2008, p. 12).

The skill of adapting and applying evidence-based practice interventions to client systems will be discussed more specifically in Chapter 10, which reviews the phase of implementing plans.

In light of the emphasis placed on evidence-based practice in the literature, it is important to note that there are possible limitations to adopting a purely evidence-based practice model, particularly given the complexity of the problems clients experience and the concern that evidence-based practice alone cannot adequately prepare practitioners to address their clients' needs (Adams, Matto, & LeCroy, 2009). That being said, Adams, Matto, and LeCroy (2009) state that, "skills in finding and interpreting research evidence are among many other very important skills for students of social work" (p. 180). They go on to say, "Good social work practice, and by extension, good social work education for future practitioners, needs to be grounded in theory and practice skills overlaid with in-depth training in selected intervention approaches" (Adams, Matto, & LeCroy, 2009, p. 180).

So you might be asking yourself, where do I go from here? The answer is to first build your evidence-based practice knowledge specific to your field site and develop your skill in evaluating research, which is accomplished by reviewing and discussing the literature (see Integrative Activity 9.2: The Literature Review). This is done by searching various databases. The two most widely recommended are Social Work Abstracts and SocINDEX. To conduct a search, identify subject terms that relate to your population, the context of the agency services, the type of service, or specific interventions. Then review all the suggested sources, develop a bibliography, and select several for a full review. To review the source, read the articles and critique them in supervision or present in class to determine those that will be useful for you in field. For those that are applicable, identify in supervision how the research informed your practice.

EP 2.1.6b

INTEGRATIVE ACTIVITY   9.2

The Literature Review

Purpose: The purpose of this activity is threefold. First, it will develop your ability to conduct a literature review that is grounded in your practice experiences, which will develop your understanding of how practice informs research. Second, by reflecting on the types of research findings your literature review generated (e.g., qualitative or quantitative), you will increase your understanding of evidenced-based practice. Third, by applying your findings from the research to your practice in field you are demonstrating your ability to engage in research-informed practice.

Directions: Identify a practice-based research question, and write in the following box. Then conduct a literature review that relates to your question. After you have developed a bibliography, select, read, and analyze several peer-reviewed scholarly research articles and books or book chapters, and discuss their applicability to your practice in field with your field instructor.

Steps to conducting a literature review:

1. Using your library website, conduct a search using Social Work Abstracts or SocINDEX database, for instance, and a book search, and create a bibliography of the results. Note: many programs' library websites have programs that can create a bibliography.
2. Select at least three from your search and read.
3. Write a brief review of the article, book, or book chapter, identifying the type of research, the findings, and their applicability to your practice setting.
4. Discuss findings in supervision and in class. Share results with agency.

Practice-based research question:

Article/Book: Cite your literature sources using the APA style guide.	Summarize the article/book, including the type of research and identify the major finding(s).	Identify how the article/book informed your practice and what questions have arisen as a result of the article/book.

As you think about the knowledge you possess, what are the sources of that knowledge? That is, where does your knowledge come from? What sources do you feel social workers need to draw on to develop their knowledge base? What criteria do you use to determine if the knowledge you hold is applicable to your practice in field?

CASE PRESENTATION

A helpful way to complement the aspects of critical thinking in field emphasized in the chapter thus far, task analysis and the literature review, is to use case presentation. Presenting cases in field can serve several important purposes and enable you to develop and demonstrate the competencies that relate specifically to this chapter.

EP 2.1.3c

In terms of the purpose, case presentation can assist you and the clients you work with in many ways. First, gathering needed information from multiple sources and presenting a case will help you gain a better understanding of that case. This is done at the agency or practice level when a case is presented in individual or group supervision, grand rounds, peer supervision, or with the agency clinical consultant. At the program or academic level this is done when a student presents a case in the integrative seminar course or incorporates case-based practice experiences in their other classes. Another purpose of the case presentation is to present the outcome of your case work. Again, at the agency or practice level, this might happen in supervision, as you are reviewing your caseload, or in a meeting, where you are presenting the outcome of research you conducted or the findings of the client satisfaction surveys you conducted. At the program or academic level, again this might happen in the integrative seminar course or in a capstone assignment, such as in a case analysis.

Whether you are presenting a case to gather more information or presenting the outcome of work you have completed, case presentation is a useful task that can help you both develop and demonstrate your competence in critical thinking, as seen by your:

1. ability to present information in an organized and thought-out manner, drawing from multiple sources,
2. ability to formulate a question based on your synthesis of the information you have gathered, and last,
3. assessment of the outcome of your work and perhaps recommendations for next steps.

To develop a case presentation, complete Integrative Activity 9.3: Case Presentation. This activity will assist you in preparing your presentation, organizing the information you plan to share, and identifying any specific questions you need answered.

INTEGRATIVE ACTIVITY 9.3

Case Presentation

Purpose: The purpose of this activity is to guide you in a process of preparing and conducting a case presentation and thus assist you in developing and demonstrating competence in critical thinking. (Remember, a case can be an individual, a family, a group-treatment or task, or a program you are developing, a policy you are writing, or research and evaluation you are conducting on behalf of the agency.)

Directions: For each area, jot down notes to prepare your case presentation. In the sections for recommendations and next steps, jot down suggestions received and your next step with regard to the case. Last, after you have presented your case in supervision or in your team or staff meeting or seminar class, assess your skill at presenting a case.

1. Describe the case you are presenting: (provide necessary background; identify if micro-, mezzo-, or macro-level case; identify how long you have worked on the case, your role, the goals, etc.)

   Micro: an individual and or family you are working with

   Mezzo: a group, task, or treatment you are facilitating

   Macro: a program, community, policy, research, or evaluation you are developing or conducting

2. Identify why you are presenting this case: (i.e., your goal in the case presentation, if you are presenting the outcome of the case, or gathering needed information)

   Goal:

   Outcome: (if presenting the outcome, include your analysis of the outcome)

   Gathering Information: (What do you need?)

(Continued)

3. If gathering information, identify the information needed and any specific question(s) you would like answered as a result of the presentation:

4. Information received, including any recommendations:

5. Next steps based on the presentation:

6. Assessment of your case presentation skills:

Suggested Field Tasks

- Review related course work.
- Analyze field tasks.
- In supervision describe and explain practice tasks.
- Present and analyze client system information.
- Demonstrate ability to conceptualize practice.
- Use reflection to explore role, tasks, and experiences of field.
- Articulate learning from tasks.
- Explain knowledge, skills, and values developed as a result of field experiences.
- Identify and discuss how research is used by agency to support activities of the organization.

- Identify at least one research question that relates to your placement setting.
- Conduct literature review on practice area, identifying database searched and search parameters.
- Read and discuss, and present findings of research, and explain how it informs practice.

Competency Notes

The following identifies where the CSWE *EPAS* (2008) Educational Policy (EP) and practice behaviors are discussed in the chapter.

EP 2.1.1b Practice personal reflection and self-correction to ensure continual professional development (p. 134): Social workers must develop the skill of reflection and self-correction in order to develop as professionals.

EP 2.1.3a Distinguish, appraise, and integrate multiple sources of knowledge, including research-based knowledge and practice wisdom (p. 132): Social workers must develop and demonstrate the ability to utilize multiple sources of information to serve client systems.

EP 2.1.3b Analyze models of assessment, prevention, intervention, and evaluation (p. 136): Social workers must develop and demonstrate the skill of analyzing his or her practice in order to serve clients.

EP 2.1.3c Demonstrate effective oral and written communication in working with individuals, families, groups, organizations, communities, and colleagues (pp. 134, 139): Social workers must be able to demonstrate effective oral and written communication skills when presenting client information.

EP 2.1.6a Use practice experience to inform scientific inquiry (p. 136): Social workers must be able to develop research questions and conduct literature reviews that are grounded in practice in order to demonstrate competence in practice-informed research.

EP 2.1.6b Use research evidence to inform practice (p. 137): Social workers must be able to apply the findings of a literature review to their practice with clients to demonstrate competence in engaging in research-informed practice.

References

Adams, K., Matto, H., & LeCroy, C. (2009). Limitations of evidence-based practice for social work education: Unpacking the complexity. *Journal of Social Work Education, 45*(2), 165–186.

Bogo, M., & Vayda, E. (1998). *The practice of field instruction in social work: Theory and process* (2nd ed.). Toronto: University of Toronto Press and Columbia University Press.

Gambrill, E. (2006). *Social work practice: A critical thinker's guide* (2nd ed.). Oxford: Oxford University Press.

Gibbons, J., & Gray, M. (2004). Critical thinking as integral to social work practice. *Journal of Teaching in Social Work, 24*(1/2), 19–38.

Hutchison, E., & contributors. (2011). *Dimensions of human behavior: Person and environment*. Los Angeles: Sage Publication, Inc.

Kiser, P. (2008). *The human services internship: getting the most from your experience* (2nd ed.) Belmont, CA: Thomson Brooks/Cole.

Lietz, C. (2010). Critical thinking in child welfare supervision. *Administration in Social Work, 34,* 68–78.

Rogers, G., ed. (1995). *Field education: A pedagogy of its own in social work education views and visions.* Iowa: Kendall/Hunt Publishing.

Rubin, A., & Parrish, D. (2007). Challenges to the future of evidence-based practice in social work education. *Journal of Social Work Education, 43*(3), 405–428.

Sheafor, B., & Horejsi, C. (2008). *Techniques and guidelines for social work practice.* Boston: Pearson Education, Inc.

Thomlison, B., & Corcoran, K. (2008). *The evidence-based internship: A field manual.* Oxford: Oxford University Press.

Vandsburger, E. (2004). A critical thinking model for teaching human behavior and the social environment. *The Journal of Baccalaureate Social Work, 10*(1), 1–11.

CHAPTER 10

The Planned Change Process in Field

Knowledge of and ability to effectively use the planned change process, also identified as the helping, problem-solving, or empowering process, is central to competent social work practice. There is much in the literature that defines this important process and identifies it as a significant part of generalist practice (Johnson & Yanca, 2007; Kirst-Ashman & Hull, 2009b; Miley, O'Melia, & DuBois, 2011; and Sheafor & Horejsi, 2008).

This chapter provides the necessary content to increase your knowledge of the planned change process particularly as it relates to your field work. Furthermore, the chapter provides resources that will assist you in the process of using the phases of engagement, assessment, contracting, intervention, monitoring, evaluation, and termination as you work with client systems.

The ability to effectively use the planned change, helping, problem solving, or empowerment process can be daunting for the student in field. The chapter content and integrative activities are designed to be used in a step-by-step fashion throughout your field experience. The purpose is to make the planned change process more manageable while also bringing to life the best of what generalist social work practice can offer, which is to competently assist your client systems in meeting their goals or resolving issues. For a breakdown of each of the five step in using the planned change process in field, see Table 10.1.

THE PHASES OF THE PLANNED CHANGE PROCESS

The first step in developing your ability to effectively use the planned change process in your practice with client systems at your field site is to review your knowledge base with respect to the phases of the planned change process. Although there are many names for the planned change process and various conceptualizations of the phases, to allow for consistency and understanding, this chapter refers to the phases defined by Kirst-Ashman and Hull (2009b).

Kirst-Ashman and Hull (2009b) define planned change as, "a process whereby social workers engage a client; assess issues, strengths and problems; and establish a plan of

TABLE 10.1	Five-Step Process of Using the Planned Change Process in Field
Step 1	Review phases of the planned change process. Identify what each phase looks like in your agency. Develop common language. Integrate understanding of contexts that shape practice. Complete Integrative Activity 10.1.
Step 2	Shadow and practice each phase at agency. Complete Integrative Activity 10.1.
Step 3	Conduct a multilevel assessment. Complete Integrative Activity 10.2.
Step 4	Develop and implement a multilevel plan based on the multilevel assessment. Complete Integrative Activities 10.3 and 10.4.
Step 5	Conduct the planned change case analysis. Complete Integrative Activity 10.5.

action, implement that plan, evaluate its effects, terminate the process, and do subsequent follow-up to monitor the client's ongoing status" (p. 29). The phases of the planned change process are,

- engagement,
- assessment,
- planning,
- implementation,
- evaluation,
- termination, and
- follow-up. (Kirst-Ashman & Hull, 2009b, p. 32)

It is critical that you first review your knowledge base of each of these phases, as well as identify what each phase of the planned change process looks like in your field agency. Integrative Activity 10.1: The Phases of the Planned Change Process in Field will assist you in this learning task.

EP 2.1.10

Furthermore, as you are developing your knowledge of what the planned change process looks like in your agency, make sure you develop common language for what you, your field instructor, and program faculty call each phase. This is important for supervision and integrating your course work with your practice experiences in the field, as well as determining how the tasks you engage in relate to the various phases of the planned change process.

Finally, as you are conceptualizing the planned change process in your agency, reflect on the agency as a whole, its history, and the larger system level issues that may be impacting the agency, such as funding, legislation, political, and societal issues. Much of the information will come from the agency analysis you engaged in, and it will assist you in developing competence in understanding the contexts that shape practice and how that impacts the planned change process at your agency.

EP 2.1.9a

Integrative Activity 10.1 first defines each phase of the planned change process and then provides an opportunity for you to discuss with your field instructor or agency designee how that phase is accomplished at your agency. For instance, the first phase is engagement. This phase includes how you begin to develop your understanding of the client system and the problem. Engagement is also important to establishing the working

EP 2.1.10a, b and c

relationship. For example, when working with an individual, in order to engage your client you must consider your preparation and effective use of empathy and interpersonal skills. This effective use of engagement is critical to developing an accurate understanding of the focus of the work and what both you and your client are hoping to accomplish.

An important part of engagement is intake. Intake refers to how a client system accesses the services of the agency, or more simply, it answers the question, How did this client system become a client system? A client system can access the services of your agency in many different ways. For instance, a client may simply walk into the agency during hours of operation, call a hotline, schedule an appointment for an intake session with an agency representative, or be referred to attend a group being run at the client's school. Or a client system might be a community that has identified a need that can be met by your agency. In fact, sometimes the client system is the organization itself, as in the example of the need to establish a new program or policy. So the client system can be many things. Therefore, it is critically important to always ask yourself and answer, Who is my client system?

As you consider the phase of intake, it is also important to determine,

- whether or not the intake is done over the phone or in person,
- whether a referral is called in or faxed into the agency by a referring agency,
- whether the social worker does the intake at your agency office or if the intake is done at another location, and last,
- whether the client system, as in the case of a community or the agency itself, is determined to be a client by the agency itself and if so, who makes that determination.

All of this information is important to ascertain, particularly in the context of the second step of the five-step process of using the planned change process in field, which is to identify specific opportunities that you will have to engage in each step of the planned change process through shadowing and practice. This is the purpose of the last column in Integrative Activity 10.1; in that column, list the specific tasks that you will engage in to practice each phase. Again focusing on engagement and particularly emphasizing intake, identify how you will be able to intake a client system at your agency. If for some reason this is not possible, I recommend that you, at a minimum, educate yourself with regard to the process and shadow that process.

For instance, say you are working at your county's children's protective services and have been placed in the ongoing unit (i.e., you will be working with families that already have a substantiated allegation of abuse or neglect). You will at least want to shadow and learn about the intake process, which most likely would be a central hotline where allegations of abuse or neglect are called in. In the best-case scenario, you will be able to work in intake, take calls, gather information, and go out with the case worker to do the investigation. As in the previous example, if for some reason, the official intake process is not available for you to conduct yourself, focus on your first contact with your client system. Your first contact is an intake and an important part of the engagement phase. The first contact you have with the client system can be very rewarding, as well as provide you with an opportunity to practice your communication skills of introducing yourself, explaining your role, demonstrating warmth and empathy, and establishing the working relationship. All of these lay the foundation for the subsequent steps of the planned change process that follow.

As you are familiarizing yourself with each phase of the planned change process, think critically about how the planned change process unfolds in your agency. It is important to realize that all social work practice regardless of the setting and the client systems served has a beginning, middle, and an end with distinct phases. This realization will provide you with the necessary structural framework to conceptualize the bigger picture of what your agency does, as well as help you identify the skills that are necessary to develop to become an effective practitioner.

As you reflect on the planned change process in your agency, ask yourself if the planned change process is long term or short term. For instance, if you are in an agency that provides social services to walk-in clients, you may use the planned change process several times a day with multiple clients. If, on the other hand, you are a social work student at an agency that provides ongoing case management services, the planned change process may take several months, with you revisiting certain phases multiple times to complete all the phases. I always tell my students that it doesn't matter what the planned change process looks like or how long it takes to complete all the phases. What does matter, however, is that you develop an understanding of

- what the phases of the planned change process are,
- what each phase looks like in your agency,
- how each phase is completed,
- what it is called,
- who does it and where,
- how the planned change process is impacted by organizational and societal issues, and
- your opportunities to practice each phase.

Last, as you are familiarizing yourself with the planned change process as it relates specifically to your agency and role, ask yourself if all the phases are equally emphasized or if some are missing or condensed. In all likelihood, the process will look different in every agency. Year after year, when I discuss and review the planned change process in class with my students, several students tell me that the process does not look like how it is laid out in their book. In all likelihood, this will be the case for you as well. However, regardless of how the planned change process at your agency may be similar to or different from what is spelled out in your textbook, all the phases should somehow be present and you need to develop your understanding of what the process entails in your field site.

EP 2.1.1c

INTEGRATIVE ACTIVITY 10.1

The Phases of the Planned Change Process in Field

Purpose: The purpose of this activity is to (1) assist you in developing your understanding of the phases of the planned change process as they relate specifically to your agency; (2) identify the specific field-based learning tasks that you will engage in to develop the ability to complete each phase; and (3) analyze the planned change process at your agency.

Directions: In supervision review each phase of the planned change process, and discuss what each phase looks like at the agency. Next, identify the various field-based learning tasks associated with each phase that you will be able to complete to develop competence. Remember, a client system can be an individual, family, group—treatment or task, organization, or community. Last, provide an overall analysis of the planned change process at your agency.

Source: This worksheet is grounded in the "GIM—the Generalist Intervention Model," by Kirst-Ashman and Hull, 2009b.

Phases of the Planned Change Process	Agency Practice Discuss the phase, and identify how the agency completes that phase.	Field Based Learning Task(s) List the specific learning task(s) to practice the phase.
Engagement: This phase is defined as either the first contact the client system has with the agency or the first contact the student has with the client system. It is a period of orientation to the situation and establishing communication and the foundations of the helping relationship.	Discuss and identify how a client system becomes a client of the agency. Identify the agency's intake process.	Identify the specific tasks you will complete to engage client systems.
Assessment: This includes all information that the student gathers about the client system so that decisions can be made about how to assist the client in solving the problem. This also includes the ability of the student to make a determination about the situation.	Discuss and identify how the agency gathers information, that is, identify the assessment process. Also, identify the assessment tool(s) that the agency uses to gather information. In this step, also define your client system. Note: If your agency does not use structure assessment tools, you may want to develop an outline of the information that you will gather from your client systems or identify tools such as an ecomap or genogram for your own use with client systems.	Identify the specific task(s) you will complete to assess your client systems, identifying any and all tools you will use in the assessment process.
Planning/Contracting: This phase involves the student together with the client system deciding what is to be done based on the determination of the assessment. The critical steps of this process involve: 1. prioritizing the problems or issues, 2. turning problems into needs, 3. determining the level of the need (micro, mezzo, macro), 4. developing goals and objectives to address the needs, and 5. formalizing a contract.	Discuss how the agency determines the needs of the clients. Discuss common needs, goals, and objectives identified by clients and how the agency develops a contract with a client (i.e., verbal or in writing).	Identify the specific task(s) you will complete to engage in planning/contracting with your client system.
Implementation: This is the phase where the student fulfills the plan (contract) by doing (intervention) various things to meet the determined goals and objectives. In this phase, the student will also monitor the progress to determine if anything has changed. It is often during the "doing" that students use the roles of social work practice, counselor, broker, advocate, case manager, facilitator, and mediator.	Discuss and identify how the agency implements the plan and contracts developed with clients. Also identify and discuss the agency-based interventions, meaning what the agency does to assist client systems to meet their goals.	Identify the specific task(s) you will complete to implement your client systems' plans.

(Continued)

Evaluation: In this phase the student considers two important things: (1) how effective the student was in meeting client needs; that is, did the plan work? And (2) consider the agency's effectiveness through program or client satisfaction evaluation measures.	Discuss and identify agency- and worker-based evaluation measures and tools.	Identify the specific task(s) you will complete to evaluate your client system interventions and the agency's level of effectiveness.
Termination: This is the final phase where the student ends the working relationship with the client system. Termination involves specific skills and planning. In the GIM, follow-up is the final stage, which involves checking up on the client system to determine if the client is still making progress.	Discuss how client systems usually terminate contact with the agency. Identify the agency-based tools involved in the termination process, such as a termination summary, discharge report, or other. Discuss how the agency gathers follow-up information on the clients served by the agency.	Identify the specific task(s) you will complete to terminate with your client systems.
Documentation/Record Keeping: A critical part of the planned change process is the documentation and record keeping that may coincide with each step. Documentation and record keeping refer to what the student writes and maintains officially, in client or agency records, about the client system and work.	Discuss and list all documentation and record keeping maintained by the agency according to each step of the planned change process. Intake: Assessment: Contracting: Implementation: Evaluation: Termination:	Identify the specific task(s) you will complete to document your work with client systems. Note: If you identify a step that does not have documentation/record keeping maintained by the agency, you may want to develop your own way of documenting that step.

Overall Analysis of the Planned Change Process: Identify your thoughts about how the planned change process plays itself out in your agency. What steps flow seamlessly, and what steps are either absent or vary?

The Planned Change Process at Multilevels

For most students in field, the planned change process is most readily conceptualized within the context of micro-level practice or work with individuals and families. The tasks involved in engaging an individual as a client, gathering information necessary to assist that client, establishing goals, agreeing on a plan of action, implementing the plan by conducting various interventions, monitoring the client's progress, evaluating the work, and ending the helping relationship, and sometimes providing follow-up, is what most students think about when they think about social work. Furthermore, it is often easier to identify and practice the phases when working with individuals and families.

However, the planned change process is also used in mezzo-level practice when working with task or treatment groups. In fact, practicing at the mezzo level is an excellent learning opportunity to deepen your understanding of the planned change process, because not only does a group, in the case of a time-limited psychoeducational group, have a beginning, middle, and an end; for example, the 8-week anger management group has a beginning session week 1, a midpoint week 4, and a last session week 8. But each session, for instance, if the group is an hour-long, has

- a beginning: the start time of group at 3:00 in the afternoon;
- a middle: the midpoint perhaps where you are implementing the plan for that week's session around 3:30; and
- an ending: with the group ending for that day at 4:00, reviewing what happened and identifying what will be happening the next week.

In this example, the student really gets to develop a comprehensive understanding of the planned change process at the mezzo level.

In terms of ongoing groups, such as those that are run at a hospital that are open, where members rotate in and out, it is helpful to develop a sense of the planned change process as it relates to the group's purpose. Even though the group is ongoing and structured such that it repeats various exercises and content on a cycle so the clients can benefit regardless of when they start or end their involvement in the group, it is still important for the student to conceptualize how the goals of the group and the planned change process relate to the overall purpose of the group. Conceptualizing the planned change process as it relates to this type of group can be challenging for a student because the group will not have a specific beginning, middle, and end as in a time-limited group. However, it is still necessary for the student to gain an understanding of what the group is trying to accomplish and how best to achieve that by using the planned change process. With ongoing groups, the student can focus on how the phases of the planned change process play themselves out in each session given each session has a beginning, middle, and an end.

Similarly, when working on task groups, using the planned change process can be helpful to (1) develop your understanding of each phase of the planned change process in a task group and (2) improve the overall functioning of the task group by increasing the likelihood that the group will meet its goals. I have found that students often miss important learning opportunities when serving on a task group and would benefit from introducing the idea of using the planned change process while serving on the task group. In the case where a student does not have control over the functioning of the group, the student can reflect on the phases of the planned change process, determine if the group is using a planned change process, and discuss his or her observations and recommendations in supervision. In order to engage a task group it is helpful to get an understanding of the membership, meaning who each member is, what agency, organization or community they represent, and what they do. If the task group member is from an outside agency, research that agency or organization so that you have a better understanding of who everyone is. If the person is from the community and is not officially representing an agency or organization, introduce yourself and tell them that you need to learn about the members and ask them to share with you how they became a member of the task group.

Last, in macro-level practice, work with organizations, communities, and at the societal level, the planned change process is equally important and necessary to accomplish the goals of larger systems. Although the process that one goes through to target change at the organization and community levels may be more complex given that, "… so many more micro, mezzo and macro systems are involved" and "… it pursues goals outside your everyday job description" (Krist-Ashman & Hull, 2009a, p. 186), the phases of the planned change process are still present and need to be used.

For instance, I had a student at an agency who recognized an unmet need of their clients. She had the opportunity to address this need and develop and implement a plan of action. The need was for a food pantry. The student engaged in a multifaceted process to engage the agency as a whole, assess both the clients' needs as well as the agency's resources and needs, set the goal of developing a new program, develop and implement a plan, monitor and evaluate the process and the program, and once the program was established and sustainable, terminate her involvement in the program. By using the planned change process, and planning for and reflecting on each phase, the student could integrate her knowledge of the planned change process at the macro level. The student also realized that by engaging in program development, she was shaping the agency to better respond to the needs of its clients. In addition, the student was able to integrate policy practice, as she needed to write a policies and procedures manual for the food pantry, thus integrating and demonstrating many different competencies within one learning task. It is often the case that when you use the planned change process, you will also be integrating and developing other competencies. It is important to identify and reflect on these additional competencies as you work through the planned change process.

REFLECTION QUESTION 10.1

Now that you have had a chance to review the steps of the planned change process and analyze how the planned change process plays itself out in your agency, do you feel that your agency is effectively using the planned change process? What are the areas of strength? What, if anything, would you recommend that the agency do differently to more effectively use the planned change process?

MULTILEVEL ASSESSMENT AND IMPLEMENTATION OF MULTILEVEL PLANS

An important conceptualization of generalist practice or the generalist approach should ground you as you apply your generalist training in field: that multilevel assessment should dictate multilevel intervention (Kirst-Ashman and Hull, 2009b; Johnson & Yanca, 2007; and Shatz, Jenkins, & Sheafor, 1990). Specifically, Kirst-Ashman and Hull's (2009b) Generalist Intervention Model (GIM) focuses on a generalist approach, which emphasizes the need to view a problem from a multilevel perspective as well as consider micro-, mezzo-, and macro-level systems as the target of change. Similarly, Johnson and Yanca (2007) define a *generalist approach* as being one that, "requires that the social worker assess the situation with the client and decide which systems are the appropriate *units of attention*, or focus of the work, for the change effort" (p. 1). Last, Shatz, Jenkins, and Sheafor (1990) state that,

> Rather than beginning with methodological commitments or preconceived notions of the interventions that will be used, the generalist approaches the assessment process with attention to the social and cultural context of each practice situation; determines if intervention is most appropriate at the individual, family, group, organization, or community level; and selects and applies skills from a range of social work methods. (p. 224)

To effectively apply your generalist training to your field agency, you must consider two important and necessary learning tasks:

1. engage in multilevel assessment, and
2. develop multilevel plans that are grounded in your multilevel assessment.

The ability to meet this expectation can be challenging in field, for a number of reasons. First, students often enter the planned change process at the point of implementation or the delivery of a service provided by the agency. For instance, a student is placed in an agency that provides a social-skills-building group at a school and is assigned to cofacilitate one of the groups. Although cofacilitating a social skills group is an excellent mezzo-level learning task, more often than not, the student's first encounter with the client system (the group) is going to be when the student goes with the cofacilitator the first day of group to run the group. When this is the case, the student has already missed several critically important phases of the planned change process that may or may not have happened prior to delivering the service (the group), namely, engagement, assessment, and contracting. The steps of engagement, assessment, and contracting are necessary to determine that for these clients, based on their needs, attending a social skills group is identified as the appropriate intervention. So although the student may be meeting the competency of developing group facilitation skills, in the context of the planned change process, the student may be missing important information necessary to consider the best way to assist each client to meet his or her goals.

We already discussed the fact that the planned change process will play itself out in the context of the group, and therefore, the student can focus on applying the phases of the planned change process to the group as a whole in the case of a time limited group or during each session of the group if the group is ongoing. Developing mezzo-level practice skills is necessary to one's development as a generalist practitioner and an important learning task. However, if the student is focusing only on the planned change process as it relates to the running of the group, he or she may be missing the bigger picture of each individual clients' situations and the need to consider all possible interventions that may be helpful for each member of the group not just attending the group and most importantly why the interventions are indicated. Therefore, the way to make running the group the most effective learning experience is for the student to become involved in the entire process of the group: interviewing and determining who would best benefit from participation in the group, following the clients through the group process to ultimately evaluate if the group was an effective intervention, and last, identifying all other interventions that may be indicated for the client. Again, if this is not possible due to agency constraints, at a minimum the student should be able to conceptualize and articulate an understanding of the preceding process and prior to beginning to cofacilitate the group, learn about how and why that particular service (the group) was developed, who the clients are and why were they referred and whether it is being effective. If the group is a task group, apply the preceding process, as well.

As you can see, it is important for you to be able to link the various tasks you are engaging in with the phases of the planned changed process and whenever possible, to engage in all steps of the planned change process with client systems. By doing so you will develop a comprehensive understanding of how the planned change process is used by your agency to assist your client systems in meeting their goals. To ground you in the two critical steps of conducting multidimensional/multilevel assessments and implementing multilevel plans, we will review each individually and discuss the integrative activities that will assist you in these learning tasks.

Conducting Multidimensional/Multilevel Assessments

As a field director for over 12 years and one who also teaches two courses in the curricular area of human behavior and the social environment, I regularly see a gap between the specific application of the content taught in these two courses with what most of my students do in field to assess their client systems. In other words, I am very aware of the time I spend teaching and helping students integrate their knowledge of the multidimensional, multitheoretical framework for assessing human behavior and development across the life span, yet I rarely, if ever, hear students talk specifically about their ability to apply that framework at their field agency and conduct a comprehensive biopsychosocial assessment. In fact, although all agencies utilize assessment, the form and process of the phase of assessment varies greatly and tends to reflect the services the agency provides. As a result, from agency to agency, there is not a consistent understanding of assessment and how best to train a student to be able to competently assess a client system. In fact, I have noticed two distinct trends, one is where an agency representative says, "Oh, we don't do assessments" and two, the agencies that do conduct detailed, comprehensive, diagnostic assessments often don't include this as a task for the student. Both of these are concerning and reflect the need to focus specifically on defining this phase and providing students with the resources necessary to conduct their own assessments regardless of how the agency operationalizes this phase of planned change. The fact that agencies do not have a consistent way of operationalizing assessment is understandable given the wide array of services provided by agencies. And, from the agencies perspective one could argue that it is not their responsibility to consistently ensure that a specific curriculum content area be applied in a specific way. But the variation that exists in how students develop and demonstrate competence in the phase of assessment can be seen as problematic and reflects my concern that a student's education and socialization as a generalist practitioner may be hampered by his or her field experience if they do not have the opportunity to engage in something as fundamentally important to competent social work practice and generalist practice as conducting a multidimensional/multilevel assessment.

Thus the third step in the process of using the planned change process in field is to conduct a multidimensional, multilevel assessment of a client system in your agency. Integrative Activity 10.2: The Multidimensional/Multilevel Assessment provides the necessary foundation for you to complete this step. Conducting a multidimensional/multilevel assessment is important because you need a way to both understand your client's "story" and help the client address the issues that he or she is bringing to you. Social work has historically paid attention to the interplay between the person and environment, and considers many dimensions when it comes to assessment. Thus the activity is grounded

EP 2.1.10d

in Hutchison's (2011) bio/psycho/psychosocial/spiritual/environmental assessment and will guide you in a comprehensive assessment process that will let you develop a rich understanding of your client.

EP 2.1.7a

The multidimensional approach to understanding human behavior across the life span is grounded in three important concepts, namely, consideration of the person, the environment, and time (Hutchison, 2011) and demands that you be able to integrate all of these concepts in your understanding of the client and his or her situation. The relevant aspects of the person are the biological, psychological, and spiritual dimensions. The environment considers the physical environment, culture, social institutions and social structure, dyads, families, small groups, formal organizations, communities, and social movements (Hutchison, 2011, p. 4). Last, time is important in that it asks you to consider, "Why now?" as well as the relationship between time and the client system's problem or need. Time can be defined in several ways; Hutchison (2011) identifies clock time, event time, and linear time. Linear time considers the past, the present, and the future, which complements the biopsychosocial approach by grounding you in considering the role that the past, present, and future have and will play in your understanding of the client.

For instance, as a part of your multidimensional assessment of an 8-year-old boy who is failing school, you will want to know about the client's past growth and development (possibly as early as conception), learn about his mother's pregnancy and prenatal care, and find out whether or not he met important developmental milestones as he was growing up. You also want to determine what specifically is going on now in the present, such as that his grandmother, who had been a major parental figure in his life, has just died, and in the future, such as where you hope this child is headed and what the future concerns are, particularly if he gets expelled due to his behavior.

Time is also relevant when we consider implementing plans and delivering an intervention, particularly when considered in the context of Crisis Intervention Theory. Crisis Intervention Theory states that providing services immediately when a client system is in crisis, that is, focusing on the present, can be effective because client systems are often more open to change in the height of a crisis.

EP 2.1.7b,
EP 2.1.10e

Integrative Activity 10.2: The Multidimensional/Multilevel Assessment provides you with the opportunity to conduct a multilevel assessment on a client system in your agency. The assessment considers three dimensions of the client—the person, environment, and time—and asks you to engage in two important tasks. First, for each dimension and corresponding aspect of that dimension, identify the questions that you want answered or the information that you feel you need to gather to better understand your client system. Second, once you have developed and identified the questions, gather that information and apply that information to your understanding of the client. Last, specifically identify the client's strengths and limitations that are impacting the current situation. A sound understanding of the client's strengths and limitations is critical when you move toward identifying interventions, as interventions are often more successful when they take into consideration the client's strengths and limitations.

As you set out to develop your assessment, it is important to first and foremost consider your role within the agency and to first discuss with your field instructor the information that is regularly gathered by the agency. You may want to revisit the assessment phase of the planned change process (see Integrative Activity 10.1). Then look at the gaps. For instance, if as a part of providing the service at your agency you gather only current information focused primarily on assessing if the client qualifies for the services offered, you may want to determine if there is a client who would benefit from a more in-depth assessment. The assessment might focus on questions that consider the past, the client's family, past services the client has accessed, the client's environment, and what the client hopes or feels needs to happen to improve his or her situation.

This was precisely the case for one student who was working at a social service agency that provided a food pantry. The student discussed the desire to get to know a client more deeply and gather information along the lines of a biopsychosocial assessment. The student was concerned he was not developing his assessment skills, because the agency gathered minimal information on the clients, in fact, just enough to see if the client qualified to be referred to the food pantry. The student's field instructor identified a client who came in on a regular basis and discussed with the client the concern that the client was not progressing to the point of creating enough stability so the client wouldn't need to access the services so frequently. This was of particular concern because many times the client was denied services when he came to the agency.

Thus the field instructor, who knew the client, asked if the client would like to sit down with the social work student and discuss the bigger picture of his current situation and determine if the client could do additional things to address the issue that seemed to be recurring. The client agreed and the student, after meeting with his field instructor to identify all the questions he was going ask, conducted a multidimensional assessment. The student reported that this became a wonderful learning experience and that the client easily shared information about his life and engaged in a process of looking at additional interventions that might be helpful beyond the services offered by the agency.

The learning task of conducting a multidimensional/multilevel assessment is best when applied to an individual; however, it can be adapted and applied to mezzo- and macro-level practice as well. From a mezzo-level practice perspective, it is important to remember that groups are made up of individuals. Similarly, when considering macro-level practice, organizations impact individuals and communities; both are made up of individuals and are impacted by those individuals. So if your primary client system is a group, an organization, or a community, first reflect on the individuals impacted by the services you are providing at these system levels and then adapt the assessment so it can be applied to the services you provide.

For instance, if one of your tasks is to be the agency representative at the monthly homeless coalition meeting, which is both a mezzo-level task, working on a task group, and a macro-level task, working to improve services at the larger system level, you could conduct a multilevel assessment of the coalition task group. Assessing the task group can prove to be a useful and interesting learning experience as you first identify what it is you need to know about the task group. Prior to conducting an assessment you will have conducted the phase of engagement in which you identify who each member of the group is, their history with regard to membership in the group and their personal stake or interest in the coalition.

Next, you will want to learn about the agencies that are represented and the services that each agency provides, as well as the current societal issues impacting the various services (environmental). For instance, you may learn that one of the members is a representative of the For-Profit Housing Company that is developing mixed-income housing and reflect on the goals that may be shared and that may conflict with those of the Not-For Profit Agency representative, who is concerned that the community is losing too many affordable housing units.

Last, gather information about the history of the coalition in terms of the past and present membership and the hopes of the coalition for the future (time). By conducting a multidimensional assessment of the task group that is engaged in macro-level practice, you are taking an often straightforward task and placing it in a context that will ultimately improve your understanding of, as well as potentially impact the overall functioning of, the task group.

INTEGRATIVE ACTIVITY   10.2

The Multidimensional/Multilevel Assessment

Purpose: The purpose of this activity is to develop and conduct a multidimensional assessment of a client system in your field agency. This will help you develop your assessment skills as well as assist you as you consider developing multilevel plans and finally implement those plans.

Directions: In supervision, identify a client system and complete the multidimensional assessment. Following the outline, first identify two to three key questions in each area and gather the information needed to answer those questions. Then, discuss and provide your overall assessment of the client's situation based on the information you gathered.

Multidimensional/Multilevel Assessment Outline

The Person:

1. **Who is your client system? Do you have more than one client?**

   Demographic: (age, sex, race, SES)

   Presenting problem: (from the perspective of you, the referral source, and client)

   Role of agency:

   Your role:

2. **Biological Dimension:** Identify and answer two to three specific questions that target the client's biological development, such as specific medical history, basic growth and development, biologically based diagnoses (remember there is strong evidence of the connection between physical and psychological health and external environmental conditions), and biophysical risks or protective factors.

   a.

   b.

   c.

3. **Psychological Dimension:** Identify and answer three to five questions that target (1) cognition(thinking): whether the client is oriented to person, time, and place; how is the client's thinking; if there is confusion; if there are thinking errors; (2) emotion (feeling): how the client expresses and manages emotions; what the client is feeling; and (3) identity (sense of self): how the client sees him- or herself in the world, what are his or her relationships like, how the client manages stress and coping, communication, personality. Lastly, consider whether or not there are any mental health issues, needs, and possible diagnoses, psychological risks, and protective factors.

   a.

   b.

   c.

   d.

   e.

4. **The Spiritual Dimension:** Develop two to three questions that target the client's sense of meaning and purpose, themes of good and bad and right and wrong, forgiveness, gratefulness, spiritual or religious affiliation, role that religion and spirituality may or may not play in their life, spiritual or religious practices that may be helpful.

   a.

   b.

   c.

The Environment: Based on your understanding of the client, identify which of the following eight aspects of the environment should be assessed, and then in each area identify two to three questions.

1. **The Physical Environment:** Consider where the client lives; if the client has a home; location of the neighborhood; if client has water, heat, electricity, lead paint, environmental toxins, overcrowding.

   a.

   b.

   c.

2. **Culture:** Consider cultural background, including race, ethnicity, social class, gender, sexual orientation, disability; consider what needs to be known about the client's cultural values, customs, practices, and beliefs that may be important to the current situation; consider any language barriers, family structure and roles, and ideas about helpers and helping process.

    a.

    b.

    c.

3. **Social Structure and Social Institutions:** Identify and answer one to three questions that consider the social institutions that may be impacting the client, such as government and politics, economy, education, health care, social welfare, religion, mass media, and family. Complete an ecomap.

    a.

    b.

    c.

4. **Families:** Identify and answer one to three questions that consider who is in the family, consider diverse families, complete a genogram, and identify relationships, rules, norms, roles, and issues.

    a.

    b.

    c.

5. **Small Groups and Formal Organization:** Identify and answer one to three questions that consider groups and organizations that the client is a member of or affiliated with that may be impacting the situation; also consider groups or organizations that may be helpful.

   a.

   b.

   c.

6. **Communities:** Identify and answer one to three questions that consider the client's membership in a community, physical or conceptual (i.e., the gay and lesbian community, their neighborhood, community issues, violence, poverty, crime, easy access to resources, and social movements).

   a.

   b.

   c.

Time: Identify any issues related to past, present, and future; consider, Why now? Consider the role of time in the context of the problem, how long the issue has been going on, and ideas of off-time and on-time life events.

Strengths and Limitations: Identify all the current and past strengths of the client and the limitations impacting the situation.

Other questions and content not included in outline but important to the client: Ask your client if there is anything you missed or need to know to assist him or her.

Overall Assessment: Identify your determination based on the information gathered of what you think is going on for your client. What are the client's protective factors, strengths, and resources? What are the risk factors and deficits? Considering problems from a multilevel perspective, what level do you consider the problem to be most focused at; that is, is this primarily a problem of an individual, a family, a group, an organization, a community, or a combination of several?

Developing And Implementing Multilevel Plans

EP 2.1.10f

Once you have completed the multidimensional assessment and determined, with the client system, the goals, the next, and fourth, step in the process is to identify and implement a multilevel plan. It is important to note that the plan should be grounded in the multidimensional/multilevel assessment and should focus on all the ways you can assist the client in achieving the agreed-upon goal(s). So as to determine the intervention that fits the assessment, rather than provide a particular intervention simply because it is what the agency does.

It is also important to demystify intervention. When I mention the word *intervention*, my students often get this deer-caught-in-the-headlights look—they often feel overwhelmed with the prospective of naming an intervention and implementing the intervention.

To reduce the anxiety that can go along with the idea of intervention, it is important to define what exactly an intervention is and place intervention in the context of the planned change process. Sheafor and Horejsi (2008) define intervention as the time "the client, the social worker, and others take the steps and complete the tasks that will implement the plan they believe will bring about the desired outcome" (p. 363). I like to refer to the phase of implementation as the time you will be "doing" what, as you have identified with your client, needs to be done to assist your client in meeting his or her goals—the intervention. An intervention can be when you use the role of brokering and refer your client to the jobs program to assist the client in getting a job so he or she has the income necessary to pay to the rent. Another can be when you refer the client to the social skills group to improve the client's social skills in the hopes of reducing the client's social isolation.

An intervention can be grounded in the roles of social work, discussed in Chapter 2, or be grounded in various theoretical perspectives. In the context of theory, the conventional wisdom with regard to social work practice is that theory directs practice. That is, the social worker should be grounded in an understanding of theory and implement plans through the use of various interventions that are grounded in that theory.

For instance, in the case of the student who is working at an agency that provides services to individuals who are experiencing domestic violence, an understanding of Crisis Intervention Theory would be extremely helpful as the student conceptualizes a plan and implements that plan by using an intervention. As mentioned in an example earlier, Crisis Intervention Theory tells us that the client is more open to change in the height of the crisis. Thus supporting the fact that the client is seeking services and facilitating her admission into the shelter becomes the most important plan to implement. Furthermore, Crisis Intervention Theory tells us that it is important to prioritize the needs of the client and address the most important one first. In the case of a client experiencing domestic violence, safety is the most important need, so the intervention used to implement the plan to meet the goal of increasing safety is to develop a safety plan. Although the student is also aware that educating the client with regard to the cycle of violence is important, it is more important to address safety first. Only after the client's safety needs have been met will the client be able to benefit from a session in which the student, in the role of educator, provides information on the cycle of violence, yet another important intervention.

It is important to review your knowledge of the various theoretical perspectives, practice theories, and models that ground social work practice (Sheafor & Horejsi, 2008; Hutchison, 2011; Kirst-Ashmann & Hull, 2009b; Johnson & Yanca, 2007; and Miley, O'Melia, & Dubois, 2011) and identify those that are useful to your practice in field. Table 10.2 provides a list of several theoretical perspectives, practice theories, and models that a student may find applicable to their practice in field, and a list of interventions that students can use that are grounded in the various perspectives, theories, and models. The list is in no particular order of importance and is not meant to be exhaustive. In fact, you may find additional theories, models, and interventions used in your agency. For instance, I have worked with an agency that trains all their students to use motivational interviewing as an important part of service delivery. That particular agency found motivational interviewing to be an effective intervention grounded in a strengths perspective and empowerment model.

Integrative Activity 10.3: Identifying Theoretical Perspectives, Practice Models, and Commonly Used Interventions in Field will assist you in the process of analyzing and identifying the interventions that are used at your agency and the theoretical perspective(s) your agency or field instructor may be grounded in. It is important for you to begin to,

EP 2.1.3b

- clarify if your agency has an overarching theoretical perspective,
- identify the theoretical perspectives and models of practice in which your field instructor and agency workers are trained, and
- identify the interventions that are commonly used by the agency when delivering services.

All of these will help you begin to identify your theoretical perspective, identify the practice models that you find beneficial, and identify appropriate interventions that you can provide for your client systems.

EP 2.1.10g

TABLE 10.2 Theoretical Perspective and Practice Theories and Models

Theoretical Perspectives	Practice Theories and Models	Interventions for Field
Generalist	The Generalist Intervention Model	Identifying and implementing multilevel plans.
Psychodynamic	Psychodynamic theory	Explore impact of childhood experiences on current issues.
Social Constructionist	Behavioral theory	
Social Behavioral	Cognitive-behavioral theory	Set up a behavior chart.
Humanist	Person-centered theory	Refer to a mentoring program.
Systems	Crisis Intervention Model	Affirm dignity and worth of client.
Ecosystems	Task-centered model	Express positive regard.
Strengths	Problem solving model	Develop a safety plan.
Feminist	Psychoeducational model	Prioritize goals/needs.
Conflict	Addictions model	Provide parent education.
Rational Choice	Solution-focused model	Educate client about cycle of violence.
Developmental	Narrative therapy model	Discuss disease model of addiction.
	Family therapies	Identify exceptions to problem.
	Small group theories	Conduct a family session to set family rules.
	Models for changing organizations	Facilitate a group.
	Models for changing communities	Conduct an agency retreat.
	Case Management Model	Review agency intake process.
	Family Preservation Model	Develop a new program.
	Self-help model	Conduct a needs assessment of a community.
	Empowerment-based practice model	Convene a meeting of community members.
	Social network theory	Monitor the progress of the case plan.
		Conduct an interdisciplinary treatment meeting to identify needs.
		Complete a genogram.
		Advocate for client's access to services.
		Refer client to AA, bereavement support group, etc.
		Complete an ecomap.
		Conduct a spiritual assessment.

INTEGRATIVE ACTIVITY **10.3**

Identifying Theoretical Perspectives, Practice Models, and Commonly Used Interventions in Field

Purpose: The purpose of this activity is to assist you in developing your understanding of the theoretical perspectives and practice models used by your field instructor, peers, and agency and how those relate to the interventions commonly used at your agency. This develops your ability to link theory to practice and analyze interventions. This will also help you begin to identify the theoretical perspectives and practice models that you are using or drawn to in your practice in field.

Directions: After reviewing Table 10.2 with your field instructor, discuss the theoretical perspective and practice models that are used in the agency as a whole, as well as those that the field instructor may use. Include identifying any specific trainings or certifications obtained by the field instructor. Do the same with the other agency staff.

1. Does the agency have a theoretical perspective or practice model that it uses in direct practice with client systems? If yes, please describe and state how this model gets translated into agency services.

2. What models or theories has your field instructor been trained in or exposed to? How was this accomplished (i.e., through reading, trainings, workshops)?

3. How would your field instructor describe her or his theoretical orientation?

4. How does this get translated into your field instructor's practice and more specifically, into the interventions they use when working with client systems?

5. Ask similar questions of coworkers.

6. What are the commonly used interventions of the agency to assist client systems in meeting their goals and needs? What does the agency and the social workers at the agency "do" to assist their clients?

7. How would you describe your beginning theoretical orientation? What theoretical perspectives and practice models are you drawn to?

8. How do these get translated into your practice in field and the interventions you use with client systems?

REFLECTION QUESTION 10.2

Now that you have had a chance to consider the role of intervention in implementing a plan, what are all the types of interventions (the things that the social worker and agency do to assist clients) provided by your agency? How do these interventions reflect the foundational roles of social work? How are the interventions grounded in theory? Are there any theoretical perspectives or practice models that you think would be helpful for your agency to use in their practice with client systems?

To develop and implement a multilevel plan, it is necessary to identify all the possible interventions that could be used with and on behalf of the client system at the micro, mezzo, and macro levels. The plan should consider what may need to happen at the individual and family level, as well as consider how group work, either treatment or task, may be helpful, and last, what needs to happen at the organization, community, or larger system level. By considering all possible multilevel interventions, you can begin to conceptualize a comprehensive plan that when implemented will be more effective than if you were to target only one system level. To develop a multilevel plan, start with the interventions commonly used by the agency (see Integrative Activity 10.3) and identify the level that intervention targets. For example, if the agency offers a parent education group and you determine that the client would benefit from the group, then that would be the intervention you would identify to target the mezzo level. Once you have identified an intervention at the mezzo level, you will also want to identify interventions at the micro level (those that target individuals and families) and macro level (those that target the organization, community, or larger system).

The importance of implementing multilevel plans can best be illustrated in the following situation. Many years ago, I was working with a student who was doing her field placement at a mental health hospital. One of the clients she was working with was due to be discharged, and the student was working on the discharge plan with the client (micro-level intervention). The student, however, began to encounter difficulties, as the client stated that he had nowhere to go. As the student began to develop the discharge plan, she learned that the client was dually diagnosed and being served by both the mental health and MRDD (Mental Retardation and Developmental Disabilities) system. The MRDD case manager was stating that the mental health system had to secure housing, and the mental health case manager was stating that the client needed to return to the MRDD community placement. The student became very frustrated with the client and unsuccessfully attempted on several occasions to develop a plan with the client. Finally, after taking a step back, the student determined that intervention at the micro level, targeting only the individual client, was not going to work, because the core issue was at the macro level. The student brought this to the attention of the field instructor, who agreed with the student's assessment of the situation and set up a meeting with the community mental health and MRDD case managers to negotiate a discharge plan. As soon as it was determined who would handle the client's placement, after much discussion and negotiation, the client's discharge plan fell into place. This is an excellent example of the need to determine the appropriate level of intervention based on the assessment. What also made this intervention exciting was the fact that the student was very proud and surprised because she never considered that she would do macro social work and yet had in fact engaged in a macro-level intervention on behalf of her individual client.

Integrative Activity 10.4: Developing and Implementing Multilevel Plans will assist you in developing a multilevel plan by identifying the possible multilevel interventions that you can implement based on the multidimensional assessment you conducted. The activity will help you consider what needs to happen at the individual, family, group, organization, community, and larger system levels to assist your client system in meeting their goals and needs. What is important to remember is that your client system may be an individual, a family, a group, an organization, or a community. So it is always important to first and foremost identify your client system, determine the problem from the perspective of your primary client, and when it comes to developing a plan, consider all the possible interventions that could be implemented at all levels. Furthermore, sometimes social workers determine that the agency needs to change to better serve the client. By considering and implementing a multilevel plan, it is more likely that you will identify if and when the agency needs to be the target of the change effort.

EP 2.1.10h, i, j, k, and l, EP 2.1.9b

To assist you in this process, I encourage you to develop what I like to call an accordion approach. When you play the accordion, you must be able to continuously open and close the bellows in order to create a sound. The opening and closing of the bellows can represent moving from the smaller system of the individual through the mid-system to the largest system of the organization, community, and society and back again. Playing the accordion also requires the ability to play the notes which represent the various theories and interventions utilized to assist clients. Thus, when you put these together, you can visualize what is necessary for effective generalist practice which is developing the skill of seamlessly moving back and forth from the individual to dyads, family, groups, the organization, communities, and society (regardless of your primary client system) as you use the necessary interventions to help your client system achieve their goals or meet their needs. Also, when identifying your client system, you may realize that you have multiple clients, such as in the case of foster care services that are contracted by the local county children's services. When determining the plan, you may need to consider what your referring agency expects to happen and factor that into the plan as much as what your identified client hopes will happen.

EP 2.1.6b

Finally, it is important to discuss the role that research plays in the development of multilevel plans. Clearly, developing your knowledge of what the research generally says about your area of practice is an important overall competence that relates to evidence-based practice. However, when you are developing a plan, you want to consider what the research specifically says are the most effective interventions to include in your plan. This develops your competence in the area of research-informed practice. As you are developing your plan, you may want to engage in a review of the literature specific to your client and the identified goals and needs, so you can incorporate that information in your plan.

A final word about developing a multilevel plan: it is my hope that you will be able to implement your plan in its entirety; however, if for whatever reason, you cannot, that is understandable. This may be due to the constraints of your agency, and if this is the case, implement those interventions that you are able to do within your agency. For those that you cannot directly implement, discuss them in supervision and in your seminar or other classes. In this discussion, include your thoughts about your plan, how your plan relates to your assessment, and how you would go about implementing the plan. This, in and of itself, will be a rich and valuable learning experience.

INTEGRATIVE ACTIVITY 10.4

Developing and Implementing Multilevel Plans

Purpose: The purpose of this activity is to assist you in developing and implementing a multilevel plan that is grounded in your multidimensional/multilevel assessment, identify needed interventions, and links those interventions to various theoretical perspective and practice models.

Directions: Develop a multilevel plan by identifying specific interventions that could be used to assist your client and discuss the plan in supervision. Once you have developed the plan, implement the plan.

1. **Identify the client system:** Who is your client? Do you have multiple clients? Remember, a client system can be an individual, a family, a group, an organization, or a community.

2. **Identify your assessment of client system problem:** Provide your determination of what you think is the problem and the important factors contributing to the problem, using the result of your multidimensional/multilevel assessment (Integrative Activity 10.2), and specifically address whether this is a problem of the individual, a family, a group, an organization, the community, a larger social system, or a combination.

3. **Identify the needs and goals:** (i.e., what needs to happen for the client system to meet their goals)

4. **Identify the client system's strengths, resources, and protective factors:**

5. **Identify the client system's risks, deficits, or barriers:**

6. **Identify multilevel interventions:** (e.g., evaluate the pros and cons; consider if an intervention is doable, if it will succeed, and the time frame needed to succeed)

   a. Micro: What does the individual and family need to do? What do you need to do on behalf of the individual and family? List all the possible interventions that could be implemented at the micro level, and link each intervention to a theoretical perspective, practice model, or both.

b. **Mezzo:** What needs to happen at the group level, either considering treatment or task groups, to assist the client? List all possible interventions that could be implemented at the mezzo level, and link each intervention to a theoretical perspective, practice model, or both.

c. **Macro:** What needs to happen at the organization, community, and larger system level to help the client meet his or her goals? List all possible interventions that could be implemented at the macro level, and link each intervention to a theoretical perspective, practice model, or both.

7. **Evaluate the multilevel plan:** What were you able to implement and how did you go about doing that? Was your intervention effective?

THE PLANNED CHANGE CASE ANALYSIS

EP 2.1.3b &
EP 2.1.1b,
EP 2.1.10m

The fifth and last step in the process of integrating and developing competence in effectively using the planned change process in field is to conduct a planned change case analysis. This activity will provide you an opportunity to pull all the steps identified in Table 10.1 together and analyze the planned change process. By taking the time to engage in a comprehensive reflection and case analysis, you will develop a better understanding of the big picture of the process in your field site, as well as have an opportunity to identify and critique specifically what you did during each phase. In addition, you will have an opportunity to consider both the multilevel assessment and the multilevel plan you developed and implemented based on your assessment, both of which are critical to generalist practice or the generalist approach. Integrative Activity 10.5: The Planned Change Case Analysis will assist you in conducting your case analysis. As in most of the activities of field, once you have completed this activity, it is important to discuss your analysis in supervision and in your course work.

INTEGRATIVE ACTIVITY **10.5**

The Planned Change Case Analysis

Purpose: The purpose of this activity is to (1) integrate your understanding of the planned change process with a client system case you have had direct involvement with while in field, and (2) analyze how the process went.

Directions:

1. Read Chapter 10, and complete all integrative activities. For additional information review the phases of the planned change or helping process in your practice textbook(s).

2. Select a client system case; remember a client system can be an individual, family, group, organization, community, or society you have had/are having direct involvement with. The emphasis is on the specific client system, not the general roles or functions of the agency. When selecting a case, choose one you have had or are having extensive involvement with where you were able to conduct all phases of the planned change process. Remember this could be a onetime contact or an ongoing experience.

3. In writing, follow the outline and in D, address each phase of the planned change process and specifically describe what you did to accomplish that phase.

   The Analysis Outline

   A. Briefly describe the client system case you are going to analyze (i.e., an individual client or family, a group—treatment or task (this could either be one specific session or an entire group), or an organization, community, or society).

   B. Identify why you chose this client system case to analyze.

   C. Given the emphasis on knowledge and the fact that the generalist field education approach is grounded in curriculum, demonstrate, through the linkage of specific courses, the knowledge you applied to your understanding of the client system case (revisit Integrative Activity 2.3: Curriculum Review). For instance, if your client is a child and you are working in a child welfare agency, you would describe your knowledge of both child development and the child welfare system gained in your human behavior or child welfare course. If you are selecting an organization and program that you designed as your client system case, you would draw on your macro practice course, and perhaps your diversity course if you are working primarily with an African-American population, as well as your human development course if the primary population is adolescents.

   D. Describe what you did in each phase of the planned change process and how the client system responded to each phase. In addition, identify any specific stage that stood out in terms of something you felt good about or found particularly challenging. In addition, given the varying nature of the settings, identify any phase(s) that differed from the book definition and discuss how your agency achieves the overall goal(s) of the planned change process in light of this difference:

      1. Engagement;
      2. Assessment;
      3. Planning and Contracting (in planning, identify a plan that targets the micro-, mezzo-, and macro-level system);
      4. Implementation;
      5. Monitoring;
      6. Evaluation; and
      7. Termination.

   E. Identify and describe any value-driven, legal, and ethical program or systemic issues that impacted the case and your work with the client system.

F. Identify how you used culturally competent practice skills and how you integrated your understanding of social and economic justice when working on the case.

G. For the Implementation phase, consider the linkage of theory to practice (revisit Integrative Activity 10.3: Theoretical Perspective, Practice Models, and Commonly Used Interventions) and identify three theoretical perspectives or practice models that you applied to the case. Briefly describe the theory, and identify at least one intervention you could use based on the theory. Then identify at least one specific intervention you implemented and the theory that guided the intervention. Last, analyze the intervention's effectiveness in assisting the client in meeting his or her goal.

4. **Last, do an overall analysis of the process, answering the following:** How did I do? What were my strengths, and what are my growth areas? How did the planned change process flow? Did I achieve the desired result? How would the client system say they experienced the process? Is there anything I would recommend to improve the process?

Suggested Field Tasks

- Present and analyze client system information.
- Review related course work.
- Develop and conduct a bio/psycho/psychosocial/spiritual/environmental assessment.
- Use knowledge of development when assessing a client.
- Demonstrate understanding of how behavior relates to and is impacted by social systems.
- Demonstrate knowledge of theories by defining and explaining at least three theories that explain development and behavior and guide intervention.
- Discuss how the planned change process looks at agency.
- Intake and engage individuals, families, groups—task and treatment, organizations and communities via phone and in person.
- Prepare for client system contacts.
- Gather information on client systems.
- Identify client system goals.
- Identify formal assessments used by agency.
- Conduct agency-based assessments (intakes, social history, ecomap, genogram, or other agency-based assessments) on client systems.
- Identify client system's strengths and limitations.
- Identify multilevel plans that help client systems resolve problems.
- Engage in interventions (implement plans) that demonstrate the roles of negotiation, mediation, and advocacy.

Competency Notes

The following identifies where the CSWE *EPAS* (2008) Educational Policy (EP) and practice behaviors are discussed in the chapter.

EP 2.1.1b Practice personal reflection and self-correction to ensure continual professional development (p. 168): Social workers must competently utilize reflection in developing their understanding of and ability to utilize the planned change process in practice.

EP 2.1.1c Attend to professional roles and boundaries (p. 147): Social workers must understand their role and how best to utilize the roles of social work in order to effectively implement the planned change process.

EP 2.1.3b Analyze models of assessment, prevention, intervention, and evaluation (pp. 161,168): Social workers must develop skill in analyzing the phases of the planned change process as well as the possible interventions that can be implemented in order to serve their client systems.

EP 2.1.6b Use research evidence to inform practice (p. 166): Social workers must develop skill in knowing and applying research to their practice with clients.

EP 2.1.7a Utilize conceptual frameworks to guide the processes of assessment, intervention, and evaluation (p. 154): Social workers must develop skills to utilize conceptual frameworks in all phases of the planned change process.

EP 2.1.7b Critique and apply knowledge to understand person and environment (p. 154): Social workers must apply their understanding of human behavior in the social environment to their practice with client systems.

EP 2.1.9a Continuously discover, appraise, and attend to changing locales, populations, scientific and technological developments, and emerging societal trends to provide relevant services (p. 145): Social workers must develop their understanding of how agencies are shaped by the context in which they operate and how that context impacts the planned change process.

EP 2.1.9b Provide leadership in promoting sustainable changes in service delivery and practice to improve the quality of social services (p. 165): Social workers must develop the skills necessary to identify when the agency should be the target of intervention on behalf of clients.

EP 2.1.10a Substantively and affectively prepare for action with individuals, families, groups, organizations, and communities (p. 145): Social workers must be able to successfully engage client systems.

EP 2.1.10b Use empathy and other interpersonal skills (p. 145): Social workers must develop and demonstrate competence in using empathy and interpersonal skills in order to effectively engage client systems.

EP 2.1.10c Develop a mutually agreed-on focus of work and desired outcomes (p. 145): Social workers must be able to identify with client systems the focus of their work and expected outcome.

EP 2.1.10d Collect, organize, and interpret client data (p. 153): Social workers must be able to gather information on client systems, organize that information, and make determinations.

EP 2.1.10e Assess client strengths and limitations (p. 154): Social workers must be able to gather information on strengths and limitations of client systems and utilize that information in practice.

EP 2.1.10f Develop mutually agreed-on intervention goals and objectives (p. 160): Social workers must be able to identify goals and necessary interventions with client systems.

EP 2.1.10g Select appropriate intervention strategies (p. 161): Social workers must be able to identify and apply interventions that are appropriate to the client situation.

EP 2.1.10h Initiate actions to achieve organizational goals (p. 165): Social workers must be able to engage in practice that reflects the goals of the organization in which they serve as well as identify the organization itself as a target of change when indicated.

EP 2.1.10i Implement prevention interventions that enhance client capacities (p. 165): Social workers must be able to engage in interventions that target prevention in order to better serve client systems.

EP 2.1.10j Help clients resolve problems (p. 165): Social workers must develop the skills necessary to assist client systems in resolving the issues that bring them to their attention.

EP 2.1.10k Negotiate, mediate, and advocate for clients (p. 165): Social workers must develop the skills necessary to engage in practice in which they can negotiate, mediate, and advocate on behalf of their clients.

EP 2.1.10l Facilitate transitions and endings (p. 165): Social workers must be skilled at assisting their client systems in the process of transitioning to other services and ending service.

EP 2.1.10m Social workers critically analyze, monitor, and evaluate interventions (p. 168): Social workers must be able to analyze, monitor, and evaluate the services provided to client systems.

References

Council on Social Work Education. (2008). *Educational policy and accreditation standards.* Alexandria, VA: Council on Social Work Education.

Hutchison, E., & contributors. (2011). *Dimensions of human behavior: Person and environment.* Los Angeles, CA: Sage Publication, Inc.

Johnson, L., & Yanca, S. (2007). *Social work practice: A generalist approach.* Boston: Allyn and Bacon.

Kirst-Ashman, K., & Hull, Jr., G. (2009a). *Generalist practice with organizations and communities.* Belmont, CA: Brooks/Cole.

Kirst-Ashman, K., & Hull, Jr., G (2009b). *Understanding generalist practice* (5th ed.). Pacific Grove, CA: Brooks/Cole.

Miley, K., O'Melia, M., & DuBois, B. (2007). *Generalist social work practice: An empowering approach.* Boston: Allyn and Bacon.

National Association of Social Workers. (1999). *Code of ethics.* Washington, DC: NASW.

Schatz, M. S., Jenkins, L. E., & Sheafor, B. W. (1990). Milford redefined: A model of initial and advanced generalist social work. *Journal of Social Work Education, 26*(3), 217.

Sheafor, B., & Horejsi, C. (2008). *Techniques and guidelines for social work practice.* Boston: Pearson Education, Inc.

Wayne, J., & Cohen, C. (2001). *Group work education in the field.* Alexandria, VA: Council on Social Work Education.

CHAPTER 11

Frequently Experienced Situations in Field

The focus of this chapter is to present frequently experienced situations in field, or what I call FESs. The situations presented and discussed in this chapter come up year after year, so much so that I felt a chapter that just focused on each situation individually would be helpful to you as you navigate through your field experience.

Each situation is a composite of several specific experiences that students have had over the years. I have narrowed down the situations to what I consider the top 10. Obviously, this list is not exhaustive and may not specifically apply to you; however, the situations lead to more general information that all students can relate to and have the potential for reflection, discussion, and learning. It is important to note that if you have a situation that you feel needs attention but is not covered in this chapter, seek out the assistance of your field instructor, field director, or a faculty member.

Each situation will be presented in the form of a question or statement. The question or statement will be followed by some background and recommendations for how to think about and approach the situation. For each situation, I will provide what I call a *best practice* way of approaching the situation, which based on my knowledge and experience has been effective for students to handle the situation. Also, I may provide additional information from the literature to ground your thinking about the situation.

One last important thing is that the recommendations presented in this chapter on how to handle a specific situation are just that—recommendations. Therefore, when you are deciding how to handle a specific situation you are dealing with in your field agency, even if it is similar to one presented in this chapter, you must always consult with your field instructor, field director, or a faculty member and follow that person's recommendations. Last, the situations presented are in no particular order of importance.

THE TOP 10 FESS

1. **My client doesn't want to work with me because I am a student.**

    "Yesterday in field, I was supposed to meet with a client and fill out some paperwork. But when I went to the meeting, the client refused to talk to me because I am a student. What should I do about this?"

This situation is very common for students to experience. It can present itself either as a client who does not want to work with you because you are a student or you cannot engage in a learning task because you are a student. This experience and even just the fear of this happening can cause students to question why they need to tell their clients they are students, or even worse, cause students to not disclose their student status to clients to prevent something like this from happening.

Indeed, having a client refuse to work with you or being told you can't do something because you are a student can be frustrating and even upsetting. However, if this happens to you, it is important to keep a few things in mind.

First of all, as discussed in Chapter 2, you, your field instructor, and the agency are ethically bound to inform the client systems you work with that you are a student. This is not negotiable. Second, in all likelihood, at some point during your field experience, this will happen, so prepare yourself now for how you will respond. The best thing to do is acknowledge that you hear the client and respect his or her wishes. If you feel that you can discuss the situation with the client, it is OK to let the client know that, yes, you are a student, but you have been trained and are receiving supervision by a social worker, and you will ensure that the client receives the best possible service. If the client insists that he or she does not want to work with a student, thank the client for meeting with you and let the client know that you will need to let your field instructor know and that someone will be with them shortly. Inform your field instructor or agency designee of the situation, and make sure that someone meets with the client. After the client has been taken care of, discuss the situation in supervision to see if you or your field instructor can do anything else to avoid this from happening in the future.

If the situation involves a learning task such as participating in a meeting, first handle the situation in a similar fashion as that suggested in the preceding example. Then meet with your field instructor to determine if the field instructor or agency director can do anything to enable you to participate in that learning task in the future.

EP 2.1.1c

A bright spot related to being a student and one that is the flip side of the preceding situation is the fact that a number of students have told me a client has opened up to them because they were a student. I have heard many stories of students saying they have met with clients who the social worker said probably won't talk much, but when they met and the client was introduced to the student, the client completely opened up. What often happens is that many clients like the idea of helping a student and thus become engaged. Or the student's status actually becomes an effective engagement tool as they talk about the school, the program, or the student's desire to be a social worker. So although sometimes your student status may become an issue for your client, there may also be times that it can be an asset. The most important thing you can do when working with clients is to be confident and have clarity about your role as a social work student in your agency, and always introduce yourself as a student. This alone will translate into competence for a client.

Finally, try not to take these things personally or overemphasize your student status, because for some clients, anything may have been used as a deterrent to the helping process. Or the client may be searching for a way to find some control in a situation that may be making them feel out of control. Or the client may have a legitimate concern that needs to be respected. So the best course of action is to acknowledge and meet the client's need and move on to the next task at hand.

2. I'm not doing what I thought I would be doing, can I get a new placement?

"I'm so frustrated; I'm not doing any of the things I thought I would be doing. To make matters worse, my field instructor keeps asking me to do things that I don't think I should be doing. Can I get a different placement?"

Although this was touched on in the discussion on multilevel tasks in Chapter 3, this is a common experience that often requires specific attention. First and foremost, anytime you have a question about the tasks you are or are not engaging in, you must discuss this openly and honestly with your field instructor.

In fact, whenever students or field instructors bring up issues about field, I ask each person if they have discussed the issue with the other party. I can't tell you how often I am told no. Then I always send each party back to discuss the situation with the other. I realize that may be easier said than done, so let's discuss how you could go about discussing your concern about tasks with your field instructor.

First of all, you can refer to your learning plan. If the task you are not getting an opportunity to engage in is on the learning plan, you can refer to the learning plan and discuss the plan for how to incorporate that task into your days at field. If the task is not on your learning plan, you can say that you have several tasks already included on the plan, some of which you are having a hard time getting to and that you won't be able to complete the requested task at this time. Tell your field instructor that you are open to discussing including the task, but then you will have to drop another task due to the time constraints of the field placement.

Finally, the student's leap to wanting to switch placements is not so uncommon. My position with the students I work with has always been that the problems that come up while in field are often important learning opportunities. If a student switched placements every time there was an issue, (1) they would be constantly switching, and (2) they would miss out on an important learning opportunity to develop professional skills that will be necessary when practicing. Those skills include assertiveness, being one's own advocate, and professional communication. If a student is particularly nervous about discussing an issue with their field instructor, I encourage the student to write down what he or she wants to say, practice with me or the other students, and fully prepare for the meeting.

EP 2.1.1d

If the problems do not get better, then you may need to discuss with your field director if the placement is appropriate. But this should be the last conversation to have, not the first.

3. Can I use my cell phone at field?

"Can I use my cell phone at my field site? It would just make everything so much easier."

This great question is very much related to the issue of contexts that shape practice. As discussed in Chapter 6, the use of technology in social work practice has grown over the years. More and more social workers and agencies are turning to the use of technology in the form of computers, Internet, cell phones, social networking, and computerized files. When I was practicing in child welfare in the 1990s, we began to use portable phones when we went on home visits. In those days, the phones were the size of a shoe box but did provide an important safety feature to increase communication between the worker and the office. Today, almost everyone has a cell phone, and many cell phones function as one's office—people receive their e-mail and perhaps surf the Internet during the day if they have a smart phone. But back to the question: is it OK for a student to use a personal cell phone at field?

EP 2.1.1d

My answer to this question is it depends on how and with whom you are using your phone. Giving your cell number to your field instructor, field director, and faculty liaison and using it in the course of your day to communicate with your agency, university, and other professionals is perfectly appropriate and can be very helpful if you need to discuss an issue, are lost, or are running late to a meeting.

EP 2.1.1c

I do not, however, recommend that you give your personal cell phone number to your clients, for several reasons. First and foremost, it is important to establish appropriate boundaries and educate your clients with regard to those boundaries. The client should have the number of the agency and your extension, if you have one; if you don't, discuss with your field instructor about giving clients your field instructor's extension. The client should also be given the emergency after-hour's number and be told how to appropriately use the emergency line. This will let the client leave you messages if necessary and receive services in a crisis. If you need to call your client, you should use the agency phone. If your agency has portable phones that you can take with you when you do home visits, you can, of course, use that phone to call your clients.

Second, if your client has your cell phone number, they could call you unsolicitedly. A client could call anytime of the day or night, and given that you are only in field part-time, unless you have a block placement, your clients could end up calling you when you are not at field, in class, or at work.

Third, a client could call in crisis when you are not working at your agency, and you may not have access to the information you need to assist the client or even contact your field instructor. As a student you never want to be the sole person responsible for your client; therefore, there should be other resources that your clients can draw on when they are in need.

EP 2.1.9a

I did have a student who was at a setting where she said everyone used their cell phones, and it didn't make sense to her why she shouldn't go ahead and do the same. It is always challenging to navigate the world of the student and the world of the agency, but it is important to remember that, first and foremost, you are a student, and just because the professional social workers engage in a particular practice at the agency does not mean that you should as a student. In the event that a student wants to use his or her phone, it is important to discuss the situation with the field instructor, field director, and perhaps faculty liaison. Together, make a decision that is in the best interest of all parties, taking into account the fact that the student is not an employee of the agency and is learning about professional practice and therefore may not have the same level of skill and expertise as the social workers at the agency.

4. My client stated that he would be better of dead and I didn't know what to say.

"In group today, my client mentioned to me that he was thinking about suicide and I had no idea what to say. Fortunately, the other social worker talked with the client, but, I mean, I kind of froze and just didn't know what to say."

Suicide assessment and intervention in field is a scary and real part of your professional development. Therefore, it should be given extra time in supervision where you can review what you learned in your practice classes prior to entering field and plan for this eventuality while in field. Anyone at anytime could have thoughts of suicide. What becomes important for you in field is developing a consistent plan of action of what to do should a client express suicide ideation. Even the most prepared student can become nervous and anxious and even stumble when working with a client with suicide ideation. That being said, it is critically important that should this happen, you put the needs of the client first and ensure that the client is served. In the preceding situation, fortunately the student was not alone. Even though the student "froze," a worker was present who could assist the client. But what if the student had been alone? How should the student have handled the situation?

This happened when I was a field instructor. The student I was supervising went out on a routine visit to update releases of information, and in the course of the meeting, the client expressed suicide ideation. The student was alone and handled it perfectly by calling—first, acknowledging what the client said; second, informing the client that she needed to call her supervisor; third, calling me; and fourth, staying with the client until I arrived. Together the student and I assessed the level of risk and discussed options with the client to ensure the client's safety.

To ensure you are prepared to manage a situation of suicide risk, let's review a few important recommendations. Incidentally, many of the recommendations that relate to your duty to prevent harm (suicide risk) can apply to situations of mandated reporting or duty to warn, so make sure you are equally prepared for those situations as well. First, discuss in supervision specifically what your field instructor wants you to do should a client express suicide ideation. Educate yourself with regard to the statistics and warning signs. Always maintain the possibility that any client during any contact could disclose information that requires you to act to ensure their safety. Review any tools that your agency uses to assess the level of risk. The S-A-D-S-P-E-R-S-O-N-S acronym developed by Patterson, Dohn, Bird, and Patterson (1983) organizes the risk factors in a manageable way to allow for assessment of level of risk. Furthermore, Sheafor and Horejsi (2008) offer several areas of consideration to determine if a person may be at high risk. They are:

- history of prior attempts
- client has a plan and access to the means
- client is in a painful situation that is getting worse
- client lacks social support
- client has changed from distressed to being calm. (p. 522)

A helpful learning tool is to role-play with your field instructor a client experiencing suicidal ideation and practice asking assessment questions and developing a plan of action.

When I worked on a suicide prevention hotline, we assessed callers to be at one of three risk levels, low, moderate, or high. If we assessed a client to be at high risk, we intervened with the goal of safety and treatment. If we assessed the client to be at low or moderate risk, we utilized contracts, linked the client with services, and often requested to speak to another person, with the permission of the client, to inform that person that the client was in distress.

Assessing the suicide risk of a client as a student can be a scary learning experience, so it is important to process the situation with your field instructor and to always inform your field instructor if you are concerned about a client.

5. **I saw my client at the grocery store and freaked. What should I have done?**

"Oh my God! I was at the grocery store yesterday and I saw my client. I totally freaked out and left. Now I feel really bad. I mean what if she saw me and I didn't even bother to say hi. I think I should have gone up to her and said hi, what do you think?"

This is one of my favorite situation to discuss with students because it happens every year, and although you may think that you are well grounded in ethical practice, when you are caught off guard by running into your client in a public setting, such as at the mall, it is very jarring and you may not react the way you think you would. What is also so interesting is how students year after year have similar reactions to this situation and initially tend to view the situation only from their perspective. They miss all the possible ways this situation can impact the client, as well as the importance of developing the skills necessary to tolerate the ambiguity that is inherent in this type of situation.

First of all, what you want to remember is a simple best practice guideline: If a client notices you in public, follow the lead of the client. For instance, if the client appears to ignore you, it is important to realize that the client may not want to say hello. This can be for a variety of reasons. First of all, the client may be with someone and not want to have to explain who you are. They may not know what to say or may think that they shouldn't say hi. If on the other hand, a client greets you in public, simply say hello and go about your business. If you are with someone else, make sure you maintain confidentiality and don't disclose that this is a client. It can be awkward, so discuss with your field instructor how you could handle this. I have said things such as, "Oh, just someone I knew from work," which is a fairly innocuous statement. The most important thing for you to remember is that it is not the client's responsibility to maintain confidentiality—it is your responsibility. Therefore, if the client says hi, its OK to say hi back. But if the client does not, do not acknowledge the client.

The part of not acknowledging a client is where students struggle the most and state that they don't want their clients to think they are rude or mean, or they think it is ridiculous that they can't say hi to a client. However, once the situation is explored in more detail and put in the context of ethical responsibility, and once they consider how the client might feel or what the client needs, most students come to realize that it is necessary to always err on the side of confidentiality.

I tell the students I work with that I, too, have experienced many instances of seeing clients in public and each situation is very different. I have had clients shout my name down a grocery store aisle or make eye contact, turn around, and quickly walk away. I always follow my client's lead. Although our values may tell us to be nice to all clients in all situations, we must develop the skills necessary to allow our professional values to guide our actions.

If you are practicing in a rural or small town, I can guarantee you this will happen. You may even want to discuss this ahead of time with your clients and let them know how you plan to operate to see if that fits with what the client would like to happen. Oftentimes, how to react to each other in public can be negotiated ahead of time, particularly if you and your clients frequent the same establishments and you have no other options.

6. **My group co-facilitator won't let me say anything. What should I do?**

"I was so excited because I was finally going to be able to run a group, but the person I was working with did all the talking. I didn't know what to do. There were so many times during the session that I wanted to say something but I couldn't. I just don't know what to do. Now I'm dreading the next group session."

This situation can be frustrating and challenging to address as a student in field, but it is important to both your generalist training and your professional development. Group work, whether with treatment or tasks groups, is an expected area of practice for the generalist practitioner, so when you have the opportunity to cofacilitate a group, it is great. That being said, identifying the learning task of cofacilitating a group is just the beginning of how to create a productive and rewarding learning task. First of all, cofacilitating anything is challenging due to the fact that you have to manage the task as well as your working relationship with the cofacilitator, which can often be the greater challenge of the two. It is important to negotiate and discuss your role and plan for how you and your cofacilitator will function. I am speaking from experience.

One of my greatest professional practice challenges was cofacilitating an incest survivor group where my working relationship with my cofacilitator became problematic to the point where it threatened our ability to continue to offer the group and required significant intervention with our supervisor. What I found most interesting was how my cofacilitator experienced my style of processing. To process a session, I would passionately discuss what happened, state my observations, concerns, and even shock with some of the content. This was the process that I would go through to debrief and figure out what to do next for the group. My cofacilitator interpreted my style and the information I shared as my not being able to handle the group. My cofacilitator reported feeling responsible to take care of me and felt that was not appropriate. Even thought I reassured my cofacilitator that I was fine and in fact enjoyed the challenge of working with this population in a group, this was not enough, and my cofacilitator discontinued work on the group. As an interesting side note, the new cofacilitator and I developed a strong and effective working relationship. So this example shows that the working relationship of the cofacilitators is critical and is an important dynamic to consider in terms of the group process.

To develop a strong working relationship with your cofacilitator, the first thing you want to do is have a planning session. Planning for group or other tasks is an area that students tell me is often lacking in their placements. Given that you will be simultaneously developing your group skills and managing a cofacilitation relationship, it is critical that you request a planning session. During the session, review the structure of the group and the materials, and discuss the plan for your training and eventual independence as a group facilitator. The plan could be structured as in week 1, you will observe; week two, you will do one part of the group; and by week 5, you will be able to run the entire group. Or it can flow more freely, where you will have the freedom to interject whenever you see fit. The latter, in my experience, is more challenging, but the former can feel too structured. I suggest a hybrid—allow for some structure and some spontaneity. Ask your cofacilitator to periodically ask you for feedback or sit back and allow for pauses to give you a chance to interject, as well as have at least one thing per session that you are responsible for. After a group session, it is equally important to process the session, share your thoughts, ask for feedback, and plan for the next session. Wayne and Cohen (2001) state that, "Co-leaders can help each other achieve greater self-awareness by providing feedback about their performance in the group. Through joint problem solving, they can be helped to sharpen their assessment and interventive skills" (p. 51).

If and when issues between you and your cofacilitator come up, it is important to be assertive and discuss them even if this causes anxiety. Remember, you can always discuss your concerns first with your field instructor, field director, faculty field liaison, or other students to gather suggestions for how to handle the situation and what to say. What is most important to remember is that if you feel your training and education are being hampered, it is critical to address the issue. One last thought regarding group work: it is my hope that you will have a chance to facilitate a group on your own, as it is a wonderful experience that is important in your development as a social work practitioner.

EP 2.1.10a

7. **My co-worker was rude to a client and I don't know how to handle this.**

"I went on a home visit the other day with one of the social workers in the agency. During the visit, the social worker was very short with the client and at one point, I mean in my opinion, was rude. I couldn't believe it. Then when we got in the car, she proceeded to tell me how much she dislikes this client. I honestly didn't know what to say. I still couldn't believe that the social worker spoke to the client the way she did. It really upset me. I would never speak to a client like that."

This is a jarring but not uncommon experience for a student. As stated in Chapter 1, as a student in field, you will be exposed to what I call the good, the bad, and the ugly. In my opinion, this particular situation, at least on the surface, may fall in the "ugly" category, but let's examine the situation in more detail.

EP 2.1.1d

First of all, one of the best things about field, as far as I am concerned, is that you get a chance to be exposed to so many different clients, workers, and situations. Along with that, you will at times observe things that you either don't understand or disagree with completely. Even if it is sometimes challenging, it is an important part of professional development because you will develop your own sense of yourself as a professional social worker through this process of observing a wide variety of professional behaviors.

I remember that when I was working in family preservation my supervisor would come up with these amazing interventions, and half the time I would state that I didn't think I could pull them off. Or I would observe a coworker working with a client in a way that I knew I couldn't, but for some reason it worked with that particular client. I have also witnessed completely inappropriate conduct on the part of a worker that fell into the category of my ethical responsibility of protecting clients, and I reported the conduct to a supervisor. As you can see, it is expected that from time to time, you will witness practices that you will question and perhaps even feel the need to discuss with your supervisor.

With regard to the given situation, any number of things could be going on. First, this could be the style of the worker, which happens to be extremely different from your style. There could be issues on the case that the worker has had to deal with that necessitates the worker being more severe—although I don't think there is ever a reason to be rude. Even if the worker states that she dislikes the client, that doesn't mean that the worker won't provide the necessary service. It is not uncommon to have clients whom you struggle with or who really challenge your skills. I suggested that the student process the session with her field instructor to get some perspective and share her concerns. The student was worried and didn't want to appear as if she was telling on the other worker. This is an understandable concern, but it is so important that as a student you can share with your field instructor what you are observing and how you are reacting to what you observe. Remember, if your field instructor is concerned, he or she will handle the situation, maintain your confidentiality, and ultimately appreciate your observations.

8. Can I give my client a ride home?

"The other day as I was leaving work, I noticed that my client didn't have a ride home. I really wanted to take my client home but didn't know if it would be OK. I mean, why can't I just be nice, why do I have to think about every little thing I do? Sometimes it just seems silly."

EP 2.1.1c

I can completely understand the student's initial thoughts about this situation and agree that oftentimes in professional social work practice the things we have to do and the way we have to do them can seem, as she said, "silly." However, in situations that involve seemingly innocuous things—such as giving a client a ride home or buying a client a drink, or extremely frustrating situations, such as when you have to fill out the seven needed forms in triplicate and wait 7 to 10 days to get a voucher to buy your client a coat, so you find yourself feeling compelled to just go out and purchase the coat—as professional social workers we have to accept the fact that we cannot just act on our own. For the student, field becomes an excellent place to realize and come to terms with this fact.

As a student, you cannot simply act in isolation. You must realize that your actions do not exist in a vacuum. Just as we are trained to view our clients within the person-in-environment construct grounded in systems theory—that is, we embrace the idea that when trying to understand our client's situation, we must consider many simultaneously and interrelated factors—the same holds true for professional practice. As a student in field, you are a representative of your university, your field program, your agency, and even the profession, and you must embrace and manage the demands and ethical responsibilities, albeit at times competing, placed on you by these interdependent systems when working with your clients.

EP 2.1.2b

The student with the question had excellent self-awareness of the issues involved in this situation. First and foremost, make sure you are aware of your university's and agency's policy with regard to transporting a client, particularly if the client is a minor and follow that policy. Second, don't assume that the easiest solution is the only solution. In this situation, there were other options, and the student was able to engage the client and problem solve, which ultimately is an excellent learning experience for the client. Last and most important, the situation illuminated what I call the potential slippery slope of ethical practice. The student came face to face with her desire to be nice, efficient, and practical, which in her mind was to give the client a ride home. To make matters worse, it was raining, but she realized that as a social work student functioning as such, the simple, efficient, and nice solution could have been disastrous. Perhaps it sounds overdramatic, but the point has to be considered. You have to confront head-on those times when you just want to do X even though it may be in direct violation of a university, agency, or ethical standard of practice or policy. It is during these times that you will ultimately develop the critical thinking and best practice skills that are necessary to be a competent professional social worker.

EP 2.1.3a

EP 2.1.2c

9. **My agency is a mess. It is total chaos. I think the agency needs some policies for how to uniformly do certain client related tasks. Should I say anything?**

"I think my agency is a mess. It is in total chaos. Everyone seems to do something different when it comes to the clients, and there are times when I disagree with how client situations are handled. I don't even think there are policies for some of the things that I think are really important and for which there should be a policy."

I love this situation; to me it comes from the heart of the student who is a budding macro-practitioner. This is a student who instinctively sees how the agency is functioning, questions the practices and their impact on clients, conceptualizes real solutions, yet is confronted with and halted by his or her student status and lack of experience. This situation also illuminates the fact that you will absolutely be impacted by your agency and that how you experience your agency and conceptualize yourself as a social worker within the context of your agency is significant and reflects the student-in-organization concept discussed in chapter 2.

EP 2.1.9b

For this student what became important was to first vent those things that were making her crazy, and second, begin to identify how she might be able to positively impact her agency (macro-practice), which is an important part of her generalist training. So the student, first and foremost, shared her observations in a professional manner with her field instructor and began a discussion of possible solutions. The field instructor was very open to the feedback and the possibility of the student working on a policy and procedures manual as part of her field experience. The field instructor discussed the task with the agency director, who also thought it would be helpful and sanctioned the student to begin to work on this task. The student was a natural at organizing and prioritizing the needs of the agency, as well as at gathering information from other agencies regarding policies and procedures. She ended up developing an outline. Once the outline was approved, the student wrote some specific policies, several of which were ultimately adopted.

This situation illustrates an important thing to remember as a student: the fact that often your reactions are right on. When your observations are confidently and professionally shared, you may have an opportunity to resolve your concerns and not only build skills but actually give back to your agency in a significant way. I always tell the students I work with that the agencies that take students tend to be open and encouraging of the observations and feedback students share about their experiences. This often becomes a way to improve service delivery.

10. I don't think my field instructor likes me.

> "My field instructor makes me uncomfortable. I don't think she likes me. I really like the agency, though. Sometimes I just don't know what we are supposed to be doing in our supervision session, so does it really matter if we meet? I get all my questions answered by the other social workers anyway; it just seems like a waste of my time."

This situation is tough because on the one hand, a student's relationship with the field instructor is important and formative; it is often what students remember the most from their education. On the other hand, sometimes a student won't have an amazing relationship with their field instructor, yet that student can learn and have a positive field experience. The latter is the most important thing to reflect on when you are struggling in your relationship with your field instructor. First and foremost, what a student needs to do when faced with this type of situation is to assess if he or she is learning and having a positive experience. If yes, then the student can work on improving the relationship. If not, then it may be important to discuss the situation with their field director or faculty field liaison.

In the given situation, the student was having a positive experience and was learning, so he didn't want to leave his agency. But he was also struggling with how to manage what he saw as a challenging relationship. He also brought up another issue in conjunction with his concerns about the supervisory relationship, which involved the supervision session. He appeared to be questioning the role of supervision and how best to use the supervision session. In all likelihood, the challenges in the relationship were impacting the supervision session, so it became important to separate these two issues and discuss each individually.

First, it was helpful for the student to express his concerns and articulate that he felt his field instructor didn't like him. By doing so, he could feel some initial relief and seek out assistance. When assessing the quality and experience of a relationship, particularly an important one like your supervisory relationship, you want to look at many different things and be cautious about making rash judgments. It was important for the student to consider that his perception of not being liked may not have been true and what he was interpreting as not being liked could have been related to several variables. First, he and his field instructor could have had very different personalities and expectations for the relationship, and what he was interpreting as "dislike" simply may have been related to his field instructor's style.

With regard to his questioning supervision, it may be helpful for him to reflect on the possibility that his discomfort in the relationship could have been affecting the supervision session, or the other way around—how he was approaching the supervision session could have been impacting the relationship. So I reviewed the importance of the supervision session and discussed ways that the student could improve the session, such as preparing ahead of time for the session, discussing expectations, and focusing on how he wanted to present himself even in light of his concerns about the relationship.

EP 2.1.1f

Last, I reiterated that developing the professional skills necessary to manage a challenging working relationship, particularly when it involves supervision, can be an excellent learning experience and one that will benefit him in his professional life.

REFLECTION QUESTION 11.1

Now that you have had a chance to review the 10 FESs, which ones stood out to you? What have you experienced similar to or different from the scenarios outlined? How have you handled challenging situations in field? Who do you consult, and how do you approach problem solving in field? How do you feel the situations you have experienced will prepare you for professional practice or advanced field?

Competency Notes

The following identifies where the CSWE *EPAS* (2008) Educational Policy (EP) and practice behaviors are discussed in the chapter.

EP 2.1.1c Attend to professional roles and boundaries (pp. 174, 176, 180): Social workers must develop an understanding of their professional role and the boundaries inherent in the role.

EP 2.1.1d Demonstrate professional demeanor in behavior, appearance, and communication (pp. 175, 176, 180): Social workers must be able to demonstrate professionalism in their actions.

EP 2.1.1f Use supervision and consultation (p. 183): Social workers must be able to utilize supervision to ensure professional practice.

EP 2.1.2a Recognize and manage personal values in a way that allows professional values to guide practice (p. 178): Social workers must be aware of and develop skills necessary to manage their personal values and allow professional values to guide their practice.

EP 2.1.2b Make ethical decisions by applying standards of the National Association of Social Workers Code of Ethics and, as applicable, of the International Federation of Social Workers/International Association of Schools of Social Work Ethics in Social Work, Statement of Principles (pp. 178, 181): Social workers must develop the skills necessary to actively utilize the code of ethics in their practice with client systems.

EP 2.1.2c Tolerate ambiguity in resolving ethical conflicts (p. 181): Social workers must develop the skills necessary to handle the difficult situations that arise in their practice such as those that do not have an easily identifiable course of action or those that create internal conflict on the part of the social worker.

EP 2.1.3a Distinguish, appraise, and integrate multiple sources of knowledge, including research-based knowledge and practice wisdom (p. 181): Social work practice is grounded in the ability of social workers to constantly manage information from varying sources and utilizing the information in their practice with client systems.

EP 2.1.9a Continuously discover, appraise, and attend to changing locales, populations, scientific and technological developments, and emerging societal trends to provide relevant services (p. 176): Social workers must develop the skills necessary to understand the contexts in which they practice and how those contexts impact service delivery.

EP 2.1.9b Provide leadership in promoting sustainable changes in service delivery and practice to improve the quality of social services (p. 181): Social workers must develop the skills necessary to know when services must be changed to better serve clients.

EP 2.1.10a Substantively and affectively prepare for action with individuals, families, groups, organizations, and communities (p. 179): Social workers must be able to engage the clients with whom they work.

References

Patterson, W., Dohn, H., Bird, J. & Patterson, G. (1983). Evaluation of suicidal patients: The SAD PERSONS scale. *Psychosomatics, 24,* 343–349.

Sheafor, B., & Horejsi, C. (2008). *Techniques and guidelines for social work practice.* Boston: Pearson Education, Inc.

Wayne, J., & Cohen, C. (2001). *Group work in field education.* Alexandria, VA: Council on Social Work Education, Inc.

CHAPTER 12

Professional Development of Self in Field

Chapter 1 introduced you to one of the important goals of field education: *socialization to the profession.* Throughout your field experience and socialization to the profession, you have had opportunities to experience and reflect on the various positions social workers hold and roles they use, the different types of agencies, and the different services offered by those agencies. You have also had an opportunity to specifically apply your generalist training to your practice at your field site.

The purpose of this chapter is to provide you an opportunity to reflect on your professional development within the context of the socialization to the profession you experienced in field. Recall that Reflection Question 1.4, at the start of your field experience, asked you to consider what being a professional meant to you, what you saw as the advantages of being a professional versus an employee, and if there were any disadvantages. It also asked you to consider what excited you or created anxiety as you thought about being a professional social worker. As you reflect on the answer you gave at the time, consider Reflection Question 12.1.

REFLECTION QUESTION 12.1

Would you answer that reflection question the same or differently based on the experiences you have had in field? Do new things come to you about being a professional social worker that did not occur to you at the beginning of your field experience? If so, what are those?

As a field director, professional development of self, in the context of field education, is an area of interest and one that I have focused on over the years with the students I have worked with. One experience in particular that stands out to me and exemplifies the transformation that students go through while in field happened several years ago, toward the end of the spring semester. The student was working in a shelter, and one of her clients violated the confidentiality of location policy. The consequence of the violation was that the client had to leave the shelter. The student shared that this was a challenging situation, but she knew she had to (1) uphold the policy of the agency, as the client was very aware of both the policy and the consequence of violating the policy, and (2) could see that she had a professional responsibility to all the client and staff of the shelter and understood why the confidentiality of location policy was so important.

Although this situation was not easy to manage, the student handled it well and was able to inform the client that she had to leave the shelter. At the end of the student sharing this situation, what really stood out to me was that the student stated she was glad the situation had happened toward the end of her field experience versus the beginning. She went on to explain that the professional experience she gained through her field experience made it easier for her do something that was very difficult. She even stated that she didn't know if she could have handled the situation had it happened at the beginning of field. Thus this situation reflects how important time and experience are to a student's professional development. It is the culmination of all the experiences of field that contribute to the development of the professional skills necessary to enable a student to handle complex client situations. But what is it to be a professional? This chapter will explore many commonly understood aspects of professionalism as well as what students need to consider as they reflect on their own professional development.

THE PROFESSIONAL DEFINED

EP 2.1.1a-f

A professional is defined as "a person whose actions are thoughtful, purposeful, competent, responsible and ethical" (Sheafor & Horejsi, 2012, p. 47). The CSWE *EPAS* (2008) states that,

Social workers

- advocate for client access to the services of social work;
- practice personal reflection and self-correction to ensure continual professional development;
- attend to professional roles and boundaries;
- demonstrate professional demeanor in behavior, appearance, and communication;
- engage in career-long learning; and
- use supervision and consultation. (p. 3)

Barker (2003) defines a professional as "an individual who qualifies for membership in a specific profession and uses its practices, knowledge, and skills to provide services to client systems, and in doing so, always adheres to its *values* and *code of ethics*" (p. 341). As a soon-to-be professional social worker, it is important to consider what the preceding definitions mean to you. Consider the Reflection Question 12.2.

REFLECTION QUESTION 12.2

What do you think it means to be a professional social worker? How would you assess your level of competence in demonstrating the behaviors of a professional as outlined by CSWE *EPAS* (2008), and how are you transitioning from the role of a student to the role of a social worker?

In all likelihood, this transition has been and will continue to be exciting, rewarding, and challenging.

At the end of every year, I ask the students I have been working with what they got out of field and if field was a worthwhile endeavor. The students, year after year, overwhelmingly agree that they are significantly different, the field experience was worth the stress and hard work, and they truly believe they got things out of the experience that they could not have gotten from the classroom. Over the years, several common themes have appeared as students described their professional development. For instance, students report feeling that they are;

- confident in their ability to assert their knowledge, values, and skills in practice;
- able to respond effectively to complex and challenging client situations, as evidenced in the story at the beginning of the chapter;
- excited and relieved about ending or advancing their education and getting closer to becoming a "real" social worker;
- anxious about licensure and job seeking, graduate school, or advanced field; and
- able to manage the complex problems faced by client systems.

Finally, one student recently told me, on the last day of class, field had helped him solidify his belief that he had made the right choice to become a social worker. Although, the preceding sentiments are only a few of the themes related to professional development and are in no way exhaustive, they do speak to the unique contribution that field makes in the professional development of the student.

ETHICAL RESPONSIBILITIES OF THE PROFESSIONAL

The NASW Code of Ethics (1999) addresses social workers' ethical responsibilities as professionals and puts forth standards that address competence; discrimination; private conduct; dishonesty, fraud, and deception; impairment; misrepresentation; solicitations; and acknowledging credit (pp. 23–24). A few need to be specifically discussed.

EP 2.1.2a & b

First, in terms of the social worker's responsibility of *competence*, this ethical standard speaks to the responsibility of social workers to work within their area(s) of expertise and engage in lifelong learning. This is accomplished by keeping abreast of the knowledge through routine review of the literature and attendance at continuing education trainings.

EP 2.1.1e

The standards that address *private conduct* and *impairment* state that social workers should (1) not let their private lives interfere with their ability to practice as social workers, and (2) when a social worker's personal conduct is interfering, that person should seek immediate action. This speaks to self-care, self-reflection, and the need of social workers to be acutely aware of how they are doing as a person first and responsible to know when they need assistance. Self-care will be addressed in more detail later in the chapter.

EP 2.1.1d

Another standard that needs to be highlighted is *misrepresentation*, which addresses the fact that social workers have an ethical responsibility to accurately represent themselves to their clients and claim only accurate information regarding their education, credentials, and expertise and practice accordingly. Although the code does not explicitly state that a social worker should be licensed, licensure is important for several reasons. First, it protects client systems through a governing body, a licensing board that monitors the actions of licensees and investigates issues of wrongdoing. Second, it advances the status of the social worker and allows for reimbursement of services. Third, it distinguishes you as a social worker who thus has a specific body of knowledge base, values, and skills to use in the practice of assisting client systems.

EP 2.1.1c

PROFESSIONAL DEVELOPMENT

Now that we have defined the professional and discussed the ethical responsibilities of a professional social worker, it is important to turn our attention to how one becomes a professional social worker, or the professional development of self. Professional development of self in field has been studied (Barretti, 2004; Cochrane & Hanley, 1999). Barretti (2004) states that the development of a professional self is more a process than an acquired set of behaviors or values and found that development begins before students enter a social work program. Barretti states,

> Because students hold well-defined conceptualizations of social workers and of the profession through previous experiences with both, it behooves social work programs to start where the "client" is by building upon students' breadth of experience rather than assuming they are blank slates on which only they will write. (p. 22)

When considering professional development of self, it is important to take a holistic perspective, considering who the student is, the student's background, how the student defines him- or herself as a social worker, what it means to the student to be a social worker, the experiences the student has had in field and the classroom, and how these experiences have impacted the student's professional development.

For the past several years, I have been exploring all of the preceding points and have expanded the discussion of professional development to include a *spiritually sensitive perspective* (Larkin, 2010). Now before you stop reading, let me explain. Note that much of the following material is adapted from an article I wrote, "Spiritually Sensitive Professional Development of Self: A Curricular Module for Field Education," published in *Social Work and Christianity* (2010).

A Spiritually Sensitive Perspective

As you may or may not be aware, spirituality in social work practice has been written about extensively for over two decades. Derezotes (2006) identifies what he calls a second phase of spirituality that is not only concerned with personal spiritual growth but also with a transformation that leads to a deeper understanding of our responsibility to care for each other. Derezotes (2006) states that, ". . . there is a growing awareness that spiritual development brings with it an increased responsibility to serve, and that personal spirituality and service are themselves interconnected and interrelated" (p. 2). In light of this, it is becoming increasingly important for students to have the opportunity to reflect on their own spiritual development and the role that spirituality may or may not play in their development as a social worker. This is supported by Barretti (2004) who found that some students, ". . . do not entirely credit social work training for their transformation and instead viewed their training as a complement to other developmental or spiritual changes already occurring" (p. 20).

Canda and Furman (1999) provide a definition of spirituality that is helpful as you consider your professional development of self from a spiritually sensitive perspective. They state that, "spirituality relates to a universal and fundamental aspect of what it is to be human—to search for a sense of meaning, purpose, and moral framework for relating with self, others and the ultimate reality" (p. 370). They go on to say that, "spiritually sensitive social workers address clients as whole persons, applying professional roles, rules and assessment labels in a flexible way that is responsive to the values of the client and his or her community" (p. 32). Derezotes (2006) distinguishes spirituality from religion by stating that,

Spirituality can be seen as the *individual's* sense of connectedness, meaning, peace, consciousness, purpose, and service that develops across the life span. In contrast, religiosity can be seen as *socially* shared rituals, doctrines, and beliefs that may or may not support and enhance the individual's spiritual development. (p. 3)

It is important to note that an exploration of professional development of self from a spiritually sensitive perspective is grounded in spirituality, not religion. This is done with intent and to be inclusive and provide a wider lens for your consideration. I do, however, realize that for some students, religion and spirituality are conceptually and experientially joined and for others any notion of spirituality may be irrelevant. Thus I have broken down the concept of spiritually sensitive professional development into three specific areas that can be explored regardless of one's particular personal identification with spirituality or religion. I found that for one particular group of students I worked with, considering professional development of self from a spiritually sensitive perspective was important regardless of their religious or spiritual or nonreligious or nonspiritual orientation (Larkin, 2010).

Larkin (2010) states that,

Spiritually Sensitive Professional Development is defined as professional development that considers the whole student, is grounded in an understanding of meaning and purpose in one's work, utilizes a process of reflection and discernment for ethical practice and emphasizes spiritually based self-care. (p. 446)

To ground your thinking and reflection, each of the three aspects of the preceding definition, *meaning and purpose in work*, *reflection and discernment for ethical practice*, and *spiritually sensitive self care* will be discussed separately (Larkin, 2010).

Meaning and Purpose in Work

The first aspect of spiritually sensitive professional development to consider is *meaning and purpose in work*. This consideration is significant in that it asks you to consider what it is about your work that brings you meaning and how that meaning relates to its purpose.

From a personal perspective, I don't think my work as a social worker is more important than other types of work, but I do feel that my work is meaningful to me and significant in the lives of the client systems I work with. As you have seen throughout your field experience, social workers often become intricately involved in the lives of their clients. It is in these moments of deep connection that recognizing and drawing on meaning can be beneficial to both the client and the worker. The same may hold for you. During your field experience, in all likelihood, you too were confronted with deep questions of life where the meaning and purpose of your work as well as your beliefs and values may have been both challenged and confirmed.

REFLECTION QUESTION 12.3

As you think about your field experience, what direct or indirect client system experiences have you had that you would consider as having meaning? How did you handle these experiences? Was it challenging, or did it come natural? What meaning did these experiences hold for you as a social work student?

Finding meaning in one's work is an idea conceptualized by Fox (1994). He states,

> Good living and good working go together. Life and livelihood ought not to be separated but to flow from the same source, which is Spirit, for both life and livelihood are about Spirit. Spirit means life, and both life and livelihood are about living in depth, living with meaning, purpose, joy, and a sense of contributing to the greater community. A spirituality of work is about bringing life and livelihood back together again. And Spirit with them. (pp. 1–2)

Developing clarity about the meaning and purpose your work holds for you can also be an important part of both your professional development and ability to sustain a professional life, or what Thomas (2005) calls composing a life in the day to day. Considering the impact of your day-to-day experiences in field is important in your ability to gain a sense of meaning and purpose. These experiences have become the foundation of your understanding of what it is to be a social worker and who you are becoming as a social worker. Reflecting on these experiences, discussed in more detail next, will help you gain a better understanding of what it means to you to be a social worker and thus determine your purpose. On the surface, a sense of meaning and purpose in work should go beyond your job description and focus more on what it means to be a professional social worker. To begin to articulate your understanding of meaning and purpose in your work, consider Reflection Question 12.4.

REFLECTION QUESTION 12.4

What drove you to want to be social worker, and what does being a social worker mean to you? Where did your desire to be a social worker come from? What do you see as your purpose as a social worker? Another way to look at this is to ask, what kind of social worker do I want to be?

EP 2.1.1b

Reflection and Discernment for Ethical Practice

The next aspect of spiritually sensitive professional development is reflection and discernment for ethical practice (Larkin, 2010). To discern is to develop the ability to more fully understand and make a determination about something within its context. Reflection is an important part of the process that leads to discernment. Engaging in reflection and discernment is important for you to more clearly define and articulate your professional development as a social worker. Three parts of professional development are important to consider:

1. who you are as a social worker, or your professional identity,
2. what you are called to do, your professional role, and
3. how you are to be a social worker in the day to day, your professional behavior (Larkin, 2010).

It is through a process of reflection that you will be able to discern these three parts of professional development.

As you reflect specifically on your professional role, I think it is important to mention that social workers can experience conflict related to the professional role they choose. This conflict seems to center around questions of, am I doing the right work, and am I doing enough. Just asking these questions can diminish the good work one is doing. So, I think it is important to remember that, according to the NASW, there are some several hundred thousand social workers in the United States who are doing all kinds of work and that when you reflect on that you realize that you are one of many and your professional role is also one of many. So, there is no right or wrong professional role. Thus, as you think about your professional identity, role, and behavior consider Reflection Question 12.5.

REFLECTION QUESTION 12.5

How would you describe your professional identity? What is/are the professional role(s) that you want to take on as a social worker? And how would you describe the professional behavior you want to exhibit in your day-to-day life as a social worker?

In terms of ethical practice, it is important to recognize that ethical practice is mentioned in all three of the definitions of a professional previously cited; thus developing the skills necessary to engage in ethical practice as a professional is critical. Reflection and discernment are two important tools to assist you in this process. Staral (2003) emphasizes self-reflection, ethical decision-making, and self-care and relates them specifically to her experiences with Ignatian Spirituality. Staral (2003) exposed her students to the Examen of Consciousness, a Jesuit spirituality practice, which encouraged students to reflect on their daily lives. As a result of the reflection, students were better able to gain insight and resolution. So the reflection and discernment the students engaged in helped them discern, or see, detect, or make clearer, what they needed to do (Staral, 2003). As you will recall, reflection is a critical part of ethical decision making, resolving ethical dilemmas and managing the ambiguity that can come along with social work practice. It is often the things that nag at us and demand our attention that we later define as a dilemma; thus reflection and discernment become important tools in resolving ethical dilemmas.

EP 2.1.2b, c &d

As you consider your experiences in field and develop your skill of reflection and discernment, you will be better able to understand who you are becoming as a social worker and manage the challenges of a professional life as well as uphold the ethical responsibilities of a professional as identified by the NASW. Canda and Furman (1999) state, "When we realize that spirituality encompasses the wholeness of what it is to be human, we become aware of the precious and wonderful nature of every moment and interaction" (p. 217).

Spiritually Based Self-Care

The last aspect of spiritually sensitive professional development that is important to consider in the context of professional development is spiritually based self-care (Larkin, 2010). This refers to those things you can do to take care of yourself and expands the options and encourages you to include relevant spiritually based practices. Staral (2003) makes this link between spirituality and self-care. It is important for you to consider what role spirituality can play, if any, in your self-care. Barton (1996) articulates the concept of "a rule of life" as an important part of the process of spiritual transformation and states,

A rule of life seeks to respond to two questions: Who do I want to be? How do I want to live? Actually, it might be more accurate to say that a rule of life seeks to address the interplay between these two questions: How do I want to live so I can be who I want to be?" (p. 147)

Take a few minutes to reflect on the preceding quote as it relates to your professional development and particularly in light of the idea of spiritually based self-care. As you may notice, the interplay (identified in the preceding definition) between who you want to be and how you want to live also relates to the three parts of professional development identified earlier: professional identity, professional role, and professional behaviors (Larkin, 2010). As you look back at your responses to Reflection Question 12.5, how do you see the idea of "rule of life" relating to how you conceptualized your professional development?

A rule of life (Barton, 1996) relates to spiritually based self-care in that it suggests that social workers identify what they need to do daily, weekly, monthly, and yearly to sustain themselves as professionals and have long careers. Spiritually based self-care practices go beyond the obvious things such as time management, making lists, attending supervision, getting enough rest, and eating right, and considers practices that transcend the surface and delve more deeply into their understanding of who they are, where they come from, and what they need to be social workers. For some individuals, they may draw directly from religious and or spiritual practices such as prayer or use of scripture; others may focus on existential practices that consider questions of human suffering and our responsibility to one another; still others may turn to nature as a way to replenish their resources; and last, others may use their creativity in the form of art or music for self-care. Regardless of the particular practice, it is important to accept and embrace self-care, particularly in light of the fact that social work is a helping profession grounded in the care of others. Consider Reflection Question 12.6.

REFLECTION QUESTION 12.6

What do you see as your needs related to self-care? What spiritually based practices can you draw on? What spiritually based practices might you develop?

EP 2.1.3a

PROFESSIONAL DEVELOPMENT OF SELF CAPSTONE PAPER

Now that you have had a chance to consider your professional development of self in general and from a spiritually sensitive perspective, it can be helpful to pull your thoughts and ideas together in the form of a capstone paper. I have been having the students I work with write professional development of self capstone papers for years. Every year students share how they find it a useful activity in that it forces them to think more critically about the big picture of their field experience as opposed to only focusing on their work with clients or their agency. More recently, as I have added the spiritually sensitive perspective to the paper, students have reported getting even more out of the activity. In fact, one student stated, "If the capstone paper had not had the spiritual focus I don't think I could have written it, I mean I would of, but I don't think it would have been as helpful or meaningful to me" (Larkin, 2010, p. 457).

To write your capstone paper, see Integrative Activity 12.1: Professional Development of Self Capstone Paper. This activity provides an opportunity to synthesize the responses to the reflection questions in this chapter. It allows you to integrate your understanding of your professional development from a holistic perspective, considering all aspects of yourself, even if some aspects are still not completely apparent. As you will recall, professional development is a process and one that involves lifelong learning. So you will spend your entire career refining and learning about who you are as a social worker and how you want to put your identity into practice.

INTEGRATIVE ACTIVITY | 12.1

Professional Development of Self Capstone Paper

Purpose: The purpose of this activity is to provide the foundation and direction for writing a capstone paper in which you explore your development as an emerging professional social worker, incorporating a spiritually sensitive perspective.

Directions:

1. To prepare to write the capstone reflection paper, use the following directions:
   - Reflect on the three areas of the definition of spirituality sensitive professional development—meaning and purpose in work, reflection and discernment for ethical practice, and spirituality sensitive self-care (Larkin, 2010)—as they specifically relate to you and your experiences.
   - Consider your own spiritual and religious development and the role that spirituality and religion have or have not played in your development as a professional social worker.
   - Reflect on how you would describe your professional identity, professional role, and professional behavior.
   - Reflect on spiritually based practice issues, including ethical dilemmas or any spiritually based practice interventions you may have used in field.
   - Discuss spiritually based social work practice and professional development with your field instructor.

2. Once you have reflected on the preceding items, consider these additional areas:
   - your professional strengths, weaknesses, and greatest successes and challenges;
   - any value-driven, ethical issues, or dilemmas related to your professional development that you encountered in the field and what you learned from them;
   - how you are coming to define yourself as a professional from a spiritually sensitive perspective, including what has been easy for you and what has been challenging; and
   - any observations of professionalism, or lapses of, in your field instructor, coworkers, peers, and agency, as well as the profession as a whole and the impact they have or have not had on your development.

Suggested Field Tasks

- Engage a mentor.
- Engage in self-care activities, and monitor stress and burnout.
- Explore your professional development of self.
- In supervision, identify and discuss personal values and distinguish personal and professional values.
- Use reflection to explore role, tasks, and experiences of field.
- Explain knowledge, skills, and values developed as a result of field experiences.
- Join your department's Social Work club.
- Join NASW or another professional organization.

Competency Notes

The following identifies where the CSWE *EPAS* (2008) Educational Policy (EP) and practice behaviors are discussed in the chapter.

EP 2.1.1a Advocate for client access to the services of social work (p. 186): Social workers must have an understanding of the services available to clients and ensure that a client is receiving all necessary services.

EP 2.1.1b Practice personal reflection and self-correction to assure continual professional development (pp. 186, 190): Social workers must develop and demonstrate the ability to reflect on their practice and development as a professional social worker.

EP 2.1.1c Attend to professional roles and boundaries (pp. 186, 187): Professional social work is grounded in an understanding of the boundaries inherent in the roles that social workers provide to clients.

EP 2.1.1d Demonstrate professional demeanor in behavior, appearance, and communication (pp. 186, 187): Social workers must develop an understanding of professional behavior and demonstrate that in their practice.

EP 2.1.1e Engage in career-long learning (pp. 186, 187): Foundational to professional social work practice is the recognition that the social worker must engage in career-long learning in order to provide the most effective practice possible.

EP 2.1.1f Use supervision and consultation (p. 186): Social workers must utilize supervision and consultation in order to be a competent professional.

EP 2.1.2a Recognize and manage personal values in a way that allows professional values to guide practice (p. 187): Professional social work practice is grounded in the ability of the social worker to manage their personal values and develop the skills necessary to allow professional values to guide practice.

EP 2.1.2b Make ethical decisions by applying standards of the National Association of Social Workers Code of Ethics and, as applicable, of the International Federation of Social Workers/International Association of Schools of Social Work Ethics in Social Work, Statement of Principles (pp. 187, 191): Social workers must know and utilize the NASW Code of Ethics and other codes of ethics to guide practice decisions.

EP 2.1.2c Tolerate ambiguity in resolving ethical conflicts (p. 191): Professional social workers must develop the skills necessary to handle the ambiguity that is inherent in ethical situations and be able to resolve ethical conflicts in a professional manner.

EP 2.1.2d Apply strategies of ethical reasoning to arrive at principled decisions (p. 191): Social worker must be able to make professional practice decisions that are grounded in the skill of ethical decision making and reasoning.

EP 2.1.3a Distinguish, appraise, and integrate multiple sources of knowledge, including research-based knowledge, and practice wisdom (p. 192): Professional social work practice is dependent on the ability of the social worker to integrate multiple sources of information into all aspects of their practice.

References

Barker, R. (2003). *The social work dictionary* (5th ed.). Washington, DC: NASW Press.

Barretti, M. (2004). The professional socialization of undergraduate social work students. *The Journal of Baccalaureate Social Work, 9*(2), 9–30.

Barton, R. (2006). *Sacred rhythms arranging our lives for spiritual transformation*. Downers Grove, IL: Intervarsity Press.

Canda, E. R., & Furman, L. D. (1999). *Spiritual diversity in social work practice: The heart of helping*. New York: The Free Press.

Cochrane, S. F., & Hanley, M. M. (1999). *Learning through field: A developmental approach*. Needham Heights, MA: Allyn and Bacon.

Conn, J. W. (1996). *Women's spirituality: Resources for Christian development* (2nd ed.). Mahwah, NJ: Paulist Press.

Derezotes, D. (2006). In Quinlin P. (Ed.), *Spiritually oriented social work practice*. Boston, MA: Allyn and Bacon.

Edwards, R. L. (Ed.). *Encyclopedia of social work* (19th ed.). Washington, DC: National Association of Social Workers.

Fowler, J. F. (1981). *Stages of faith: The psychology of human development and the quest for meaning*. San Francisco: Harper.

Fox, M. (1994). *The reinvention of work*. New York: Harper Collins.

Furman, L. (2001). *An integration of religion and spirituality into social work practice: An emerging trend for the new century* (conference handout).

Larkin, S. (2010). Spiritually sensitive professional development of self: A curricular module for field education. *Social Work and Christianity, 37*(4), 446–466.

Okundaye, J. N., Gray, C., & Gray, L. B. (1999). Reimaging field instruction from a spiritually sensitive perspective: An alternative approach. *Social Work, 44*(4), 371–383.

Popple, P. R., & Leighninger, L. (1999). *Social work, social welfare, and American society* (4th ed.). Boston: Allyn and Bacon.

Sheafor, B., & Horejsi, C. (2012). *Techniques and guidelines for social work practice,* (9th ed.). Boston: Pearson Education, Inc.

Sheridan, M. J., Bullis, R. K., Adcock, C. R., Berlin, S. D., & Miller, P. C. (1992). Practitioners' personal and professional attitudes and behaviors towards religion and spirituality: Issues for social work education and practice. *Journal of Social Work Education, 28,* 190–203.

Sheridan, M., & Hemert, K. (1999). The role of religion and spirituality in social work education and practice: A survey of student views and experiences. *Journal of Social Work Education, 35*(1), 125–141.

Staral, J. M. (2003). Introducing Ignatian spirituality: Linking self-reflection with social work ethics. *Social Work & Christianity, 30*(1), 38–51.

Thomas, T. (2005). *Spirituality in the mother zone: Staying centered, finding God*. Mahwah, NJ: Paulist Press.

Thompson, M. (2005). *Soul feast: An invitation to the Christian spiritual life* (2nd ed.). Louisville, KY: Westminster John Knox Press.

CHAPTER 13

Endings in Field Education

If you are reading this chapter, it means you are either the kind of person who likes to read the last chapter first, to see how the book ends, or you are approaching the end of your field experience. I suspect it is the latter. Completing your field experience is a wonderful accomplishment and one that is multifaceted. Every year as the students I work with get toward the end of field, I tell them I am big on endings. This means I think it is critically important for you to,

1. develop your understanding of the role endings play in social work practice and field education, and
2. be present with and experience your endings.

In this chapter, we will discuss both and provide reflection questions and integrative activities for you to use while in field.

ENDINGS IN SOCIAL WORK PRACTICE

EP 2.1.10l

As you will recall, termination is the final phase of the planned change process and is defined as, "when the worker guides concluding activities of the process in a manner that is sensitive to issues surrounding the ending of a relationship" (Sheafor & Horejsi, 2008, p. 449). Let's look more closely at this definition and discuss the two important aspects of the definition.

First, the definition states that termination involves the worker guiding activities; that is, the worker is doing something or having a role in the process and experience of the ending. In micro-level practice, with individuals or families, this might include a final session in which the worker reviews the accomplishments of the client, acknowledges that the work is ending, and provides any final recommendations. In mezzo-level practice with a treatment group, the worker may use a ritual or activity to mark the final group session. One such activity could be having each member of the group identify one thing that he or she got out of the group that the member will continue to use in day-to-day life. Last, when it comes to macro-level practice with an organization, and more specifically program development, the worker may write a final report documenting that the program is up and running, that all agreed-upon tasks with regard to developing the program are completed, and who or what entity is taking over the running of the program.

As you can see in the preceding examples, the worker was active and engaged in a specific activity to mark the ending, and the ending often reflected the role the social worker played in the client's service. So consideration of your professional role and the boundaries inherent in that role are also important when considering endings. For instance, some students state that they do not have an ongoing relationship with clients, so individually informing clients that they are leaving the agency may not be necessary. If that is the case, then it may only be important for the agency staff to be made aware that the student is leaving. That way, if anyone asked about the student, the staff could let that person know the student was no longer with the agency.

EP 2.1.1c

With regard to the second part of the definition, it is important that you develop the skills necessary to ensure that the ending activity reflects the relationship and is sensitive to how the client system may experience the ending. This is most apparent when working with individuals and families. It is very important that you develop an understanding of the endings that the clients you work with have experienced; then make sure your activities take that into consideration. A common anxiety that the students I have worked with have expressed to me, particularly when working with children, is the fear that they will be letting the child down or become yet another person who is walking out of the child's life. This anxiety is even greater when the student is initiating the ending due to field placement ending. This situation is common; it requires planning and discussion in supervision and can be handled well.

EP 2.1.3a

For instance, one student I worked with had this exact concern, and in fact, the client expressed this as well. To address this concern, the student was very direct and honest with the client. The student stated that the client was indeed correct that the student would be ending their work together soon because his field placement was ending. The student even stated his concern about this fact and questioned in supervision whether or not they should work together at this time. By first acknowledging the reality of the ending, affirming the concern of the client, and expressing his own concern, the student was able to engage the client and actually address termination in the first meeting. Thinking about the ending really should start at the beginning of the work. The client and student together were able to negotiate what they felt they could accomplish in the time they had and planned ahead for the ending. By the time the last meeting occurred, both the client and student were well prepared; the student emphasized how the client could use the relationship with even a short time frame to accomplish the goal. This turned into the client's successful use of the helping relationship. The student asked the client how he could use what he learned in future relationships with other social workers. The client was able to identify his success and translate what he did with the student into possible future relationships.

This is exactly what I encourage the students I work with to do, which is to help clients focus on what they did, how they were able to use the relationship, and the planned change process. By doing so, this deemphasizes the worker and in turn, emphasizes the process and the client's ability to effectively use the process. Finally, one thing I always did when I ended work with children was to reframe the ending to help them see that by working with different people, even if it seems overwhelming, they are gaining valuable experience and skills and that each person who comes into their life brings something different that the client can use. Again, the goal is to acknowledge the fact that helping relationships end and create an experience that honors the needs of client and maximizes the potential outcome of the ending.

EP 2.1.1f

When considering how best to terminate contact with client systems, it is important to discuss all the possible ways this can be handled in supervision with your field instructor. Effective use of supervision and consultation can make a difference in how well thought out the termination is and how that ending will impact clients.

However, before you can adequately assess the role of endings in the lives of your clients and then ensure that your termination activities reflect that understanding, you must first reflect on how you experience endings in your life currently and in the past. As you have most likely been told in your social work program, strong social work practice skills begin with self-awareness. Consider Reflection Question 13.1.

REFLECTION QUESTION 13.1

How have you handled endings in your life? As you think about ending field, what does that bring up for you? As you think about ending your work with your clients, your agency, and your program, how do you feel about that? What do you need when you experience an ending, and how can you translate that into your practice with your clients, agency, and field program?

Types of Endings in Practice

Gelman (2009) identifies three types of endings with clients that are important to consider. They are, "natural terminations . . . client-initiated . . . and forced" (p. 183). In her study of 54 MSW students, Gelman (2009) found that forced termination, or a termination that occurs as the result of field ending, was the most often experienced at 93% of students, with 24% of students experiencing natural termination, when the work ended because goals are met, and 35% when the client initiated the ending (p. 183). It is also interesting to note that for 44% of the students surveyed, forced endings were the only type of termination experienced (Gelman, 2009, p. 183). Gelman (2009) also found that although the students studied had received training in their course work, they would have benefited from earlier discussion of termination in their supervision session and emphasis on planning for termination. Baum (2006) also found that students experienced distress due to "untimeliness of the end-of-year treatment termination" (p. 649) or what Baum defined as a "forced termination" (p. 639). So considering the types of endings you will likely experience and the impact these endings will have on you and your clients is an important part of the termination process.

REFLECTION QUESTION 13.2

As you begin to think about termination and specifically the client systems with whom you are working, what are the possible activities that you could use to facilitate the ending? Next, what are the specific needs of your client systems that you should take into consideration as you plan for the ending? Last, what are the types of endings you are likely to experience at your field site, and what impact will these endings have on you?

ENDINGS IN FIELD EDUCATION

For some students, the previous reflection question may illuminate the fact that due to the nature of their work at their field site, the impact of their ending field will be minimal on the clients they serve. For example, for the student who works at the local social services agency that provides primarily emergency-based service, such as rent and utility assistance and referrals to the food pantry, he or she has not established ongoing working relationships with clients; in fact, he or she may see many different clients each day. For this student, the focus on termination will be more on the field experience as a whole, which is the second area of consideration and important for all students to consider.

Ending Your Relationship with Your Agency

As you approach ending your field experience, the first thing to reflect on is the fact that you are ending your working relationship with your agency. This involves acknowledging all of the contributions the agency has made in your development as a social worker, as well as the contributions you have made to the agency. The latter is what I call, your legacy. It is important to reflect on the contributions you have made to your agency and acknowledge them as a part of the termination process.

Next, it is important to acknowledge the impact the relationships you have formed with all the staff of the agency, excluding your field instructor, as that relationship will be discussed separately. Reflect on all the relationships you have developed, positive and negative, and consider the role that each of these relationships has played in your development as a social worker. Think about what you would like to share with these coworkers before you leave. Just as we have emphasized planning in all aspects of social worker practice, planning for your last week and day is important. In fact, so much so that I tell the students I work with that you don't want your last day to be like any other day—you do want this day to be significant.

EP 2.1.3c

As part of considering your ending with your agency, you also want to demonstrate appropriate professionalism in that you have cleaned out your office, completed all necessary work tasks, informed your coworkers and field instructor of the status on all current projects and tasks, and, of course, said all of your good-byes.

EP 2.1.1c, d

REFLECTION QUESTION 13.3

As you think about ending your working relationship with your agency, including coworkers, and tasks, how do you want your last week and last day to go? To help you answer this question, consider the following visualization: Visualize yourself coming home from your last day of field, and answer the following questions. What do you hope happened? What specifically do you hope you did so you can say you had a good last day and feel good about how that day went?

Ending Your Relationship with Your Field Instructor

Ending your relationship with your field instructor is often significant for students, particularly given the multifaceted nature of the student–field instructor relationship. It is important that you engage in a focused reflection and prepare for the ending of this relationship. In all likelihood you will have strong feelings about this relationship and realize its significance in your development as a social worker. It is also important to realize that this sentiment is most likely shared by your field instructor. I can speak only for myself, but when I was a field instructor, I really enjoyed the unique relationship I could build with the student I was supervising, and I acknowledged that this relationship was important to me. I also always shared with the students I supervised how much I learned

EP 2.1.1b

from them and appreciated the opportunity to serve as their field instructor. This is often because students and field instructors are encouraged to engage in the larger discussions about the profession, what being a social worker means, and their development as a social worker. On the other hand, you may not feel a strong attachment to your field instructor and that is OK. However, it is still important to acknowledge the ending of this experience and unique relationship.

There is no right or wrong way to go about ending this relationship, except to be present and acknowledge that the relationship is indeed ending.

REFLECTION QUESTION 13.4

As you think about acknowledging your relationship with your field instructor, what would you like to say or do? What would you like your field instructor to say or do?

Ending Your Field Education Experience

The last thing to reflect on as you consider endings in field education is the fact that you are ending your field education experience. This entails several things worth looking at. First of all, for those of you in a BSW senior field placement, this means the end of being a student, the end of your field curriculum, and the end of your undergraduate BSW education. That is a lot of endings. For those of you in a foundation MSW field placement, this is the end of this part of your field program.

These endings are often experienced with mixed emotions. I have had students tell me they feel relieved, sad, excited, and petrified all at the same time. As you learned when you studied the Life Course Perspective, transitions are important to consider and how transitions are experienced shapes one's future. Ending field and possibly your current social work program is absolutely a significant transition that often brings with it new stressors and questions. But before we explore those new stressors and next steps, it is important to sit with this accomplishment and relish in all that you have learned and the contributions that you have made to all the client systems you have worked with.

In fact, this is an important critical thinking and professional development of self task. It is necessary that you develop the ability to articulate verbally and in writing what you have learned, what you have accomplished, and what you realize you need to work on next. It is also important that you can describe the work you have done so that it relates to the overarching competencies needed by a generalist social worker. Developing this skill and being prepared to share your thoughts about the preceding information will be extremely helpful to you as you think about what is next.

EP 2.1.3c

Curriculum Analysis

An important part of articulating what you learned in field is reflecting on the knowledge, values, and skills you have internalized from your curriculum as well as how you integrated that curriculum in your practice in field. Just as you engaged in curriculum review as a part of your orientation when you began field, you will want to engage in curriculum analysis as a part of ending.

The purpose of analyzing your curriculum is to solidify your understanding of it and identify any gaps that may have existed. If you identified any gaps, it is my hope that first, you could close that gap while in field, and second, you will provide that information to your program, either through your course evaluation or exit survey. It is very important that field education not exist in a vacuum: that students' experiences and curriculum evaluation, either in terms of the areas that seamlessly integrate with the practice experiences of field and those where there were gaps, be incorporated into the social work program. Integrative Activity 13.1: Curriculum Analysis will provide you the opportunity to conduct this analysis and consider what the areas of strength are and where the gaps are. Last, in light of your field experience, what, if any, recommendations would you make with regard to your program's curriculum?

INTEGRATIVE ACTIVITY 13.1

Curriculum Analysis

Purpose: The purpose of this activity is to provide an opportunity for you to analyze your curriculum in the context of the core competencies and practice behaviors to solidify your understanding of your curriculum and preparation for practice. This will also help you identify any gaps in your training and thus inform your program's curriculum.

Directions: The first column lists the 10 core competency areas identified by CSWE *EPAS* (2008). In the second column, identify the course(s) that provided the most relevant content; in the third column, provide feedback regarding your level of preparation and how the content informed your practice in field. In the fourth column, identify any gaps in the curriculum, that is, areas in which you were not well prepared. Last, provide an overall analysis of your curriculum, answering the foundational questions: How has your curriculum prepared you? What were the seamless points of integration, and what, if any, gaps existed between your preparation and the expectation of your field agency from a generalist perspective?

Note: Specialized curriculum is not necessarily a gap; it is just that—specialized. Only include content that relates to the core competencies or you feel should be included.

EPAS (08) Core Competency (to review a description and the practice behaviors see Integrative Activity 1.1.)	Program's Courses (refer to Curriculum Review)	Feedback Regarding Preparation and Applicability to Field Tasks	Gaps in curriculum
2.1.1—Identify as a professional social worker and conduct oneself accordingly.			
2.1.2—Apply social work ethical principles to guide professional practice.			
2.1.3—Apply critical thinking to inform and communicate professional judgments.			
2.1.4—Engage diversity and difference in practice.			

(Continued)

2.1.5—Advance human rights and social and economic justice.			
2.1.6—Engage in research-informed practice and practice-informed research.			
2.1.7—Apply knowledge of human behavior and the social environment.			
2.1.8—Engage in policy practice to advance social and economic well-being and to deliver effective social work services.			
2.1.9—Respond to contexts that shape practice.			
2.1.10(a)–(d)—Engage, assess, intervene, and evaluate with individuals, families, groups, organizations, and communities.			

Overall Curriculum Analysis: In this section, provide your overall analysis of your program's curriculum and how prepared you were for practice. Also, include areas of strength, gaps, and any suggestions you have for improving the curriculum. Last, identify the areas of the curriculum that were seamless in terms of integrating into the practice experiences of field and those that were more challenging.

PULLING IT ALL TOGETHER

EP 2.1.3a

We have discussed the importance of articulating your understanding of your field education experience in terms of the knowledge, values, and skills you have integrated into field. We also discussed the role that curriculum analysis plays in solidifying your understanding of your curriculum and identifying gaps. Now it is time to pull this all together and develop your ability to articulate what you have learned, what you have accomplished, how you applied your generalist training to your field site, and what you see as the next step in your development as a competent social worker. Integrative Activity 13.2: Pulling It all Together will assist you in this task. The outcome will be invaluable as you consider the next step, which we will discuss in more detail later. Regardless of what you decide to do next, Integrative Activity 13.2 will provide an excellent foundation for you to articulate your accomplishments in field, your understanding of generalist practice, how you applied your generalist training to your particular agency, and how best to apply your knowledge, values, and skills to whatever you do next, whether that is at a job, in graduate school, as a volunteer, or in your advanced field placement.

INTEGRATIVE ACTIVITY 13.2

Pulling It All Together

Purpose: The purpose of this activity is to assist you in the process of articulating your learning by translating your understanding of the knowledge, values, and skills integrated and developed in field into the larger, overarching competencies of a generalist social worker.

Directions: For each question, jot down your thoughts and be prepared to explain your answers verbally. For the latter, think about how you would describe what you did in field to someone who has no understanding of social work and your particular area of practice.

1. Describe your agency, its program and services, and whom it primarily serves.

2. Identify the primary multilevel tasks and roles you engaged in at your field site.

3. Identify the specific knowledge you drew on and developed in field.

4. Identify the specific personal and professional values that you used and that were tested and realized in field.

5. Identify the specific practice skills you integrated and developed in field.

6. The Council on Social Work Education's (CSWE) *Educational Policy and Accreditation Standards* (*EPAS*) states that the, "BSW curriculum prepares its graduates for generalist practice through mastery of the core competencies. The MSW curriculum prepares its graduates for advanced practice through mastery of the core competencies augmented by knowledge and practice behaviors specific to a concentration" (p. 3). The CSWE *EPAS* defines generalist practice as follows:

Educational Policy B2.2—Generalist Practice

Generalist practice is grounded in the liberal arts and the person and environment construct. To promote human and social well-being, generalist practitioners use a range of prevention and intervention methods in their practice with individuals, families, groups, organizations, and communities. The generalist practitioner identifies with the social work profession and applies ethical principles and critical thinking in practice. Generalist practitioners incorporate diversity in their practice and advocate for human rights and social and economic justice. They recognize, support, and build on the strengths and resiliency of all human beings. They engage in research-informed practice and are proactive in responding to the impact of context on professional practice. BSW practice incorporates all of the core competencies (pp. 7–8).

Whether you are completing your BSW senior field or your MSW foundation field, reflect on the preceding definition of generalist practice, as well as, the core competencies identified in Integrative Activity 13.1, and identify how you would describe yourself as a generalist practitioner and what specifically you did in field to apply your generalist training to your practice.

7. Identify the ways in which you can translate the generalist training you applied in your field to the next role you take on, whether that be employment or your advanced education.

8. Identify what you see as the next step in your development as a social worker.

WHAT'S NEXT?

The last question in Integrative Activity 13.2 asked you to identify the next step in your development as a social worker. This can mean finding a job and beginning to practice or continuing in your education. Or you may decide that you want to do something altogether different. Let's review the options that are available in order to discern what the next best step is for you.

Finding a Job

If you are completing your BSW degree and you plan to work in a state that licenses the BSW, then you may decide that you want to work before you go on to graduate school. In the 10 plus years that I have been a field director, every year approximately a third of the students pursue work which may entail pursuing licensure. To determine if your state licenses the BSW degree, go to the Association of Social Work Boards (ASWB) website and find your state to see the licensing regulations. This same site can give you all the information you need to take the exam. If you know the state you will be practicing in, you can also contact that state's licensing board directly to gather information regarding licensure. The advantage of working before attending graduate school is that you will gain experience you can draw on later in your advanced coursework. Also, you may have a better foundation from which to decide about what concentration area you want to focus on as an advanced practitioner.

Going to Graduate School

If you are completing your BSW degree, you might want to consider going straight on to graduate school. Again, there is no right or wrong thing to do, it is just important to consider all your options. As discussed in Chapter 1, most MSW programs offer some advanced standing to students who have a BSW degree. This can be a deciding factor in terms of the time commitment. When looking into programs, you will want to determine if you indeed qualify for advanced standing and what type of program you are looking for. As you recall, the BSW degree emphasizes generalist practice, whereas the MSW degree emphasizes advanced practice in a concentration area. It will be important for you to know the type of advanced practice you want to focus on in your graduate program. When looking at programs, it is important to educate yourself with regard to the program, the concentrations the program offers, the course work, and the faculty. Also, if you have the opportunity, it can make a huge difference to visit the programs you are interested in and meet with students. I have seen an increase in the number of students deciding to go straight on to graduate school; this may be due to the thinking that they will have better job opportunities with the MSW degree. Others state they enjoy learning and feel that continuing their education while they are still in the student mode is the best way to go.

What About Something Completely Different?

I also see several students each year pursue something completely different after their BSW degree and before employment or graduate school. This often takes the form of the Peace Corps, AmeriCorps VISTA, Jesuit Volunteer Corps, Teach for America, or even travel. Again, there is no right or wrong decision; it is more important to consider the step that is the best fit for you and your goals.

Advanced Field Education

If you are completing your MSW foundation field, where you emphasized applying your generalist practice skills in preparation for advanced field, then in all likelihood you will be pursuing your advanced field placement. As you think about the concentration you have selected for advanced practice, you will want to consider your field opportunities. Again, it is important to discuss the placement process and go on interviews to determine the agency that can provide the best fit for your professional goals.

REFLECTION QUESTION 13.5

As you think about the preceding options, what do you see as your next step and why? What, if anything, do you need to realize your next step?

Suggested Field Tasks

- Explain knowledge, skills, and values developed as a result of field experiences.
- Demonstrate ability to conceptualize practice.
- Use reflection to explore role, tasks, and experiences of field.
- Articulate learning from tasks.
- Plan for and implement agency and client termination.
- Evaluate progress in meeting goals and objectives of field and core competencies and practice behaviors.
- Discuss next steps after field with supervisor.

Competency Notes

The following identifies where the CSWE *EPAS* (2008) Educational Policy (EP) and practice behaviors are discussed in the chapter.

EP 2.1.1b Practice personal reflection and self-correction to assure continual professional development (p. 199): Social workers must utilize reflection when considering endings in practice.

EP 2.1.1c Attend to professional roles and boundaries (pp. 197, 199): Social workers must consider their professional role and the boundaries inherent in that role when making practice decision with regard to ending services with clients.

EP 2.1.1d Demonstrate professional demeanor in behavior, appearance, and communication (p. 199): Social workers must demonstrate professionalism in their behavior when ending services with client systems.

EP 2.1.1f Use supervision and consultation (p. 197): Social workers must utilize supervision and consultation when considering endings in practice with client systems.

EP 2.1.3a Distinguish, appraise, and integrate multiple sources of knowledge, including research-based knowledge, and practice wisdom (pp. 197, 202): Social worker must consider multiple sources of information when ending services with client systems.

EP 2.1.3c Demonstrate effective oral and written communication in working with individuals, families, groups, organizations, and colleagues (p. 199, 200): Social worker must be able to draw on and utilize effective oral and written communication when ending services with client systems.

EP 2.1.10l Facilitate transitions and endings (p. 196): Social workers must develop and demonstrate the skills necessary to assist clients in making transitions and ending services.

References

Baum, N. (2006). End-of-year treatment termination: Responses of social work student trainees. *British Journal of Social Work, 36,* 639–656.

Gelman, C. (2009). MSW student's experience with termination: Implications and suggestions for classroom and field instruction. *Journal of Teaching in Social Work, 29,* 169–187.

Ginsberg, L. (2001). *Careers in Social Work*. Boston: Allyn and Bacon.

Rubin, G. (1968). Termination of casework: The student client and field instructor. *Journal of Education for Social Work, 4*(1), 65–69.

Sheafor, B., & Horejsi, C. (2008). *Techniques and guidelines for social work practice* (8th ed.). Boston: Pearson Education, Inc.

Shulman, L. (1994). *Teaching the helping skills: A field instructor's guide.* Alexandria, VA: Council on Social Work Education.

Walsh, J. (2002). Termination and your field placement. *The New Social Worker, 9*(2), 14–17.

INDEX